MW01252848

Criminal Justice
Recent Scholarship

Edited by
Marilyn McShane and Frank P. Williams III

A Series from LFB Scholarly

Sanctioning Bias Crime
A Public Perspective

(6 1 0 0 (

Terrylynn Pearlman

LFB Scholarly Publishing LLC
New York 2008

Library of Congress Cataloging-in-Publication Data

Pearlman, Terrylynn, 1971-
  Sanctioning bias crime : a public perspective / Terrylynn Pearlman.
    p. cm.
  Includes bibliographical references and index.
  ISBN 978-1-59332-265-6 (alk. paper)
  1. Hate crimes--Pennsylvania--Public opinion. 2. Hate crimes--United
States--Public opinion. 3. Public opinion--United States. I. Title.
  HV6773.53.P4P43 2008
  364.150973--dc22

2007050634

ISBN 978-1-59332-265-6

Printed on acid-free 250-year-life paper.

Manufactured in the United States of America.

To My Husband

Table of Contents

CHAPTER 1

Bias Crime Legislation and Public Opinion – An Overview

The United States has been home to prejudice and discrimination in a variety of forms and degrees since its founding. However, only over the past 20 years has illegal activity motivated by bias been defined as a crime. In that time, bias crime legislation has been passed in some form by nearly every state as well as the District of Columbia and the Federal Government. The relatively recent legislative recognition of bias crime has been credited to the social movements of the preceding decades, including the civil rights and women's movements, which by substantiating the political victimization of minority groups and acknowledging victims of crime provided the basis for an anti-hate crime movement. That movement generated the social awareness and pressure necessary for the current proliferation of legislative responses to bias crime (Grattet and Jenness 2001) even while academic debate on the prevalence of such crime, the need for a special response, and the potential effects of such legislation continues.

In general, ongoing legislative efforts and academic debate have gone on independent of the views of ordinary citizens. Only since the adoption of bias crime legislation in most States has citizens' views been tapped and then in only the most superficial manner or in the narrowest of contexts. Thus, the current research was designed to explore public views on bias crime emphasizing how it should be sanctioned. The limited research on the topic and theoretical perspectives derived from research on public punitiveness and public opinion on other criminal justice policies were used to inform that exploration.

Bias Crime and Bias Crime Legislation

In general, bias crime, or hate crime, denotes a crime perpetrated against a person based on his/her actual or perceived status, or in other words an offender's prejudice. In 2005, the last year for which official statistics are available, 7,163 bias crimes were reported nationwide. Since collection of bias crime data began in 1993, the number of such crimes reported has fluctuated from a low of almost 6,000 in 1994 to a high of nearly 10,000 in 2001 (U.S. DOJ 1993-2007). The official statistics indicate that bias crime based on racial motivation is generally the most common, followed by religion, sexual orientation, and ethnicity/national origin (U.S. DOJ 2006). However, analysis reveals that per capita reported bias crimes are most frequently committed against gays followed by Jews and blacks (Rubenstein 2004). The majority of bias crimes are against persons, intimidation being by far the most common, followed by property destruction or damage and vandalism. White males are the most common perpetrators of such crime (U.S. DOJ 1993-2007). In the broader context of crime, bias crime data suggests that the number of such crimes is minuscule compared to other offense categories and generally less serious in nature (Jacobs and Potter 1998).

Regardless of the numbers, over the past two decades bias crime has been the object of a prolific legislative response. Although legislation has taken many forms, including reporting statutes, substantive crimes, and civil rights statutes, the form most legislatively popular and judicially approved is the sentence enhancement. A bias crime sentence enhancement upgrades the degree, or increases the authorized penalty of, a previously legislated substantive offense if it is proven to be motivated by prejudice. Unlike a substantive bias crime, it does not establish a new or aggravated offense and a finding of bias is not relevant to an individual's guilt or innocence only his/her sentence. For example, the Federal Hate Crimes Sentencing Enhancement Act (U.S. Congress 1995) provides for an "enhancement of not less than 3 offense levels for offenses that the finder of fact at trial determines beyond a reasonable doubt are hate crimes." Thus, an offender convicted of attacking citizens within a national park for instance (a Federal offense) could receive a punishment applicable to a crime three levels higher if the court proves that it was "a crime in which the defendant intentionally selects a victim...or property that is the object of the crime, because of the actual or perceived race, color, religion, national origin, ethnicity, gender, disability, or sexual orientation of any person."

Across states, bias crime sentence enhancements, and thus the definition of a bias crime, vary in terms of (1) the predicate offenses–or underlying crimes–for which a possible enhancement is authorized, (2) the status provisions–or types of prejudice–that are covered, (3) the factual determination required to show prejudicial motivation, and (4) the permitted magnitude of the enhancement. However, the most widely accepted enhancement applies to crimes of intimidation and harassment committed, or its victims "intentionally selected," "based on," "by reason of," or because of" race, religion, or ethnicity/national origin, and authorizes two to ten years of additional punishment (Jacobs and Potter 1998). National polls document that sixty to seventy percent of Americans support bias crime sentence enhancements. Such polls generally ask respondents whether they would favor imposing a tougher sentence for someone who commits a crime "in which they [perpetrators] specifically target their victim as a member of a minority group" or "because of the victim's race, religion, background, or sexual orientation" or "because the criminal hates the group of people to which the victim belongs." Similarly strong support is found when people are asked whether racial minorities, religious and ethnic minorities, women and homosexuals should be included in the groups protected by such enhancements. However, when support for sentence enhancements is measured by willingness to apply an enhancement to a hypothetical bias crime, it drops below fifty percent. This pattern mirrors findings for other criminal justice policies and is consistent with research demonstrating variation in public opinion based on the specificity of the question (Applegate et al. 1996b; Cullen et al. 2000; Hutton 2005; Roberts and Hough 2005). It suggests that abstract support for bias crime sentence enhancements may not adequately reflect citizens' preferred sanctions for bias crime.

Importance of Understanding Public Opinion

While clear gaps exist in public opinion research on bias crime, the current research was not designed solely with the issue of bias crime in mind. Rather, bias crime serves as a case study of citizens' views on criminal justice issues, the factors that influence them, and the effects of both on their perceptions of appropriate policies for addressing crime. Its particular importance resides in its potential for informing, and perhaps improving, criminal justice policy, while enhancing public education and discourse.

While debate continues as to whether "public" opinion exists and what, if any, impact it does, could, or should have on policymaking, governments and other social agencies continue to elicit citizens' thoughts on a variety of issues, including criminal justice policy, often through the use of opinion polls. However, polls may not capture the context and substance of those opinions and their relevance. For example, knowing that someone generally supports bias crime sentence enhancements says nothing about his knowledge of bias crime, his reasons for supporting or opposing such legislation, or the nature of, or his commitment to, that legislation. Such information might indicate to politicians whether support for such legislation would be political suicide but it fails to offer the insight that more in-depth data might provide. For instance, comprehensive data may reveal values, beliefs and attitudes that may provide new or clearer understandings of an issue that in turn might suggest more effective and politically feasible policies. Understanding the nature and intensity of support for particular policies may suggest variations on them or alternative policies that might be better received and have more of an impact on the issue. Or, it might provide policymakers with the knowledge necessary to better address the concerns of the public relevant to a particular issue. Finally, even if detailed public opinion is unnecessary for the development of policy and passage of legislation, it may offer the opportunity to better educate the public and potentially raise the nature and sophistication of public discourse on the topic. Thus, whether or not a representative democracy requires actual or even perceived responsiveness to the public, familiarity with public opinion may offer valuable insights for addressing social issues both through the law and the promotion of open and more informed dialogue.

In addition, how policies are understood and received by the public may influence the overall impact of such policies. Citizens' ability to identify a bias crime and their willingness to report and support the prosecution of a bias crime are likely to affect the overall use and legal success of bias crime legislation. These behaviors are likely to be influenced by citizens' perceptions and knowledge of bias crime and bias crime legislation. They also are likely to influence the decisions of criminal justice actors regarding how to respond to bias crimes. For example, if victims and/or witnesses are uncooperative or if judges or juries are unwilling to convict defendants of bias crimes or apply bias crime sentence enhancements, prosecutors may be less willing to charge or request them, and police less likely to investigate the possibility of a crime's potential biased motivation. At the same time, citizens' opinions may further affect the impact of legislation by nullifying any intended symbolic message of the legislation. For instance, the possible intention of bias crime legislation to send a message condemning intolerance may be negated by the public perception that such legislation provides special treatment or promotes inequality, which may result in hostility towards and potential intolerance of those it is designed to protect. In the end, legislation may not function as expected if the public fails to support or respond to it as expected.

In all, public opinion could play an important role in the formation, implementation and impact of criminal justice policy. In-depth opinion research, by revealing more than just the general level of support or opposition to a particular policy, may provide insight into what nature and direction that role may or could take and its potential impact for policies and the issues they seek to address.

Importance of Bias Crime as a Case Study

Given the potential influence of public opinion on criminal justice policy, exploring views on crime issues other than bias crime may provide similar benefits. However, bias crime legislation represents a category of criminal law defined by controversy and conflict related to concerns beyond those of pure crime and punishment. Thus, examining opinions on it offers the possibility of identifying highly salient social values and their influences on criminal justice policy.

Bias crime legislation may be perceived by the public as substantively different from legislation that addresses typical street crime. The punishment of a brutal physical attack is for the most part unquestioned, even expected or demanded. Absent concerns regarding legal guilt, there is perhaps common sense consensus that such behavior must not go unpunished. However, the criminalization and punishment of other behaviors is not so clear cut, particularly those that raise potentially conflicting concerns and reactions. For example, abortion may raise concerns regarding the definition of life and death, morality, equality in terms of the protection of unborn fetuses, or liberty in terms of a woman's right to choose. People may vary in the concerns they deem relevant; the conflicts those concerns raise, if any; and what measures they feel are necessary to address them. For instance, one may believe that abortion should not be used as a method of birth control, a fetus is a human being, and that a woman should have the right to say what happens to her own body. These beliefs, depending on their precise nature and relative importance, could justify support or opposition to legislation designed to prohibit abortion. Exploring perceptions of and responses to these sorts of issues provides an opportunity to identify values people recognize as most salient and their relative dominance when issues place them in conflict for either individuals or society as a whole, offering a telling statement as to the role and strength of particular social values.

Bias crime offers a host of potentially conflicting concerns beyond those of traditional crime and punishment. In particular, it highlights social issues regarding the nature and harm of prejudice, and how far society has gone, and should go, to support tolerance and condemn bias and hatred. More specifically, it raises questions as to the appropriate treatment of potential targets of bias crime, whether and how their status or views should influence that treatment, and whether protecting them based on those considerations represents equal or special treatment. It also evokes consideration of perceived perpetrators, the offensiveness of their views and the actions they motivate, and at what point their actions are "biased" and in need of governmental control. Such issues pose potential conflicts even before they are considered in the threatening context of crime. In all, bias crime presents numerous issues regarding how people should treat one another and at what point the government should step in to promote and/or prohibit a particular line of behavior through criminal justice legislation. What issues or values people perceive as relevant and how they influence their support for or opposition to bias crime legislation could offer insight into public opinion concerning other criminal justice issues that highlight important social issues as well as providing an assessment of the nature and strength of various social values.

In sum, bias crime provides an interesting and potentially complex case study of public opinion on criminal justice policy. It represents a crime, although not commonplace or well understood, for which most citizens support more punitive legislation. At the same time, it provides an example of the phenomenon of reduced support for the application of such legislation. Qualitative research into citizens' opinions about bias crime and bias crime legislation offers an opportunity to explore the dimensions and structure of these opinions. In addition, it provides a foundation for future research on the potential influence of those opinions on policymaking and the impact of public policy. Further, given that consideration of bias crime is likely to raise concerns beyond crime and punishment, such research offers a chance to explore those concerns, the values behind them, the relative importance of both, and how they influence support for bias crime legislation and other criminal justice policies involving potentially controversial and/or conflicting issues.

Theoretical Perspectives for the Study

No theory currently exists regarding public opinion on bias crime legislation, and the available literature and research do not provide sufficient information on which to base a coherent, comprehensive, theory and hypothesis-driven model of such views. Academic literature on the issue focuses primarily on one of two arguments. The first deems bias crime legislation as an unnecessary and potentially harmful response to a socially-constructed epidemic. The second recognizes bias crime legislation as a necessary response to a crime that is different, worse, and deserving of a more serious penalty because of its greater culpability and harm. Public opinion polls on the issue reveal majority support for bias crime legislation but reduced support for actual application of more severe sentences for bias crimes and provide no explanation of either finding leaving the meaning and potential ramifications of such support for criminal justice policy unclear. Available scholarly research on public opinion of bias crime and bias crime legislation suggests that some of the issues raised by academics are reflected in public opinion – specifically that bias crime is a different, more serious crime because of its hate-based motivation, which results in greater harm to its immediate victim and beyond. At the same time, studies suggest that the public may not be all that familiar with bias crime or that they do not perceive it in the way expected by researchers. In addition, most of the studies tap only the views of college students or people involved with the issue, and the narrow and directed focuses of the individual studies leave unexamined a comprehensive, more self-guided view of individuals' thoughts on the issue. Designing a theory and hypothesis-driven study based on such disjointed data creates a substantial risk of prompting public opinion that fulfills expectations rather than discovering actual views. It is for this reason that the current study is exploratory in nature.

However, research on public punitiveness and public opinion on the death penalty and three strikes legislation provides a reasonably sound basis for determining the appropriate breadth of that exploration. Such research offers instrumental and symbolic perspectives of public opinion on criminal justice policy that identify a range of constructs potentially relevant to public opinion on bias crime. Given the lack of research on bias crime, situating a study solely within these perspectives would be in appropriate. However, given their potential relevance, the current study ensures a broad enough exploration to capture both instrumental and symbolic issues related to views on bias crime. Even though the current study is not designed to specifically test the theories or perspectives they offer, a brief summary of both is offered as well as an explanation of how each might impact public opinion on bias crime.

Instrumental Crime Concerns and Punitiveness
In her work *Crime and the Public Mind*, Kathryn Taylor Gaubatz (1995) explores and provides strong evidence for an American consensus on the need for harsh policies toward crime and criminals and determines that it is grounded in fairly instrumental concerns. She concludes that people's concerns regarding security, desert, social compassion for offenders, and society's faults strongly influence their views on the appropriate sentencing goals of the criminal justice system, which in turn affect their willingness to support more punitive criminal justice policies such as increased use of incarceration, longer sentences and the death penalty. In general, people who are concerned with security and desert tend to favor retributive and deterrence-based goals and support more punitive policies. People whose security concerns are tempered by considerations of social compassion and society's flaws favor more preventive and rehabilitative goals and support punitive policies, such as lengthy incarceration, only for the purpose of incapacitation. Based on Gaubatz's conclusions, public support for bias crime legislation, which authorizes a more punitive penalty for bias crimes, may be influenced by such instrumental concerns either as they affect people's reactions to crime in general and/or bias crime in particular.

Given the seemingly consistent influence of security concerns-the "desire for protection from loss or harm to self, family or community" (Gaubatz 1995, 45)-on support for punitive policies, people's opinions on bias crime legislation may be affected by factors that contribute to their evaluations of the danger posed by crime and/or bias crime. People's perceptions of crime and punishment, the harm crime poses, their personal vulnerability to crime, and the vulnerability of others whom they desire to protect may be of particular importance. These factors have been shown to be associated with people's perceptions of crime seriousness as well as their general criminal punitiveness, both in terms of perceptions of crime in general and particular offenses. In addition, public opinion polls and research on bias crime have tapped some of these perceptions, and the findings indicate that people may be unfamiliar with the typical nature of bias crime. They also suggest that people may have greater security concerns regarding bias crime primarily because of its perceived violent nature and greater physical and psychological harms to its victims, their communities and society. These beliefs, which stem in large part from perceptions of the effects of the "bias" in bias crime, may further influence people's security concerns by providing a basis for their assessments of the vulnerability of themselves and others and the need to support punitive measures to protect either. In all, bias crime may generate greater security concerns beyond those associated with comparable non-biased crimes, and thus punitive bias crime legislation may garner greater public support even from people generally less inclined to be punitive. The to-date narrow context of research on public opinion on bias crime makes it difficult to suggest whether or how the public's sense of social compassion or the role of society in promulgating bias crime might serve to temper that potential for greater punitiveness.

Symbolic Crime Concerns and Punitiveness
Tom Tyler and his colleagues (1982, 1997) suggest that people's opinions on criminal justice policy are based more on symbolic rather than instrumental crime concerns. They report that people's opinions on three strikes legislation and the death penalty are influenced by their views on the social condition of society, specifically their perceptions of the social and moral cohesion of society. People who believe that social ties are breaking down or that a shared set of moral values is being diluted are pessimistic about society's state. For such people, crime is symbolic of society's deterioration, and punishment must not only reassert social control but reaffirm the social and moral values necessary to strengthen society's cohesion and stability. They also tend to believe that responses to crime that require strong social ties and moral consensus will be ineffective given the questionable state of both, and so they generally support more punitive criminal sanctions.

Tyler and his colleagues also claim that people's views of society are strongly influenced by their socio-political values–their beliefs about, or philosophies of, the appropriate relationship between people and their government. People who favor the concentration of power in a few and the absolute submission to elites and the government tend to view society as less cohesive and, as a result, they tend to be more supportive of three-strikes legislation and the death penalty. Other research suggests that people's values of freedom, equality and justice (Gaubatz 1995)–their opinions on the appropriate limits on governmental social control and individual liberty, the application of uniform treatment and outcomes, and the administration and fairness of justice–may further influence their perceptions of society's cohesion and thus their willingness to support punitive legislation.

These findings suggest that citizens' views on punitive bias crime legislation may reflect their perceptions of society's cohesion, based in part on their values, and its influence on their perception of crime and appropriate responses to crime. In fact, their opinions' on bias crime legislation may be especially subject to such symbolic concerns. Tyler and his colleagues' (1982, 1997) research suggests that people who view social diversity as a problem are more likely to perceive society as less cohesive and to support punitive legislation. The possible perception of bias crime as an act of intolerance may serve to prompt more individual consideration of social diversity than non-biased crime and thus more punitive measures from those who view social diversity as problematic. However, the connection between diversity and punitiveness may be more complex in the context of bias crime. For people who view social diversity as a benefit to society, and especially those who also hold negative views on the current state of social tolerance-society's ability to endure beliefs and values that are different, bias crime may be perceived as an even greater threat to social cohesion than for those who view social diversity as problematic, prompting support for punitive bias crime legislation to assert or reaffirm the value of social diversity and tolerance. In all, people's opinions on bias crime legislation may reflect what they perceive crime in general or bias crime specifically to symbolize for the condition of society. Thus people may be more inclined to support punitive legislation to the extent that crime or bias crime is perceived as a reflection of social deterioration or a threat to social cohesion.

Overall, citizens' opinions on bias crime legislation may reflect their instrumental and/or symbolic concerns related to crime or bias crime. In turn, their willingness to apply bias crime legislation to hypothetical bias crimes may reflect how well a particular incident mirrors the concerns that motivate their general support for such legislation. While some people's opinions may be solely dependent on security concerns or perceptions of, and threats to, social cohesion, many are likely to reflect a relative weighing of both. The greater people's perceptions of the seriousness and harmfulness of crime or bias crime and their own and others' vulnerability to it, the more security may trump symbolic concerns. People who are less concerned with security—perhaps those who are familiar with the generally non-violent, low-level nature of the typical bias crime—may hold opinions influenced more by concerns related to social diversity and tolerance, although their instrumental concerns still will likely impact the nature of their support or opposition to bias crime legislation. The exploratory nature of the current study provides an opportunity for the relevance of such issues to be revealed.

The Current Study

Unfortunately, given the nature of the research on the topic of study and thus the inability to more strongly connect the theoretical perspectives offered to views on bias crime legislation, the testing of a structured, hypothesis-driven model of public opinion on the issue was not warranted. Testing such a structured model might run the risk of prepackaging views the content and direction of which are currently unknown. Thus, the current research is exploratory in nature relying on open-ended in-person interviews to more comprehensively explore the possible landscape of adult public opinion on bias crime and bias crime legislation. That said the theoretical perspectives do provide broad domains of thought that may be relevant to such views and thus were incorporated into the interview through general questions on crime and punishment and social diversity and tolerance in addition to questions on bias crime, bias crime legislation, and hypothetical bias crime vignettes. It was the hope that the former might shed light on the public's views on the target issue without limiting their content and direction and help identify key constructs and hypotheses necessary for the future development and testing of a model of those views. Unfortunately, data collection on the questions designed to tap views on social diversity and tolerance was inconsistent because of time constraints and thus such issues are discussed only to the extent that they were independently raised in response to bias crime-related questions.

A purposive sample of 40 residents of rural, western Pennsylvania was recruited for participation. The interviews were conducted between November 2004 and September 2005. All were transcribed and manually coded and analyzed based on the primary areas of interest - views on crime and punishment, bias crime and punishment, hypothetical crime and bias crime vignettes, and bias crime legislation. Each individual interview also was analyzed in terms of the participants' overall view in each area allowing for investigation of influencing factors, comparisons across areas including issues of consistency and contradiction, and an overall interview assessment. Patterns, themes, consistencies, and contradictions were examined across interviews.

CHAPTER 2

The Emergence and Legality of Bias Crime Legislation

To date, some form of bias crime legislation has been enacted by nearly every State as well as the District of Columbia and the Federal Government (Anti-Defamation League-ADL 2007).

Bias Crime Legislation

Legislation used to prosecute bias crime generally takes one of two forms: substantive crimes or sentence enhancements. Substantive bias crimes establish either new crimes that specifically entail an element of prejudice or aggravated offenses that authorize a more severe penalty for a current crime that is proven to be motivated by prejudice, meaning old offenses are re-criminalized into more serious and more harshly punished offenses based on their biased motivation. Such legislation varies in title and language. However, regardless of its content, a biased or prejudicial motivation is considered an element of the offense and must be proven to the finder of fact beyond a reasonable doubt before a defendant may be convicted. In addition to statutes that focus on the biased-motivation of an underlying crime, some states have anti-Klan statutes and/or laws that criminalize behaviors deemed inherently biased such as cross-burning and mask-wearing (ADL 2007; Jacobs and Potter 1998). In the past 10 years, both forms of substantive bias crime legislation have undergone constitutional challenge that has limited the form that such legislation may take and led to greater State reliance on sentence enhancements.

In fact, sentence enhancements account for the majority of bias crime laws (Jacobs and Potter 1998) owing in part to their faring better in the legal arena. Rather than establish separate or new offenses, sentence enhancements upgrade the degree of a current offense or increase its maximum penalty if it is motivated by prejudice. Whereas for a substantive bias crime a defendant is charged with an offense that

13

includes an element of prejudice, for a sentence enhancement no such element is present. Instead, once a defendant is convicted of an offense, the court may increase the sentence within the minimum and maximum sentencing parameters for that offense by demonstrating a biased motivation or sentence the defendant to a penalty beyond that maximum if the biased motivation is proven beyond a reasonable doubt. The biased motivation is relevant only to sentencing, not the determination of guilt or innocence.

Sentence enhancements vary based on the predicate offenses and prejudices to which they apply and the magnitude of their penalties. Currently, most States consider only intimidation or harassment as predicate offenses, while some allow any offense to be eligible for a bias crime enhancement. Still other States enumerate a list of possible predicate offenses ranging from very low-level offenses to rape and murder (Jacobs and Potter 1998). Prejudice based on race, religion and ethnicity/national origin is covered by such legislation in the majority of States. A minority of States cover bias based on sexual orientation, gender, or transgender/gender identity.   In addition, a number of other prejudices, including bias based on sensory handicap, age, marital status, and political affiliation, are included by a handful of States (ADL 2007).   In States with both substantive and enhancement legislation, the prejudices included are generally the same. Finally, the magnitude of bias crime sentence enhancements ranges on average from two to ten years of additional incarceration (Jacobs and Potter 1998).

Another aspect of bias crime legislation similar to both substantive offenses and sentence enhancements is the factual determination required to show prejudicial motivation. Although the level of proof and finder of fact may differ, both types of legislation generally define and interpret the motivation in the same way. However, across States, those definitions and interpretations differ, reflecting one of two dominant forms. The first requires that some level of prejudice be manifested or demonstrated.   Prior to 1993, wording such as "precipitated by animus, hostility, maliciousness or hatred" or "intent to harass and intimidate the victim" was common and both implied a "high degree of emotional intensity behind the offense" (Grattet and Jenness 2001, 678). Legislation so worded often is referred to as a racial animus statute because it requires a direct showing of hate (Lawrence 1999). The second form is the "because of" motivation, which gained popularity in a majority of States after 1993 given its much less stringent criteria and the legitimacy it was granted by the

Supreme Court in *Wisconsin v Mitchell* (1993). In fact the move toward greater use of such statutes partly accounts for the general shift from a focus on "hate" crime early in the development of the issue to "bias" crime in the 1990's (Grattet and Jenness 2001). Generally "because of," or similarly worded statutes, require only that the crime be committed or the victim be "intentionally selected" "based on," "by reason of," or because of" an enumerated prejudice. Because such legislation generally requires no direct showing of hate but rather only biased selection they are often referred to as discriminatory selection statutes. Regardless of the necessary motivational showing, State interpretation determines whether bias or hate must be evident in the current crime or may be based on character evidence or prior prejudiced activity or speech (Lawrence 1999).

In the end, whether the criminal response to bias crime takes the form of a substantive statute or a sentence enhancement, the end result is generally the same-a higher penalty than would have been received for the underlying offense if not for the biased motivation. Together, these two types of legislation serve as the backbone of the criminal response to bias crime although both receive support and backup from civil rights and bias crime reporting statutes.

Emergence of Bias Crime Legislation

According to Grattet and Jenness (2001), the bias crime issue as it emerged in the 1980's was the result of an anti-hate movement born out of the social movements of the preceding decades, which brought increased awareness and understanding of the nature of discrimination and its relation to violence. In brief, the civil rights movement of the 50's, being primarily concerned with the problem of discrimination, identified minority marginality with violent repression and thus focused on the establishment and enhancement of opportunities for minorities throughout society. Relying strongly on its foundation, the civil rights movement of the 60's strove to extend those opportunities beyond the lines of race to religion, national origin, and ancestry. The women's and gay and lesbian movements of later decades redefined the boundaries of who constituted legitimate victims of discrimination and was therefore deserving of the opportunities afforded the victims recognized before them. However, throughout each of these movements groups fought not only for enhanced opportunities for their constituents but also against discriminatory violence. With each passing movement, the understanding that such violence was not only a symptom of marginality but also a tool for its maintenance grew and so to did the emergence and survival of anti-violence projects. The crime victim's movement brought the needs of victims, especially those of violent crimes, to the forefront of the criminal justice system, demanding both legal and extralegal strategies for providing victims with justice. By the early 1980's concerns with the discriminatory victimization of minority groups, established by the earlier liberal, progressive movements, and the victimization of violent crime and a criminal justice system that ignored victims, documented by the primarily conservative victim rights movement, converged. Together these concerns highlighted the issue of bias-motivated violent victimization and the need for a legal response that would come to define the anti-hate movement.

Like the movements from which it grew and whose strategies and goals it reflected, the anti-hate movement evolved piecemeal. In the mid-1980's, racial, religious and ethnic violence took center stage, reflecting the concerns of the mobilized advocacy groups, including the Anti-Defamation League and the Anti-Klan Network, the International Network for Jewish Holocaust Survivors and the Institute for the Prevention and Control of Violence and Extremism. Such groups made bias crime legislation a priority and strongly promoted a Federal hate crime reporting statute based on bias against their primary constituents (Grattet and Jenness 2001). Initially proposed in 1985, the Hate Crime Statistics Act (HCSA) was passed in 1990 (U.S. Congress) and became the first Federal law to directly recognize hate crime. Prior to that time, the only Federal legislation highlighting the victimization of particular groups was 18 USC 245 (U.S. Congress 1968). Passed in 1968, it authorizes Federal jurisdiction over crimes of force or threat of force committed against people because of their participation in Federally-protected civil rights. Although the law covered all citizens equally, it specifically referenced crimes committed because of the victim's "race, color religion or national origin" that interfered with their federally-protected civil rights. Unlike today's designated hate crime statutes, 18 USC 245 based its punishment on the nature of the underlying crime rather than the status of its victim.

The Hate Crime Statistics Act authorizes the Department of Justice to compile data from local law enforcement agencies across the country on crimes manifesting specified prejudices. Early drafts of the Act focused solely on crimes motivated by race, religion and ethnicity, reflecting those groups at the forefront of the anti-hate movement and those already recognized as legitimate victims under Federal anti-discrimination laws. However, the final version included nationality and sexual orientation as Asian and Arab American and the Gay and the National Gay and Lesbian Task Force (NGLTF) joined the effort and convinced Congress that the violent experiences of their constituents were similar to those of more traditionally recognized victims (Grattet and Jenness 2001; Fernandez 1991). For similar reasons, in 1994 disability was added to the Act through the Violent Crime Control and Law Enforcement Act (U.S. Congress 1994). As of 2007, legislation was pending to further include prejudice based on homelessness (U.S. Congress, 2007a).

However, all groups seeking inclusion in the Act are not included without controversy and some are not included at all. Fearing that the inclusion of sexual orientation would signal approval of homosexuality and justify future substantive rights for gays and lesbians, Congress included an "American Family" provision in the Act, which stated in part that "nothing in this act shall be construed...to promote or encourage homosexuality" (U.S. Congress 1990). In addition, gender was rejected as a provision of the initial Act not by Congress but the coalition lobbying for the Act based on its belief that violence against women was qualitatively different and that data on rape and domestic violence was already collected. Scholars contend that the coalition also likely was concerned that the prevalence of gender-based violence would overshadow the victimization of other groups (Grattet and Jenness 2001). In 1994, women's advocacy groups successfully lobbied for the passing of the Violence Against Women Act (VAWA), which stated that "crimes motivated by the victim's gender constitute bias crimes in violation of the victim's right to be free from discrimination on the basis of gender." However, in *U.S. v Morrison* (2000) the Supreme Court ruled the law unconstitutional finding it violated the 5th and 14th Amendments to the Constitution. In 2007, legislation is pending that once again seeks to include gender in the HCSA (U.S. Congress 2007b).

Although the Hate Crime Statistics Act only permits collection of data, it was initially perceived by advocates and Congress as a vital first step in addressing bias crime. It not only would allow the extent of the problem to be assessed but would send a strong message likely to increase awareness and sensitivity on the part of the public, politicians and law enforcement and create a solid foundation for improving understanding and legal responses to such crime (Jacobs and Potter 1998). After its initial passage, the continued pressure of social movements, and a concerned Congress ready to send a stronger message condemning bigotry and violence, led to the Federal Hate Crimes Sentencing Enhancement Act (Grattet and Jenness 2001). Effective as of 1995, it provides a Federal sentencing commission guideline authorizing a three-level sentence enhancement when a Federal hate crime is proven beyond a reasonable doubt. It defines hate crime as "a crime in which the defendant intentionally selects a victim or in the case of a property crime, the property that is the object of the crime, because of the actual or perceived race, color, religion, national origin, ethnicity, gender (excludes sex crimes), disability, or sexual orientation of any person" (U.S. Congress 1995) The inclusion of the previously controversial sexual orientation and gender provisions has been accounted for by the enormity of the Violent Crime Control and Law Enforcement Act of 1994 of which the Act was a part as well as by the desire of the U.S. Sentencing Commission to align its provisions with those of current Federal civil rights offenses (Jacobs and Potter 1998).

Since 1999, the Federal Government has unsuccessfully attempted to pass legislation that would expand its ability to address bias crime by helping States with their efforts. Currently pending in the House of Representatives, the Local Law Enforcement Hate Crimes Prevention Act of 2007 would authorize the Federal Government to provide state, local and Tribal law enforcement, at their request, with "technical, forensic, prosecutorial" and other forms of assistance to investigate and prosecute violent felonies causing death or serious bodily injury "motivated by prejudice based on the actual or perceived race, color, religion, national origin, gender, sexual orientation, gender identity or disability of the victim" or that violate the jurisdiction's hate crime laws. It also would permit the Federal government to "impose a fine and/or prison term of up to 10 years" on anyone who willfully attempts or causes bodily injury because of the actual or perceived status categories identified above (U.S. Congress 2007c). Similar legislation, entitled the Matthew Shepard Local Law Enforcement Hate Crimes Prevention Act of 2007, has been proposed in the Senate (U.S. Congress 2007d).

State bias crime legislation preceded Federal efforts, emerging in the late 1970's, but in response to the same social movements and advocacy groups that eventually pressured Federal action. Initially, States experimented with various approaches to such legislation, however, as precedent emerged and the ADL put forth its own model legislation in 1981, their approaches began to converge but not without variation particularly with regards to status provisions. Race, religion, ethnicity/national origin, and disability are recognized in almost every State with such legislation but sexual orientation, gender and disability, while included by 40 to 50 percent of those States, still face open opposition in many States based on controversy similar to that at the Federal level. Additional provisions such as age, political affiliation and military status are recognized by States haphazardly primarily because of their newness as recognized victims and their lack of advocacy (Grattet and Jenness 2001). As previously indicated, State laws also vary in terms of the type of bias crime legislation and the magnitude of its penalty. To date, Wyoming is the only State without any form of bias crime legislation (ADL 2007).

Constitutionality of Bias Crime Legislation

In addition to the influence of advocacy groups and social movements, courts have impacted the bias crime legislation passed by both the Federal and State governments. Bias crime legislation has undergone substantial legal scrutiny with over 40 cases reviewed by the U.S. appellate courts alone. However, the Supreme Court's decisions in *R.A.V., Black, Mitchell, and* Apprendi have set the legal parameters for constitutional bias crime legislation shaping and legitimating the legal response to bias crime. And more recently, Supreme Court rulings in Blakely, *Booker* and *Cunningham* have addressed sentencing enhancements in ways that may further impact bias crime legislation.

To date, the nature of constitutional substantive bias crime legislation remains less than clear. Such legislation was first challenged in 1992 in the case of *R.A.V. v City of St. Paul* in which the court ruled unconstitutional, as a violation of the First Amendment, legislation that attempted to criminalize fighting words in a manner that was not content neutral. The court argued that criminalizing symbolic speech that reflected certain viewpoints, such as burning a cross, without similarly criminalizing all such symbolic speech "creates the possibility that the city is seeking to handicap the expression of particular ideas" (391).[1] It also acknowledged the wide discretion sentencing judges traditionally possess in determining appropriate sentencing factors and the traditional status of motive as one such factor, suggesting that bias crime legislation might encounter less constitutional difficulty as a decision of sentencing rather than guilt or innocence, which led to the increased use of sentence enhancements over substantive bias crime statutes. However, in 2002 in the case of *Virginia v Black et al* the court noted that even under *R.A.V.* a particular type of content discrimination does not violate the First Amendment when the basis for it consists entirely of the very reason its entire class of speech is prohibited and thus ruled constitutional legislation that banned cross burning carried out with the intent to intimidate.[2] Although the ramifications of Black are yet unclear, they could 1) increase the use of substantive bias crime offenses or 2) continue the move toward greater use of sentence enhancements, which seem to involve less constitutional confusion.

The Supreme Court first reviewed the constitutionality of bias crime sentence enhancements in 1993 in the case of *Wisconsin v. Mitchell* in which the defendant was sentenced to seven years for a crime with a two-year maximum sentence because his victim was intentionally selected because of race. The court held that "the First Amendment does not prohibit a state from providing enhanced punishment for a crime based on the actor's discriminatory purpose in committing the crime" and that "the First Amendment...does not prohibit the evidentiary use of speech to establish the elements of a crime or to prove motive or intent" (489). Its ruling served as official approval of "because of" bias motivational standards that require only discrimination rather than hate; defined enhancements as more severe punishment for conduct rather than speech, making it possible to avoid First Amendment concerns by choosing enhancements rather than substantive crimes to punish bias crime; and permitted additional punishment based on a showing of bias by a preponderance of the evidence. Thereby, it made it possible to avoid First Amendment concerns and prove bias more easily through use of enhancements rather than substantive offenses.[3] However, in 2000, in the case of *Apprendi v New Jersey*, the Court increased the legal standards of proof for enhancements such as the one in *Mitchell*. It ruled that, "the Constitution requires that any fact that increases the penalty for a crime beyond the prescribed statutory maximum, other than the fact of a prior conviction, must be submitted to a jury and proved beyond a reasonable doubt" (2362).[4]

Since *Apprendi*, the last Supreme Court case to directly address a hate crime enhancement, the Court has made several rulings on enhancement legislation in general. In 2004, the Supreme Court ruled in *Blakely v Washington* that "a prison sentence within the statutory maximum for the conviction offense could also violate *Apprendi*". The case involved a sentence based on a guideline system that identified a standard guideline sentence based on "facts reflected in the jury verdict or admitted by the defendant" but then allowed judicial departures based on "statutorily enumerated" factors (Frase 2007, 416). Although under such guidelines the top of the standard sentence is the statutory maximum, the Court ruled that not only did *Apprendi* apply to departures above the statutory maximum but also any fact that increased the sentence within the statutory maximum that required a finding beyond the jury verdict or defendant plea. In *United States v Booker* (2005), the Court held that the *Apprendi-Blakely* requirements also applied to the Federal sentencing guidelines. In 2007 in *Cunningham v California*, the Court further ruled that such requirements also apply to State statutory determinate sentencing systems with discretionary upper levels if the system "does not authorize use of the upper term unless further facts [are] found" (Frase 2007, 421).

   To date, the impact of *Apprendi* and the newer enhancement cases on bias crime sentences has not been studied, however Frase (2007) notes that it could potentially influence prosecutorial charging and plea bargaining, as they offer methods of avoiding compliance with *Apprendi*. As a result, they could influence bias crime sentencing decisions. Fearing the risk of taking the bias crime issue to juries that may resist or not be convinced beyond a reasonable doubt as to *Apprendi* facts, prosecutors may avoid it through increased charging or severity of charging or greater use of consecutive sentencing to maintain or possibly increase an "enhancement" comparable to that authorized by bias crime legislation. Or, they may be more willing to bargain such cases, perhaps resulting in less severe sentences to the extent that defendants are threatened by the possibility of bias crime enhancements and/or the jury's exposure to the relevant facts. At the same time, Frase points out that such tactics could be avoided all together if State and Federal hate crime legislation is changed by adopting indeterminate sentencing or an advisory guidelines system, both of which are immune from the *Apprendi* and follow-up case rulings. Either way, such rulings provide increased protection for defendants threatened with hate crime sentence enhancements on certain sentencing schemes but not others and thus could result in disparity in such sentences and/or a move towards sentencing schemes that allow for fewer protections or a shift back to greater use of substantive hate crime legislation.

It also should be noted that bias crime legislation has been challenged on due process and legal protection grounds, although neither has been successful. Thus, the Supreme Court's influence on such legislation has been primarily on how it has shaped governments' decisions whether to use substantive bias crimes or sentence enhancements and the nature those laws have and continue to take. In so doing, Courts are critical to defining how governments can and will execute their desire or need to protect victims of bias crime through bias crime legislation.

CHAPTER 3
Scholarly Perspectives on Bias Crime Legislation

Whatever the legality of bias crime legislation, advocacy groups, legislatures, and the public have championed it. However, academics continue to disagree about the reasons and need for such legislation. One train of thought is that bias crime legislation is a symbolic response to a socially-constructed hate crime epidemic that serves the instrumental needs of those involved but otherwise is unnecessary (Jacobs and Henry 1996; Jacobs and Potter 1998). Another is that bias crime legislation is necessary as an instrumental response to a "different" crime that has heretofore been ignored, thereby denying justice to both its victims and perpetrators (Lawrence 1999). These perspectives capture potential justifications that perhaps propelled the demands of social movements into legislative reality and may offer insight into ongoing support for bias crime legislation.

The Socially-Constructed Hate Crime Epidemic

The theory of a socially-constructed hate crime epidemic is presented most comprehensively by James B. Jacobs and his colleagues (1998, 1996) who claim that rather than originating from a strong and objective foundation, the belief since the mid-1980's in a hate crime "epidemic" that requires a response rests primarily on the constant reiteration of such by advocacy groups. They argue that the term "epidemic" has been adopted by such groups to persuade others of the immediate need for attention, resources, and action both in the social and political arenas. The worse the problem presented, the more likely and more quickly groups are to gain support and progress in their attempts to gain clout for their constituents, through symbolic acknowledgment of their status and plight as potential or actual victims, and to eradicate bias. The perception of bias crime as an out-of-control crime threat presents an obvious vehicle for motivating public concern and demand for a response regardless of whether it offers an accurate depiction of the problem.

As defined by Webster's Dictionary and the Center for Disease Control and Prevention, an epidemic by nature is "excessive, prevalent; contagious" and/or "occurs when the incidence of a condition is higher than normal or higher than what health officials expect" (Jacobs and Henry 1996, 366-367). To date, the validity and reliability of official and unofficial data on bias crime by which to assess the hate crime "epidemic" is questioned (McDevitt, Balboni, et al. 2001),[5] and Jacobs and his colleagues (1996, 1998) claim that the evidence presented by advocacy groups as to the hate crime epidemic fails to support the use of either definition with regards to bias crime. They cite problems that plague the validity of unofficial bias crime data reported by advocacy groups including the breadth of their sources and their definitions of bias crime, which may lead to the reporting of non-crimes.[6] In particular, they emphasize the domination of "low-end" (non-violent) incidents in the data as well as the use of data on biased attitudes as evidence of the epidemic. Jacobs and Potter (1998) also provide examples they believe demonstrate a contradiction between the epidemic lingo and data presented, citing the National Gay and Lesbian Task Force's continued claims of an epidemic on the heels of reporting a substantial decrease in hate crimes and the inability to reconcile a survey of student violence reported by the National Institute Against Prejudice and Violence (NIAPV) with figures even within the ballpark of those presented by official data. The authors do not claim that unofficial, or official, data are off the mark but rather only that when fully analyzed and reported there is no evidence that bias crime is increasing at a geometric rate and thus no validity to the epidemic label it has received that has supported the need for bias crime legislation. Their conclusions receive confirmation from Byers and Zeller's (2001) analysis of UCR hate crime data from 1991-1998 that led them to refute the existence of a hate crime epidemic.

But what may be a loose use of data to demonstrate the crisis has been enough for the media, academics and politicians to join the cause (Jacobs and Henry 1996; Jacobs and Potter 1998). The media has had no problem relying on advocacy groups' recognition of bias crime as an epidemic and conveying that perception to the public. In fact, Jacobs and his colleagues (1996) report that fifty-six news articles referred to the "epidemic of hate crime" between 1993 and 1995 alone, articles that often relied on questionable statistics or simply made the assertion without evidence. This media attention has been identified as crucial to the publicizing of the hate crime issue and both public and political support for advocacy demands for a legal response (Grattet and Jenness 1996) as well as the creation of a moral panic – a disproportionate reaction to a perceived social threat – in the late 1990's (Colomb and Damphousse 2004). Colomb and Damphousse's research revealed a "dramatic increase in the number of stories about hate crime...even as the numbers of hate crime offenses declined" from 1997-1999 and a "heightened level of concern and consensus about the "problem" of hate crime," when in fact during those years hate crime numbers actually where on the decline and were primarily low-level, non-violent offenses (7). The researchers concluded that the media "acted as the primary claims-maker by allocating considerable news space and resources to a crime category that constituted less than 1% of all crimes annually...and it drew support for its position from activist groups by using them as sources to support their position" (8).

Jacobs and Potter (1998) note that such a response to the problem is not surprising given that both crime and hate sell. They further suggest that scholarly work on the topic of bias crime reflects authors who may "create a theory in search of a problem," citing for one Levin and McDevitt's (1993) economic and social-psychological explanations of what their book's title aptly refers to as "The Rising Tide of Bigotry and Bloodshed: Hate Crimes." According to Jacobs and Potter (1998), the problem with such works is that they often rely on anecdotal evidence of horrific hate-based crimes but provide very little strong evidence for the perception of the problem as overwhelming and out of control. Again, the authors (1996) searched and found that between 1992 and 1995 thirty-one journal articles referred to and accepted without question the term "epidemic" as an appropriate description of the bias crime issue. They concluded that there is little doubt that constant reinforcement of the advocacy groups' epidemic by the news and scholarly arenas helped motivate or at least justify the prolific legislative response to bias crime in the 90's. According to Jacobs and Potter, once the issue became public domain there was great incentive to follow it through as bias crime legislation provides a perfect, even if only symbolic, opportunity to oppose and respond to crime and bigotry while sending a powerful political message to minority constituents. In the end, Jacobs and Potter account for the comprehensive social and political acceptance of and response to the "epidemic" not necessarily in terms of external groups' inability to judge the scope of the problem but in the lack of the need to do so. The epidemic "worked" for all involved.

According to Jacobs and Potter (1998), the problem with the social construction of the hate crime epidemic is that it supports the assumption that hate crimes require a different response than similar underlying crimes otherwise motivated when in their opinion the data do not support such a response. In fact, they point to historic support for the claim that marginalized and minority groups experience much less violent status-motivated crime today than in the past, and suggest that the cry of epidemic has more to do with an increased intolerance of prejudice and decreased acceptance of bias crime than any uncontrolled plague sweeping the nation. In the end, they and others fear that the hyperbole surrounding the issue may do more harm than good. First, it may result in the misallocation of scarce resources across the arenas addressing or affected by the bias crime issue. Second, as Grattet and Jenness (2001, 692) argue, hate crime may become so "normalized" that its ability to grab attention will be lost as well as any symbolic force bias crime legislation might have. Finally, the vision of the nation as beset by hate-based social division portrayed by the hate crime epidemic may become a self-fulfilling prophecy by endorsing "identity politics" (Jacobs and Potter 1998). The overemphasis, if not exaggeration, of the current state of inter-group conflict that the claim of a bias crime epidemic supports might encourage individuals and groups to define themselves by their differences and their victim status in the competition to be acknowledged as deserving of special protection-a competition bound to increase resentment "that in turn contributes to the balkanization of American society, not to its unification" (131). Jacob and Potters' recommendation, "repeal the new wave of hate crime laws and enforce the generic criminal laws evenhandedly and without prejudice" (145). However, there are scholars who certainly advocate such an approach.

Hate Crime – A Different Crime Demanding Greater Punishment

In criticizing the epidemic depiction of the bias crime issue and posing its potentially negative consequences, authors such as Jacobs and Potter come into conflict with scholars who strongly support the current legislative response to the issue as "beneficial and consistent with the aims of the criminal law" (Levin 1999, 12). However, such scholars do not rely primarily on the prevalence issue but rather justify their stance by contending that bias crime is somehow "different", "worse by definition," making it more severe and thus worthy of harsher punishment. For them, the uniqueness of bias crime revolves around its biased motivation, which for various reasons they argue legally justifies differential and harsher treatment. Motive, whether recognized as an element of a crime or a factor in sentencing, traditionally has been accepted as a legally valid means of distinguishing and treating differently otherwise similar crimes, a claim most recently reaffirmed in the context of bias crime in the Supreme Court's *Mitchell* (1993) opinion. To many proponents of bias crime, the prejudicial motivation of such crime speaks directly to its legal culpability and/or greater harm, both of which criminal law doctrine traditionally has relied upon in determining crime seriousness and setting appropriate criminal punishment (Lawrence 1999).[7]

Legal Culpability
Based on a legal culpability argument, hate crimes deserve a greater punishment because the biased offender is more blameworthy than the offender who commits a parallel non-bias motivated crime. In essence the offender's biased motivation acts as a second tier mental state above that required for culpability for the parallel crime. According to Lawrence (1999), "the culpability associated with the commission of parallel crimes and bias crime is thus identical in terms of *what* the offender did and differs only in respect to *why* the offender did so. The relevance of this difference to the calculation of crime seriousness" is that greater culpability reflects either a greater harm, lesser "social value of activity resulting in bias crimes" than those resulting in non-bias crimes, or because it violates society's equality principle (60).

Hurd and Moore (2004) question the idea that differential treatment of bias crime is or should be based on its impact on an offender's culpability, and argue that a calculation of culpability based on hateful motivation is different than traditional analyses of blameworthiness. First, they note that extreme emotional states traditionally related to culpability, such as provocation and passion, have generally been used not as enhancers, as is the case with bias crime legislation, but as defenses allowing mitigation or exoneration under the assumption that such states "suspend the sort of reasoned judgment that is required for full responsibility" (20). This argument fits well with Jacobs and Potter's (1998) suggestion that even if the relative reprehensiveness of motives could be assessed, which they doubt possible, a hate-based motivation could be used to lessen culpability, particularly if an offender's hate is the result of childhood indoctrination. Second, Hurd and Moore (2004) claim that in instances in which measures of viciousness have been used in culpability assessment, such as premeditation/deliberation, they only provide a basis for demonstrating a motivation for offenders' actions and thus pointing to their level of culpability rather than the need to know the specific reason for the crime in order to determine blameworthiness as proponents of the culpability justification for bias crime legislation suggest.

Finally, Hurd and Moore (2004) argue that the traditional use of motivations, in the sense that specific intents are often considered in assessing culpability, are based on the need to understand the instrumentality of one's acts rather than to punish an offender for his emotional or dispositional state, which is the case if bias is a basis for greater culpability. The former denotes an offender's desire to "bring about a future state of affairs," whereas the latter identifies an "emotional state rather than end to which actions are means" (19). While it is possible that some biased offenders commit their crimes for purposes of future goals related to their biased or prejudiced dispositions, it is also true that many may commit their crimes harboring bias or prejudice because it is their natural state but without it serving as a the basis for some future goal of their offense. This is especially true for discrimination selection statutes for which offenders can be convicted based on selection unrelated to actual hateful or prejudicial motivations.   Adams (2005) notes that the nature of discriminatory selection statutes fails to accurately distinguish between crimes based on hatred or bigotry and those based on false perceptions of certain groups that make them more appealing as criminal targets that may have nothing to do with hatred or bigotry (ex. belief that gay men are weaker and thus less willing to successfully resist an attack). Taking this argument a step further, all crimes involving discriminatory selection may not be motivated by bigotry or hatred but merely be motivated by a conventional criminal incentive that offers an opportunity to discriminate. Messner, McHugh and Felson's (2004) research on bias and conventional assaults indicates that biased offenders may be more versatile than specialized, meaning that "their crime is more a reflection of criminality than of their extreme hatred for particular groups" suggesting that the "role of bigotry as a motivator of bias crime is more limited than often suspected…Bigotry may serve as a factor in the selection of the particular victim rather than as the catalyst to the criminal act" (16). They also conclude that many bias crimes are similar to conventional crimes in that they are based more on instrumental concerns than hatred. Thus, statutes that net such versatile offenders rather than specialized hate-based offenders would seem to have less justification for the unique classification of bias crimes based on bigotry and hatred and its ramifications. Hurd and Moore (2004) contend that in such instances bias crime legislation punishes biased offenders more severely for their "bad character" rather than their underlying bad act or bad intention, and assert that such punishment is inappropriate because it punishes for a trait rather than a choice. Finally, they make the point that motivations resist easy rankings and that to justify picking out offenders of hate based offenses for differential treatment based on culpability requires acknowledgement of arbitrary treatment or "revising our culpability doctrines so as to take into account, and dish out punishment in proportion to, all culpable emotional and dispositional belief states that motivate defendants to do criminal deeds" (25).

Greater Wrongdoing – Greater Harm
However, as Lawrence (1999) argues, greater punishment for bias crimes also can be justified based on its greater level of wrongdoing – its greater harm. The concept of harm, though less developed in criminal law doctrine than culpability, is intuitive and demonstrated by the focus on consequences in determining crime seriousness. The relevance of greater harm to hate crime encapsulates the belief that the discriminatory or biased nature of bias crime results in more extensive damage. Enhanced punishment therefore can be justified by proportionality requirements of punishment under retributive punishment theory and more consequentialist theory that emphasizes deterrence and education limited by just deserts. Advocates of the greater harm principle argue that bias crimes have greater physical and psychological impacts on their immediate victims, and that they result in greater victimization of the status group(s) of their victims and society at large than do their parallel non-bias crimes.

Some evidence exists to support the claim that bias crimes are more physically and psychologically harmful to their immediate victims than non-biased crimes. Along with Lawrence (1999) who documents that physical assaults are more common in bias-motivated than their parallel crimes, Levin and McDevitt (1993) report that hate crimes are more likely than similar non-hate-based crimes to be personal rather than property based, and if involving assaults are more likely to be excessively brutal and/or involve multiple offenders, and/or victim hospitalization. In fact, Weisburd and Levin (1994) report that "bias crimes…are four times more likely to involve assaultive behavior," and that such assaults are "twice as likely to involve injury to the victim and four times as likely to require hospitalization" (23). The involvement of more serious injuries in bias crimes also was revealed in Messner, McHugh and Felon's (2004) research comparing bias and conventional assaults, a finding they suggest may result from the fact that such offenses are more likely to be unprovoked and thus require stronger violent and antisocial proclivities to commit. Bias crimes also have been found to more often involve serial attacks that tend to increase in seriousness overtime (Barnes and Ephross 1994; Wexler and Marx 1986). Relatively little research exists on the psychological and emotional impacts of bias crime and even less directly compares the bias and non-bias victim impacts. However, research has documented some greater psychological and physiological symptoms of bias crime victims (National Institute Against Prejudice and Violence 1986, 1989), including nervousness, anger, loss of friendships, interpersonal skills and ability to sleep and concentrate (Ehrlich et al. 1994), anxiety, depression, and traumatic stress (Herek, Cogan, and Gillis 1999) lack of will to live, and more difficulty dealing with, and recovering from, victimization (McDevitt et al. 2001). Most recently, research has demonstrated the greater severity of psychological effects of bias crime in terms of their number, intensity and duration (McDevitt et al. 2001).[8]

However, findings on the physical and psychological impacts of bias crime on victims are by no means consistent nor do studies that find differences reveal that they exist across the board or that bias crimes are more different than similar to conventional crimes in a way that would easily distinguish them. For example, Martin's (1996) findings contradict Levi and McDevitt's (1993) findings as to greater injury for victims of bias assaults. In addition, McDevitt and his associates (2001) found no significant differences for bias and non-bias assault victims across 12 indicators of post-victimization behavioral changes. Similarly, a Barnes and Ephross (1994) study that compared their own findings on the reactions of 72 hate crime victims to similar previous findings for general crime victims found none of the significant differences in the manner and degree of victim suffering suggested by the aforementioned studies. And, Messner, McHugh and Felson (2004) concluded that while there are differences between bias and conventional assaults, bias offenders are more versatile than specialized and their bias crimes are not all that unique compared to their non-bias offenses. Of course, some differences across studies seeking to distinguish bias crimes can be attributed to methodological issues, some of which place the reliability and generalizeability of the reported findings themselves in question and emphasize the need for replication and/or stronger designs. Such issues include comparative conclusions based on research without comparison groups (NIAPV 1986-1989), non-representative and/or small samples (Barnes and Ephross 1994; Herek, Gillis, et al. 1997; McDevitt et al. 2001), low response rates (McDevitt et al. 2001) and measurement issues related to victim self-reporting/identification of crime as bias-motivated (Herek, Gillis, et al. 1997).

One interesting finding on the psychological impact of bias crime is that victims of bias assault are less likely than their non-bias counterparts to experience decreased self-esteem (Barnes and Ephross 1994), a finding likely related to the facts that bias-crime victims are more likely to be attacked by strangers, view their attack as unprovoked, accept no responsibility for the crime, and point to the community's responsibility to prevent further attacks (McDevitt et al. 2001). However, it also provides a more comprehensive, though more theoretical and anecdotal, demonstration of the relatively unique quality of bias crime on which much of the greater harm argument relies - the general irrelevance of the particular victim in bias crimes. Scholars argue that because of this unique element, bias crime has a more destructive impact on the individual, community and society than most crimes. Some scholars base this conclusion on bias crime's inherent discrimination, an element that the Supreme Court has recognized as "...a unique evil that government has a compelling interest to prevent" (*Roberts v United States Jaycees* 1984) and has backed in terms of its support of laws punishing its existence in housing, public education and employment. Discriminatory attacks may "trigger the history and social context of prejudice and prejudicial violence against the victim and his group" (Lawrence 1999, 41). The resulting racial stigmatization and the harm it manifests are but one explanation for the increased psychological trauma of bias crime victims (Lawrence 1999).

A closely related argument is that of victim interchangeability, which recognizes that targets are chosen for their actual or perceived status rather than their personal identity (Lawrence 1999; Levin and McDevitt 1993; McDevitt et al. 2001). Interchangeability is important because it signals to victims their powerlessness to ward off future attacks because of the usually permanent nature of that status, another reason offered for the findings of increased psychological trauma for bias crime victims (Lawrence 1999). Further, it signals to victims' wider communities-groups of individuals who share the victim's status-that they too have been and can be further victimized. Beyond sympathy and empathy for the immediate victim, individuals within the community may themselves experience the fear and intimidation of the threat reflected in the previous crime (Lawrence 1999). In fact, it is believed by some that the secondary or vicarious victimization of bias crime is not accidental but intended given that in a pure bias crime the actual victim does not matter only their status (Levin and McDevitt 1993; McDevitt et al. 2001).

The impact of vicarious victimization may lead to problems more severe than increased anger, fear, behavioral changes, and a sense of loss of freedom by immediate and secondary victims. The Supreme Court in *Mitchell* (1993), relying on the words of the State of Wisconsin, identified, in addition to distinct emotional harms on their victims, an increased likelihood of bias-motivated crimes to "provoke retaliatory crimes, and incite community unrest" (488-498). Thus, bias crimes are expected to exacerbate inter-group tension and promote potentially violent conflict resulting from the need of the attacked group to show solidarity against the perceived group of the offender. More abstract, but no less critical, are the claimed social harms of bias crimes. Lawrence argues that, "Bias crimes implicate a social history of prejudice, discrimination, and even oppression. As such, they cause a greater harm than parallel crimes to the immediate victim of the crime, the target community of the crime, and the general society" (1999, 44). Specifically, bias crimes may serve to isolate individuals and communities, violate egalitarian ideals, and thus polarize American society. More generally, Weisburd and Levin (1994) point out that bias crime, in part owing to these greater social harms, may lead to fear and anxiety prompted by a public perception of the breakdown of social order and security.

Overall, findings of the greater wrongdoing-harm resulting from bias crime, whether resulting from physical brutality or psychological aspects related to interchangeability, discrimination and inequality, and striking at the individual, community or society, are presented as justifications for the need for separate and more severe sanctions for bias crime. However, opponents of the greater wrongdoing or harm theory question both the evidence and arguments provided to justify such differential treatment.

Jacobs and Potter (1998) question the greater physical brutality of bias crime. They point to the use of bias crime figures alone to make comparisons between bias and non-bias crimes as well as the use of physical injury and threatening words as proof of the excessive brutality of bias crime. Even assuming that future research demonstrated such a physical distinction between bias and non-bias crimes, Hurd and Moore (2004) argue that hate or biased motivation is an "over and under-inclusive" proxy for "more provable facts" of harm (3). Concurring, Adams (2005) argues that if it is the case that bias crimes compared to non-bias crimes are "excessively brutal, involve torture, or…tend to be committed by multiple offenders" then if there is a desire to have specific hate crime legislation, it should be based on the presence or absence of these specific objective factors – the crimes actual harm – rather than the "hostile or prejudiced beliefs" that motivated them (22). Reliance on the latter also would address concerns regarding first amendment freedoms and equal treatment that are often raised about bias crime legislation. And Jacobs and Potter (1998) similarly claim that there is no need to address any differences between bias and non-bias crimes because current law in fact already allows for considerations such as violence level, multiple attackers, risk of future offending, and level of victim and public injury in determinations of crime seriousness and sanctioning.

As far as the enhanced psychological damage of bias crime, opponents again critique the evidence and overall argument. Jacobs and Potter (1998) specifically point to the non-comparative nature of frequently cited data claiming to demonstrate such injury and argue that it actually only supports the finding that victims of bias crime experience psychological injury and nothing more. They also highlight the few comparative studies that have been conducted that found no differences in the psychological effects of bias and non-bias crimes, such as research by Barnes and Ephross (1994). Similar to their argument concerning physical harm, Hurd and Moore (2004) note the ill fit of hateful motivation as a proxy for the psychic harm to the victim. Given that psychic harm is a result of the perception of a hateful motivation and not necessarily the actual motivation, they suggest that a better though still problematic proxy would be the victim's perception of the defendant's motivation. Better yet they support actually assessing the actual psychic harm of the crime. Both sets of researchers also point out the fact that the actus reus of current criminal law often already takes into account greater collateral harms of crime, and victim impact statements are also often provided as a means of assessing such harms.

Although the same arguments apply for secondary/vicarious victimization, Jacobs and Potter (1998) further argue that such impact is in no way unique to bias crime, and they point to polls that show Americans consistently rank crime in general as a primary problem facing the country. More specifically, they argue that in most crime scenarios the impact of the crime once reported is bound to affect those closest to the particular crime and/or victim and/or its specific context.[9] They also question whether third-party anguish should be relevant to sanctioning, arguing the unacceptability of punishing as a bias crime a black-on-white robbery more severely because of the terror of black robbers in a predominantly white neighborhood and the resulting white flight and lowered tax base, and claiming that the reverse in the guise of a bias crime is no less acceptable. Hurd and Moore (2005) reiterate their bad proxy argument suggesting the need to avoid over or under-inclusive measures of vicarious harm and rely instead on more direct indices such as victim impact statements.

As for the greater harm to society in general argument often put forth by opponents of bias crime legislation, numerous counter-arguments are made. As far as the possibility of group conflict, from which retaliation could result, Jacobs and Potter argue that to make such considerations legally relevant divorces "criminal responsibility and blameworthiness from its roots in the defendant's culpability" (1998, 88), and conceivably bases punishment on the willingness of the attacked "community" to take the law into their own hands. Hurd and Moore (2004) agree stating that the appropriate action is not greater punishment for the original offender but punishing the vigilantes for their own crimes. As far as the potential for a perception of a breakdown in order and security, they note that the same problem exists in the presence of all crimes, particularly perhaps those that are violent or celebrated. Finally, in terms of polarization, they counter by pointing out the equally possible likelihood that hate crimes will result in a sense of social unity against such hate, and Jacobs and Potter (1998) add that bias crime legislation itself could actually serve to polarize or balkanize society by promoting identity politics.

Considering many of these counterarguments, much of the greater harm argument when broken down seems to be about more than the sum of a hate crime's tangible harm. Such concerns are often referred to as a deontological greater harm argument. In essence the problem is not a greater harm based on the particular hate-based crime but the greater inherent harm of such crime. According to Hurd and Moore (2004), four aspects of hate crime are cited as explanations for this more organic harm: greater vulnerability of hate crime victims, targeting based on immutable characteristics, the historical and thus repetitive nature of such crimes, and the message of hate sent to victims' peer groups. However, Hurd and Moore argue that even if these are aspects of hate crime that make it somehow worse and appropriate for greater punishment, than once again hateful motivation is not the best proxy for the same reasons as heretofore presented. However, aside from that, even if they do, basing greater punishment on such aspects is problematic.

According to Hurd and Moore (2004), the greater vulnerability of hate crime victims in part simply acknowledges their increased susceptibility to the harms previously discussed and is thus an objective harm-based argument. Taken further, it becomes an argument for greater punishment of all crimes with vulnerable victims and since that category goes well beyond hate crime victims the argument cannot be used to distinguish hate crimes and justify only its greater punishment. A slightly more extreme version of the vulnerability argument is put forth by Harel and Parchomovsky (1999) often referred to as the equality thesis or principle. From this perspective, differential treatment for bias crimes is based on a perceived duty of society to the equal protection of citizens from crime. Harel and Parchomovsky contend that since some groups are more vulnerable to criminal victimization based on their status, equalitarian protection demands different punishments for those who choose such victims. However, Adams (2005) argues that to punish a biased-offender more because his crime targets a particularly vulnerable group would justify the crediting of non-biased offenders for choosing their victims randomly. Since "we attach no moral significance, per se, to eliminating disproportionate victimization by bringing about a more equitable distribution of criminal harms" it should not be the basis for greater punishment unless we are also willing to recognize it as a basis for mitigated punishment (6). He also contends that basing differential treatment of biased crimes on the increased vulnerability of its victims is unsustainable because it disregards to key issues: 1) that there is no basis on which to distinguish the status provisions of such legislation and the range of additional factors demonstrated to place individuals at greater risk of victimization, such as poverty, and 2) that it would actually justify the enhanced punishment of all crimes committed against the vulnerable populations rather than just those based on bigotry and hatred that bias crime legislation is designed to prevent. In fact research suggests that for racial minorities the risk of becoming a victim of a bias assault is similar to the risk of a conventional assault, suggesting little basis for treating the victim of a bias crime any differently (Messner et al. 2004).

In terms of the other organic harm elements, Hurd and Moore (2004) argue that they too cannot be sustained as a basis for greater harm for bias crimes. As far as the immutable basis for selecting a bias crime victim, they suggest that distinguishing hate crime and making it worse because the victim cannot change the motivating factor is akin to saying that innocent non-bias crime victims, who can change a motivating factor for a crime against them, should be required to do so, in essence making such people blameworthy for crimes committed against them. To those who argue that punishing hate crimes more harshly is akin to punishing recidivists more because of the history of hate-based crime, they argue that the two are distinct because the latter is actually responsible for both the historical and the current crime whereas the hate-based offender is only blameworthy for his offense and cannot be deemed a bad character based on the historical actions of others. And if the argument is that hate-based offenders should be held to a higher degree of awareness of the evil of their actions because of such history, it is hard to conceive of why the same could not be said of all violent criminals.

Finally, Jacobs and Potter (1998) critique the overall greater harm argument for bias crime legislation because of its ramifications for the First Amendment. They claim that "the greater harm hypothesis is most plausible at the margin of the criminal law where speech blends into criminal conduct," meaning it cannot easily be separated from the highly offensive nature of the conduct inherent in the message it is intended to send (84). It is in the hate, which just happens to be conveyed through a criminal act, that the expected greater harm of bias crime exists. It is the extra punishment for that hate that evokes First Amendment concerns with bias crime legislation. To date the Courts have overruled legislation that strives to avoid the harm of hate by directly denying the right of speech or expression in the guise of group libel or campus speech codes and even some bias crime laws. In so doing they have recognized the threat to the First Amendment posed by content-based or non-viewpoint-neutral legislation even in the face of the potentially traumatic effects of hate. While "viewpoint-neutral" bias crime legislation has passed challenge by the Supreme Court, which distinguishes speech and expression from the act of conveying it through crime or victim selection, Jacobs and Potter argue that such is "a distinction without a difference" (129) in that in the end such laws seek through additional punishment of bias-motivated crimes to denounce "prejudiced and bigoted thought and expression" protected by the First Amendment (128).

Other Arguments – Deterrence and Expressivist Theory

Although the greater wrongdoing argument seems to have become the backbone of justification for bias crime legislation, other arguments have been put forth. Three such claims rely on deterrence and expressivist theories. The deterrent justification for bias crime legislation claims that a harsher sentence for a crime will stop current and/or would be offenders from committing such crime by sending the message that the legislated act is taken seriously and deviants will be caught and punished severely. Unfortunately it raises the same questions with regard to its significance to bias crime as to more generic crimes including how many bias crimes will be deterred. To date, no relevant research has been conducted, and thus deterrence advocates rely on the potential of such an effect. Jacobs and Potter (1998) doubt its relevance given that the underlying acts of bias crimes are already punished and the most serious of crimes already receive more severe sentences. They and others question how much of a deterrent effect a bias crime enhancement could have beyond the punishment for an already serious underlying crime (MacNamara 2003). In addition, there are valid reasons for claiming the likely failure of such legislation to deter most bias crimes. According to Jacobs and Potter (1998), teenagers are responsible for the majority of bias crimes and in most States unless transferred to adult court they are not eligible for bias crime enhancements. For adults, the same scholars question the ability of a law to change potentially "fully formed and incorporated" biases (89) so as to have a marginal deterrent effect beyond the punishment for the underlying crime. Another consideration is the possibility that some biased offenders may avoid prosecution simply by avoiding the verbal behavior that often is used to demonstrate a bias crime thereby potentially suggesting a deterrent effect where one does not exist (Jacobs and Potter 1998; McNamara 2003). Finally, according to Jacobs and Potter a deterrence-based justification for punishing bias crime more severely than non-biased crimes requires evidence that bias crimes are more amenable to deterrence that currently does not exist. Otherwise why not simply enhance punishments for all crimes?

According to Kahan (1996) the expressivist argument for treating certain crimes more harshly than others is that: 1) such crimes send a message that devalues their victims and their class and 2) that criminal punishment is necessary to send a message condemning that message and in turn restoring value to those victims. As such, Hurd and Moore (2004) argue that hate crime legislation is acceptable under this theory only assuming that hate crimes include such messages, that hateful messages are more wrongful than other messages, and that the criminal response adequately repudiates that message. They contend that such assumptions cannot be made. First, all bias crimes do not involve a calculated message of hate from the offender, particularly in cases susceptible to discriminatory selection statutes, which require no demonstration of animus. Nor can it be said that all legally identified hate crimes involve the perception of such a message by the victim, especially where no words are passed between victim and offender or an offender's general description is not available. Second, even if the message is intended, perceived by the victim, or even just suggested to the victim or greater society by the nuances of the incident, the issue is why it makes greater punishment necessary if not for the worsened culpability or greater harms stemming from it, making the expressivist argument a proxy for, or redundant of, the culpability and greater harm arguments already put forth. Third, even if, as supporters of such theory contend, a crime can possess social meaning beyond that intended and perceived, punishment for such would be based on the appearance of the act and its motivation rather than the actual act or motivation and again the problem with that appearance would seem to be but a designated proxy for the greater culpability or harm such an actual act or harm would cause.

Perhaps more in line with many proponents of bias crime legislation is the belief that such legislation is justified because it sends a contradictory message to that of the hateful offender, thereby supporting the victims of such crime. However, Hurd and Moore (2004) argue that the problem with this argument lies in its inability to justify sending such a message intrinsically – without basing it on or limiting it by some other instrumental value based on retributive or utilitarian theory of punishment. They further contend that to accept the condemning message as its own justification for greater punishment would be to punish people solely to express acceptable social attitudes,.

which would seem to punish protected views and expressions, since as Jacobs and Potter (1998) acknowledge, messages related to the social condemnation of the crime and discrimination are already sent out through generic criminal, civil and constitutional law.

Hurd and Moore (2004) do point out that expressivist support for bias crime legislation often may be based on the message sent by the existence of the legislation itself rather than its implementation. However, failure to enforce such legislation makes it purely symbolic, and to the extent that is recognized its message of condemnation is degraded if not eliminated. Finally, Hurd and Moore question whether sending a message of condemnation through greater punishment can be justified if a less punitive method is possible. In addition, Jacob and Potter (1998) suggest that symbolic legislation may be more harmful than beneficial because it may lead to fewer instrumental attempts at addressing bias crime; its questionable legality may lead to an erosion of the First Amendment; and/or it may support the growth of identity politics potentially exacerbating the social divisions in which biases are bred and to which social solidarity is antithetical. It also may send out the inverse of the intended message, "suggesting that some people are more important than others" (McNamara 2003, 531).

Finally, even if expressivist theory or any of the other arguments put forth justified the greater punishment authorized by bias crime legislation, concerns have been raised that the implementation of such legislation could in fact have a disproportionate, negative impact on some of the populations it is designed to protect, which could lead to arbitrary and discriminatory implementation of such legislation to address the problem. In particular, According to Adams and Toth (2006), Federal statistics indicate that the vast majority of interracial violent crimes (roughly 10:1) are black on white crimes, owing in large part to the vast population differences, and comments by the Southern Poverty Law Center indicated a concern in the early 90's that in fact black-on-white hate crimes were on the rise. This, they indicate, suggests a strong likelihood that those offenders accused of racial hate crimes may be disproportionately black. In addition, some research suggests that people are more likely to identify interracial rather than intra-racial crimes as hate crimes and thus based on probability again blacks may be more likely to be accused of such crimes (Gerstenfeld 2003). It has been suggested that such realization could "encourage arbitrary application of hate crime statutes involving crimes against groups the legislation was intended to protect" (Adams and Toth 2006, 33).

In all, academic discussion over the need for and value of bias crime legislation continues even in light of support for such legislation by advocacy groups, politicians and seemingly the public. However, until recently public support has received minimal attention. While national polls document majority support for such legislation, research has just begun on what that support represents, whether it reflects the arguments put forth by academics, and what its potential ramifications are or should be for bias crime legislation.

CHAPTER 4

Public Opinion Research on Bias Crime and Legislation

While advocates, political leaders and courts have defined the concept of bias crime and scholars have debated its scope, prevalence and seriousness, its justifications and rationalizations, relatively little research has explored the public's understanding of, and thoughts on, the issue. In most instances in which public opinion has been sought, the approach has taken the form of poll questions, which while indicating majority support for bias crime legislation reveal little about how the public defines and views bias crime, how those perceptions might influence their support or opposition to such legislation, or what their support or opposition to such legislation signifies.

Public Opinion Polls on Bias Crime

Public Concern for Bias Crime
According to Gallup Polls (1999a, 2000a) only a small minority of the public, 13-17 percent, reports frequently or occasionally worrying about becoming the victim of a hate crime, and the last time "hate crimes" was raised as "the single most important problem facing the United States today" was in 2001 and then by less than half a percent of survey respondents (2001). However, in 1999 14 percent of a national sample of 506 adults offered "racism, prejudice/hate crimes" as the greatest remaining problem the people will have to deal with in the 21st century, significantly above any other issues offered including crime and financial problems (ABC News Poll). And in 1998, the year Matthew Shepard, a 22-year-old gay college student from Wyoming, was robbed, pistol whipped -his skull smashed- and left tied to a fence, 68 percent of a national sample of adults believed that a Matthew Shepard-type scenario could happen in their own community (Yankelovich Partners-CNN Time Poll 1998c), perhaps suggesting an

explanation for consistent strong public support for bias crime legislation as indicated by numerous national polls.

Public Abstract Support for Bias Crime Legislation
In 1998, Kiley and Company reported that 50 percent of a national adult sample favored, and 18 percent somewhat favored, "imposing a tougher sentence for someone who commits a so-called hate crime in which they [perpetrators] specifically target their victim as a member of a minority group than for someone who otherwise commits the same crime." Another 28 percent split on somewhat and strongly opposing such sentences.   In 1999, Hart and Teeter Research Companies reported that 61 percent of a similar sample strongly favored, and 14 percent somewhat favored, "passing legislation against hate crimes that would increase the punishment for crimes committed against a person because of the victim's race, religion, background, or sexual orientation." And Gallup that same year found that 70 percent would favor and 25 percent would oppose a "hate crime law in their state that provided harsher penalties for crime motivated by hate of certain groups," when hate crime was defined as "those crimes committed because the criminal hates the group of people to which the victim belongs" (1999b). In 2000(a), the same question received 65 percent support and 31 percent opposition. However, a Gallup poll (2000c) that year asking a national sample of registered voters whether "assuming they could vote on key issues as well as candidates on election day" they would vote for a law that would provide harsher penalties for hate crimes, resulted in 83 percent answering affirmatively.

Also in 2000, 48 percent of a national adult sample indicated that "combating hate crimes-crimes directed against people because of their race, ethnicity, religion, gender or other social characteristics"-should be given top priority by the government, and another 29 percent indicated that the topic should receive above average priority, although respondents were not forced to choose between this and other priorities (Princeton Survey Research Associates, 2000a). A 2000 Garin-Hart-Yang survey found that 66 percent of a sample of registered voters said they would be "less likely to vote for a candidate who voted against hate crimes legislation," when hate crimes were defined as "crimes motivated by prejudice against race, religion, gender disability or sexual orientation of the victim."   The majority of republican, independent, suburban and women sub-samples of voters also indicated they were less likely to support such a candidate. In 2007, the most recent Gallup Poll to measure public support for bias crime legislation found 78 percent of the public in favor, only 18 percent opposed. It defined hate crime as "those crimes committed because the criminal hates the group of people to which the victim belongs" and informed respondents that Federal law "currently allows prosecution of hate crimes...based on the victims' race, color, religion or national origin."

Public Belief in the Deterrent Effect of Bias Crime Legislation
Aside from fear of bias crime questions, the only direct attempt by polls to discover possible explanations for majority support for bias crime legislation comes from one 1999 question that directly asked respondents their thoughts on the potential deterrent effect of such legislation. Seventy percent of a national adult sample responded that they believed increasing penalties for people who commit hate crimes-crimes directed at people because of their race, religion, ethnic background or sexual orientation-would be very or somewhat effective in discouraging others from committing such crimes (Princeton Survey Research Associates). However, such a question leaves unclear whether this belief actually prompts public support for bias crime legislation or is simply viewed as a possible benefit.

Public Identification of Bias Crime Victims
Polls provide a little more information on the public's view of the scope of bias crime protection. Some pollsters have followed up generic bias crime legislation support questions with questions that probe the public's thoughts regarding which victims should be protected by such legislation. In 1999(c) and 2000 (b) Gallup asked respondents, "if a hate law were enacted in your state, which of the following groups do you think should be covered?" In 1999 the majority of respondents indicated that each of the three categories provided (race, religion/ethnicity, sexual orientation) should be covered, and the same pattern held for 2000 when respondents also were asked about, and by majority supported the inclusion of, women. Racial minorities received the strongest support (85/81% - 1999/2000) followed by religious and ethnic minorities (84/79%), women (78% only 2000) and homosexuals (75/71%).

Most polls questioning victim acceptability in the late 90's focused on protection for gays and lesbians. In 1998, 61 percent of a Hart and Teeter Research Company phone survey of nationally registered voters believed it was a good idea to "expand hate crime laws to include crimes committed on the basis of a victim's sexual orientation." And a survey of voters in the 1998 election found that 28 percent believed that "passing laws to protect gays and lesbians from hate crimes should be a top priority for Bill Clinton and Congress," 37 percent believed it was important but of lower priority, and 16 percent felt it was not too important. Only 16 percent felt it should not be done (Princeton Survey Research Associates). Polls in 1998 also indicated that 75 percent of a national sample of adults believed the problem of violence against gays and lesbians in this country today is very or fairly serious, and 75 percent would "favor federal law that mandates increased penalties for people who commit crimes against homosexuals out of prejudice against them similar to those federal laws that mandate such action for blacks and other minorities" (Yankelovich Partners/CNN/Time Polls 1998b, 1998a), a finding replicated by Princeton Survey Research Associates in 2000 (b) and a Kaiser and Princeton Survey in 2000 (73% support). Polls also indicate that an even higher percentage (77-88%) of young adults from 18 to 24 years of age favor hate crime laws to protect gays and lesbians (Hamilton College 2001; Kaiser Family Foundation 2000). Most recently, testing the waters for the pending Local Law Enforcement Hate Crimes Prevention Act of 2007, Gallup (2007) asked respondents whether they would be willing to favor expansion of the "Federal hate crime laws to include crimes committed on the basis of the victim's gender, sexual orientation, or gender identity". Though the percentage favoring did not reach that favoring hate crime law related to the traditional victim groups, 68 percent of respondents favored such expansion, with majorities supporting it regardless of political affiliation or leaning, or religious affiliation or commitment. Only 27 percent of respondents opposed it (Newport 2007). Thus overall, polls suggest majority support for protection against all the traditional anchoring provisions of such legislation as well sexual orientation and gender, which have experienced greater legislative controversy than race and religion, and most recently gender identity.

Public Support for Application of Bias Crime Legislation
Regardless of support for bias crime legislation and protection of a range of potential victims, responses to more probing bias crime questions suggest that support for bias crime legislation does not necessarily translate into willingness to apply a bias crime enhancement to a bias crime. In 1999 a Gallup/CNN/USA Today poll presented a national sample of adults with the news that Buford Furrow

was charged with an attack in Los Angeles that killed one postman and wounded several workers and children at a Jewish daycare facility. When asked whether they believed he, if convicted of murder, should receive greater or similar punishment than others convicted of a similar crime because he was motivated by racist and anti-Jewish beliefs, only 34 percent supported greater punishment, the vast majority (64%) similar punishment. This result was somewhat surprising given that in response to the previous poll question 70 percent of the same respondents indicated that they would favor a special law in their State that would "provide harsher penalties for crimes motivated by hate of certain groups than the penalties for the same crimes if they are not motivated by this kind of hate." Overall, while most polls suggest straightforward majority support for bias crime legislation covering the most frequently targeted minority groups, that support does not hold when respondents are asked to apply that legislation to a real-life felony bias crime, a phenomenon documented with other criminal justice policies. The seeming inconsistency may lie in the expected penalty for the underlying crimes, not previously investigated in polls. If poll respondents believe that life imprisonment or death is the appropriate or expected sanction for the underlying crime than there is no room or need for additional punishment for the hateful motive. Thus, specific scenarios may include context and details that make moot or override abstract support for bias crime legislation. It also may be the result of different questions provoking distinct issues relevant to citizens' views.

In all, poll data on bias crime suggests only low levels of public fear of, or concern with, bias crime but strong support for bias crime legislation, the protection of the traditional victims of bias crimes by such legislation, and its potential deterrent effect. However, it also indicates that such strong support for bias crime legislation might not translate into public willingness to apply more punitive penalties in the face of an actual bias crime. Unfortunately, the scant nature of such data leaves explanations unexamined. In addition, the fact that the majority of the questions were asked in the aftermath of the 1998 Matthew Shepard and James Byrd Jr. incidents, two highly publicized and heinous bias crimes, leaves open whether the high levels of support for bias crime legislation might have been an immediate but passing phenomenon. However, the 2007 poll on Federal bias crime law may suggest otherwise.

Research Studies on Public Opinion on Bias Crime

Unfortunately, very little public opinion research on bias crime and bias crime legislation beyond polls has been conducted that might shed light on the issue, and what research has been done is based on small, non-representative samples, and lacks comprehensiveness, which perhaps should be expected in such a relatively new area of study. However, the available studies do begin to tap citizens' perceptions of bias crime, its perpetrators and victims, and the justifications and rationalizations for bias crime legislation, mirroring some of the main elements of scholarly debate on the issue, including greater harm and the relationship between motivation and crime severity. Further, they examine citizens' ability to recognize bias crime and factors that influence their determinations of severity and appropriate sentencing. In all, research to date provides but a glimpse into dimensions of opinion on bias crime.

Public Knowledge and Perceptions of Bias Crime
The wording of generic bias crime poll questions would seem to provide the public with a basic definition of what a bias crime is. In addition, other polls suggest that the public's understanding of bias crime should be quite informed. For example, polls in 2000 revealed that 77 percent of a national adult sample claimed following the news about hate crimes very (33%) or somewhat (44%) closely. Forty-two percent said they had "heard a lot about laws concerning crimes committed out of prejudice or anger toward minority groups, sometimes referred to as hate crime laws," and an additional 30 percent had heard some (Center for Survey Research and Analysis-University of Connecticut). However, research conducted to explore ninety-six young adults' perceptions of bias crime suggests that at least for young adults the general dynamics of the issue remain unclear or unknown.

In 1996, Craig and Waldo asked 113 students from a large mid-western university to complete five phrases designed to tap their understanding of bias crime and the motives behind them. Responses were coded based on the typical profile of a bias crime, its victims and perpetrators. The findings did not fit expectations. In response to "the typical hate crime involves..." only 48 percent of respondents referred to the demographic status of the perpetrator or victim, while 68 percent answered violence or assault. When asked to complete "the typical hate crime is committed against..." and "the typical victim of hate crime can be described as..." only a bare majority (54%) made reference to a specific minority group relative to the former, and while innocence was the most frequently cited victim description, it was only espoused by 23 percent of respondents. When asked how "the typical hate perpetrator of hate crime is/can be described..." only 22 percent made reference to a perpetrator's demographic status, 17 percent indicating male and 19 percent white. Finally, in response to "the typical hate crime is committed because...." students indicated ignorance (38%), fear (19%), and anger (10%). Overall, the researchers concluded that respondents, and in many instances white respondents more so than respondents of color, simply were not aware of what bias crime actually entails. While bias crime is a complex crime possessing many objective as well as subjective components, the fact that respondents are generally unfamiliar with even its basic details suggests that opinions do not necessarily reflect familiarity with the issue. However, it also may be that the researchers' use of "hate" rather than "bias" crime tapped respondents' perception of crimes based on violence and aggression rather than prejudice and discrimination. In addition, the statements they asked respondents to complete may have been too vague to capture the specific answers they expected. Either way, the findings suggest that people or agencies relying on or trying to address or influence public opinion on criminal justice issues and policies should not assume that the public perceives an issue in a certain way.

Public Opinion on the Seriousness of Hateful Motives
However, regardless of their knowledge or perception of what bias crime is, the public generally believes crime motivated by bias to be more serious and harmful than other crimes. Working from the premise that "judgments about culpability and appropriateness of punishments must fit the public's perceptions of crime seriousness," Vogel (2000) conducted an exploratory study of 450 undergraduate students in criminal justice and political science classes at a large, racially and ethnically diverse university in California to examine whether they perceived hate-based crimes to be more serious than similar crimes. Respondents rated the seriousness of seven criminal incidents-pushed, verbally harassed, threatened, fist assault, knife assault, gun injury, gun homicide-in the form of vignettes on a 10-point scale from "not serious at all" to "extremely serious." The crime vignettes, in addition to reflecting the most frequently reported bias crimes (intimidation, simple assault, aggravated assault and murder), reflected five categories of motive including potentially-justified (self-defense, intoxication and retaliation), no apparent reason; emotional

(jealousy and anger); external (dare); and hate (personal bias against victims racial/ethnic group, religious beliefs or sexual orientation).[10]

Holding constant both respondent and vignette characteristics,[11] Vogel found hate motives to be perceived as the most serious crime motives (with sexual orientation the most serious) and to be statistically significant predictors of students' perceptions of crime seriousness, second only to crime type. He concluded that, "the motive of hate [including hate against race/ethnicity, religion and sexual orientation] is perceived as more serious than other motives" (2000, 20). Surprisingly, such findings were not found to "translate into overwhelming support for enhanced penalties for individuals convicted of committing hate crimes" (21). Only 51 percent of the entire sample favored penalty enhancements for bias crimes, and the variable was not a significant predictor of perceived crime seriousness. In the end, the role of motive on perception of crime seriousness, which had yielded mixed results in past research (Sebba 1980), was found to be significant, and hate motives were perceived as statistically more serious than others.

Another relevant insight noted by Vogel (2000) was that his sample viewed verbal harassment as more threatening than being pushed, somewhat counter to previous seriousness research that found seriousness to be related to physical harm or financial loss (Sellin and Wolfgang 1964). He conjectured that the sample "recognized a more complex, non-traditional definition of harm...a kind of harm that transcends physical contact" (Vogel 2000, 9). Although Vogel's comparison may not be appropriate given that the older studies did not include behaviors like verbal abuse, threats and harassment, empirical support does exist for the notion that the public perceives the harm associated with hate crime in ways that expand and surpass physical injury.

Public Opinion on Bias Crime Perpetrators and Victims

Rayburn, Mendoza and Davison (2003), conducted a vignette-based study to assess "Bystanders' Perceptions of Perpetrators and Victims of Hate Crime." This study was a follow-up from an earlier study from which they concluded that hate crimes led to more positive perceptions of hate crime victims and bystander intentions to protect victims and aggress against its perpetrators (Rayburn and Davison 2002). The current experiment used the person perception method to examine college students' perceptions of victim and perpetrator culpability for similar hate and non-hate crimes based on vignettes. The vignette was a multi-attacker assault that varied based on the event the victim was leaving at the time of the attack (rally, black history month, gay pride or Jewish community center meeting) and the expletives of the assailant signaling particular victim groups (nondescript, black, Jewish, or gay). Analysis supported their earlier findings. Overall, hate crime perpetrators were perceived as more culpable than their non-hate crime counterparts, and the victims of bias crime were perceived as more innocent. However, this was primarily a result of men's perceptions as women were more likely to differentially assess all perpetrators and victims in this way. In addition, the specific motivation of the hate crime was statistically irrelevant to the findings. Although the study did not explore the basis for bystanders' views, the researchers suggested that the immutable characteristics on which hate crime victims were selected might incline bystanders to perceive the blaming of such a victim as unreasonable whereas the victim of a more ambiguous crime might lead to greater consideration of what brought on the crime and whether the victim may have been in part to blame. Interestingly, they did not discover that people with prejudiced attitudes assessed hate and non-hate victims and perpetrators differently. Rather, the holding of such attitudes were "associated with more blame for all victims and less blame for all perpetrators," (2003, 1069) although they recognize that this could be a result of their measurement of attitudes. In addition, no differences were found between the perceptions of minority and non-minorities. However, interactions between the latter two factors led to the conclusion that prejudiced non-minorities "may be more likely to blame the victim of a hate crime" (2003, 1070). They concluded that the while bystanders have unique reactions to hate crimes, their actual perceptions of hate crime are not likely explanations for greater psychological harm to victims of bias crime.

<u>Public Opinion on the Harmfulness of Bias Crime</u>
In 1999 a purposive sample of 18 elite informants from Boston, Massachusetts, representing law enforcement, city and State government, courts and advocacy groups involved in hate crime policy were interviewed on their views of the harm of hate crime (Iganski 2001). From their qualitative responses, the general consensus emerged that hate crime is unique because of the greater harm above and beyond that of its underlying crime that results from its hateful motivation. In addition, this greater harm served as the dominant

justification for extra punishment for hate crime perpetrators. Citizens'
conceptualizations of the harm were diverse including harm brought
upon the initial victim, the victim's group in and beyond the
neighborhood, other targeted communities, as well as societal norms
and values.

Iganski's (2001, R6: 628) interviewees focused on hate crime as a
"violation of really a person's essence" because of the lingering
vulnerability brought by the victim's inability to change their targeted
characteristic and the effect that interchangeability can have on the
victim's group.

> But now I know I was targeted and I was chosen for
> something about myself that I can't change, that is at the core
> of my being, that I wouldn't want to change, that is unique to
> who I am (R7: 628). These crimes are also far more damaging
> to the community because you are not just targeting one
> person, you are targeting every other person within that
> victim's group (R3: 631).

They also addressed the potential "ripple effect" of hate crime,
resulting from its ability to "polarize a community" and even
potentially lead to retaliation, an effect enhanced by the distribution of
bias crimes by the news media.

> A single case can polarize a community...The reason is
> because hate crimes are viewed as message crimes, and so the
> victim group is sending back a message to the perpetrator
> group 'we're not going to stand for this..; you're going to
> suffer as we are (R8: 630). The Matthew Shepard case, or the
> James Byrd case, can in fact affect racial relations in this
> country...And I think that's why it is special and it's different
> (R8: 631). It's not just one simple thing that's done and gone.
> It stays, it lingers and has potential to cause all kinds of
> problems which come back and haunt the whole community,
> the whole neighborhood (R5: 630).

And they commented on the effect of hate crimes on the nation's core
social norms and values.

> All crime may be offensive in a democratic society....but to
> harm someone or hurt someone because of who · they

are...racially motivated hatred or bias-motivated hatred is offensive to society (R6: 632). It really rips at what this country was founded on and...It polarizes communities, it pulls us apart (R5: 632).

Respondents further defended hate crime legislation against First Amendment concerns. Their defenses relied predominantly on the idea that a greater harm is being punished rather than an expression of hate, and that it is necessary to determine the motivation to determine the type of crime committed and its resulting harm. In the end, motivation and the speech generally used to decipher it were not believed to be punished by bias crime legislation.

...you are not penalizing somebody because of their words, their thoughts. You're punishing them because of what they did...They assaulted you...and we enhance that because as they did that their words indicated an intent to do more" (R1: 632). And I don't think that we are punishing the thought so much as we are punishing the act that flows from the thought. We are using the thought to show what motivated the crime (R6: 632).

Legal scholars have argued that if the greater harm is in response to the ideas/thoughts behind the crime, more severe sanctions might actually constitute punishment of expression (Grey 1997 in Iganski 2001). While most respondents failed to follow through to this possible conclusion, some did find extra punishment for hate crimes offensive.

I think that it may be true in some cases that a racially or ethnically motivated attack offends or hurts members of a community or a subset of the population in a way that an "ordinary" attack wouldn't do but....I'm sure that it shouldn't make a difference to the criminal justice system...Look at two victims lying on the ground and bleeding from their wounds and tell one of them we the government will take your wounds more seriously than his...It's not enough of a reason to invoke the punitive arm of the state to say that a group of people find something painful. In a free society there will always be tensions, that's part of what freedom entails (Iganski 2001, R1: 633-634).

While the views of Iganski's respondents are far from generalizeable, they do suggest that the notion of greater harm may be relevant to thoughts on bias crime. According to his respondents, bias crime is viewed as more harmful than non-hate-based crimes based on a diverse range of effects on the victim, community and society at large. For many, that greater harm serves as a dominant justification for more severe punishment for its perpetrators.

Perhaps more intriguing is the fact that the public's justifications for deeming bias crime more harmful include rationales similar to those offered by academics-bias crime violates a "person's essence" and may have psychological and physical ripple effects throughout the victim's community and society by compromising national moral codes and increasing inter-group tensions and/or affecting civil rights and freedom of speech. These similarities may be a reflection of the slightly more elite nature of Iganski's sample or of a common view of bias crime held by the public. It may be that the mass public acquires such views from elites directly or through the mass media or it may be that they have directly or vicariously experienced the effects of bias crime or are able to foresee them given their own understanding of inter-group relations. Either way, Iganski's findings suggest the importance of tapping the public's justifications for viewing bias crime as more harmful and the sources of those views.

Public Opinion on Application of Bias Crime Legislation

In 2000, Johnson and Byers (2003) explored public views on hate crime legislation through an annual survey of a sample of 630 citizens expected to vote in the 2000 presidential election from Muncie, Indiana, a moderate-sized city thought to be representative of national political views. At the time, Indiana did not yet have hate crime sentence enhancement legislation, however the findings revealed that 75 percent would approve - nearly 40 percent strongly - a law that authorized more severe sentences if a "major reason a defendant in a trial committed a criminal act was because he or she was prejudiced toward the victim" (6). Responses to related questions documented that 66 percent supported the inclusion of homosexuals under such legislation and believed that hate crimes were on the rise, and 72 percent believed that "hate crimes created fear in other minorities" (7).

Also in 2000, Cohen, Rust and Steen (2003) conducted a study entitled "Measuring Public Perception of Appropriate Prison Sentences." The survey study yielded the perceptions of 1,300 U.S. adults. In 2004, Steen and Cohen examined these data as they specifically applied to the "Public's Demand for Hate Crime Penalties," namely citizens' responses to one of four versions of a hypothetical robbery without injury. The first involved a male victim with no indication of the defendant's motivation; the rest identified the victim as a male member of a group traditionally targeted for hate crimes – homosexual, black or Jewish - and indicated that the defendant waited to rob the first member of that particular group who left a group-based facility (i.e. first black man to leave a black church). As such, the researchers were trying to assess the public's willingness to apply harsher sentences for discriminatory-selection based hate crimes.

The findings revealed no statistically significant differences in the overall sample's selection of sentence type (prison, supervision, fine/restitution, electronic monitoring, home confinement) or length of sentence (recorded in months) for the hate and non-hate based crimes. However, regression analysis revealed significant differences within particular groups. Although pro-punishment participants were more likely to assign prison sentences for non-hate crimes than others, they were less likely than others to do so for hate crimes. Pro-treatment participants were less likely to assign prison for non-hate crimes than others but offered similar sentences for hate crimes. Similarly, participants who believed that minorities have too few rights were less likely to assign prison for non-hate-based crime, however they assigned prison for hate crime twice as often as those who did not. Although such participants' general sentences were two years shorter, their average sentence for hate crimes was two and a half years longer. The researchers' explanation for this later finding was that such respondents may have been more concerned with the offender in the non-hate vignette, specifically with regard to their treatment by the criminal justice system, but the victim in the hate crime vignette.

In all, Steen and Cohen concluded that there is "minimal public support for harsher penalties for offenders who commit hate crimes than for offenders who commit identical crimes with no specific motivation" (2004, 118). Their explanation is that, while they would assume that the majority of their respondents would on principle support bias crime legislation, citizens' sentencing in particular cases reflects greater concern with proportionality and fairness based on the severity and immediate harm of the offense rather than its larger ramifications for society or the message a harsher sentence might send. They also note that their findings may have been affected by participants' ability to recognize the appropriate vignettes as hate crimes, their lack of familiarity with what bias crime legislation authorizes, or the purely symbolic nature of their potential abstract support for such legislation, issues which were not under study. However, their study clearly indicates that it is not enough to assess the public's support for bias crime legislation without further examining their support for its application.

However, in 2006 Saucier, Brown, Mitchell and Cawmen found that students were significantly more likely to authorize longer sentences for assaults against minority victims compared to white males or females. The study was based on college introductory psychology students' responses to court case vignettes that varied according to the severity of the crime (simple or aggravated assault) and the victim's status, signified in the vignettes by the name of the victim and the nature of a derogatory slur used by the perpetrator. Interestingly, a significant sentence difference across vignettes was only related to the simple and not the aggravated assault, even though crime severity did not influence the perceived justifiability of the crime or blameworthiness of the victim. Also of note, although all crimes targeted against minorities were found to be a closer fit to the definition of a hate crime than those against white targets, the aggravated assault was deemed a closer fit than the simple assault. In addition, the researchers found that respondents with more frequent personal observations of discrimination were more likely to report hate crime as a larger problem and those with personal experience and observation were more likely to indicate that minority groups were at higher risks for hate crimes. Participants reporting that hate crimes were a larger problem were more likely to assess crimes designed to be hate crime as fitting the definition of a hate crime. Finally, within individual bias victim vignettes, respondents were asked how they would sentence the offender if the victim had been a white male to which respondents recommended significantly shorter sentences. In addition respondents indicated that the vignette offenses would be less justified in a discriminatory selection scenario in which the perpetrator committed the crime after losing his job to someone of his victim's status. In all, the researchers concluded that respondents "did believe that hate crimes were more severe than crimes not motivated by hate and enhanced penalties accordingly" explaining the lack of enhanced penalty for the aggravated assaults as a ceiling effect (905).

In all research directly assessing the public's views on bias crime and bias crime legislation suggests majority support for bias crime legislation and willingness to protect a wide range of potential victims.

It further provides evidence that such support may be based on perceptions of bias-based crimes as more serious than others based on their hateful motivation and the resulting greater harm, which is often offered as justification for enhanced punishments. Yet at the same time, general support for bias crime legislation does not seem to consistently translate into application of more severe penalties for specific bias crimes.

Research on Correlates of Public Opinion on Bias Crime

Although socio-demographic characteristics have been documented as having minimal influence on public attitudes towards criminal punishment (Applegate et al. 1996a), bias crime studies reveal that social background factors such as race and sex of respondents and crime victims and perpetrators as well as tolerance attitudes may influence public opinion on bias crime.

Influence of Sex and Race on Opinions of Bias Crime
In Craig and Waldo's (1996) study of beliefs about bias crime and the motivation behind them, significant differences were found between white respondents and those of color. In particular, the latter were more likely to make reference to a specific victim group when asked about typical bias crime victims, identify perpetrators by demographic status (male and white), and identify group membership as the motivation for such crimes more frequently than ignorance. In other words, respondents of color appeared more familiar with, or willing to note, the inter-group hostility often present in a typical bias crime.

In addition, Vogel (2000) discovered social background effects on bias crime opinion in his study of the seriousness of hate-based motives for which the results were presented for the entire sample and four racial/ethnic sub-samples (Latino, Asian American, Caucasian and African American). He found that African Americans rate verbal harassment in public as the least serious crime compared to pushing, which was so identified by the other samples. In addition, for the African-American sample only a biased motivation based on sexual orientation was found to be more serious than the other motives, whereas for the other samples all four bias crime motives were determined to be more serious. In all, higher seriousness ratings across all crimes, bias-motivated or not, were found to be statistically associated with respondent characteristics (women, Catholics and those indicating no religion compared with Protestants, victims of property crime) and crime, victim and offender characteristics (previous history of similar offense, all threats and personal crimes compared to verbal harassment, Hispanic victim, and victim unknown to offender compared to knowing the victim well). Lower seriousness ratings also were statistically related to respondent characteristics (Jewish, lower concern about crime, middle class socioeconomic status) and crime, victim and offender characteristics (incidents involving being pushed and female offender). Overall, Latinos, who were predominantly Catholic, ranked hate as more serious than did the other samples.

As previously indicated, polls suggest that in general a majority of the public is willing to support the inclusion of minorities of race/ethnicity, religion, gender and sexual orientation under the protection of bias crime legislation. But a recent study of student perceptions of hate crime (Miller 2001) suggests that respondents may not identify as bias crimes incidents labeled as such by the FBI, and this may be based on the influence of the type of victim involved.[12] Respondents' sex and race were predominant and significant predictors of whether they identified incidents as bias crimes and the only factors that distinguished the opinions of criminal justice majors and others. Compared with males, females defined more acts as bias crimes regardless of the type of victim. For non-criminal justice majors, white males were less likely to identify crimes against Jewish, sexual minority, female and African-American victims as bias crimes, while criminal justice males were less likely to identify incidents with sexual minority or female victims as bias crimes. In addition, white criminal justice students were less likely to view crimes with Jewish victims as bias crimes. These findings suggest that how respondents identify bias crimes may be affected by their own race and sex, regardless perhaps of their knowledge of bias crime and bias crime legislation (although use of major to reflect such knowledge is a weak control given that the students were in introductory classes) and the status of the bias crime victim. Polls that indicate majority support for bias crime legislation may not capture what students perceive of as bias crime either by under- or over-defining the crime in terms of victim status. Polls that question bias crime victim worthiness may mask differences based on the gender and race of respondents, fail to address issues that may differentially affect bias crimes perpetrated against different victim types, and/or reflect social desirability. However, interpretation of this study's findings is made difficult by the lack of overall statistics, the lack of study detail, and its primary emphasis on criminal justice curriculum. However, the effects of socio-demographic and crime factors on perceptions of bias crime have been demonstrated elsewhere. In 1996, based on their previous findings that students lack knowledge of what a bias crime typically entails, Craig and Waldo hypothesized that a college student sample would be unlikely to respond differently to bias crime vignettes based on the type of prejudice/victim involved. One hundred and twenty-five students, aged 18-27, were provided with an assault scenario that varied by victim gender and crime motivation (racial, religious, sexual orientation and ambiguous). As expected, all bias-motivated assaults were perceived as highly disruptive to their victims, and the perpetrators of all such assaults were believed to be significantly more likely than those of ambiguously-motivated assaults to be punished if apprehended. However, differences in perceptions based on respondents' sex and race were discovered. Women viewed the ambiguous assault as most disruptive to victims, while men so viewed the assault motivated by sexual orientation and were much less likely than women to view the racially-motivated assault as disruptive as the other assault types. Women also were more likely to report knowing the victim of an anti-Semitic assault, while men were more likely to report knowing the victim of an ambiguous assault. Finally, women were significantly more likely than men to indicate support for specific laws that guarantee prosecution against hate crimes. In terms of race, the researchers found that participants of color were significantly more likely than Whites to report knowing a victim of a similar type of assault as the scenario depicted. While Craig and Waldo's results fall short of any concrete conclusions about the workings of race and sex effects, they do suggest the importance of further investigating such differences in terms of definition, perceptions of seriousness, and harm of bias crime as compared to other crimes. They also indicate that 1) previous victimization or vicarious victimization, 2) the likelihood or fear of falling prey to bias crime, and 3) perceptions of potential psychological ramifications of particular types of bias crime may influence public opinion toward such crime and in some instances differentially based on race and sex.

Finally, Marcus-Newhall, Blake and Baumann (2002) conducted three experiments to explore the role of extralegal (non-legal) factors in mock jurors' perceptions of the guilt and punishment of bias crime perpetrators. The first studied the effect victim and perpetrator race and respondent political orientation have on the perceptions of college students, the second replicated the first on a non-college sample,[13] and the third explored the influence of peer influence on bias crime perpetrators on respondents' views. Experiment one revealed an interactive effect of victim and perpetrator race on determination of guilt and sentencing whereby an incident involving a Caucasian perpetrator and an African-American victim resulted in a more negative view of the crime resulting in a greater certainty of guilt and harsher sentence. Victim and perpetrator race also had main effects on guilt. Particularly, greater certainty of guilt resulted when the victim was African-American or the perpetrator was Caucasian. Finally, an interaction effect between perpetrator race and political orientation was revealed. Self-identified liberals were more certain than conservatives of the guilt of Caucasian perpetrators and were generally more certain of the guilt of Caucasian perpetrators; conservatives demonstrated no such difference.

Experiment two confirmed the finding of an interaction effect between victim and perpetrator race for certainty of guilt but not sentencing and found main effects on certainty of guilt only for perpetrator race. Also, contrary to experiment one, an effect of self-identified political orientation was discovered only as it interacted with victim race-liberals sentenced the perpetrator to more years in prison than conservatives when the victim was African-American than Caucasian. No such differences were discovered for conservatives.

Experiment three[14] revealed a two-way interactive effect of participant and victim race on perceived severity of the crime; minority respondents rated a crime more severely than Caucasians when the victim was African-American but no difference existed when the victim was Caucasian. In addition, a marginal interaction effect between peer influence and participant race emerged whereby Caucasians perceived an attack as more serious when discouraged by a peer group compared to minorities who rated the incident more severely when the perpetrator was encouraged. In terms of sentencing, a three-way interactive effect of victim and participant race and peer influence was discovered; Caucasians sentenced perpetrators more severely when they were encouraged to attack African-American victims rather than Caucasian victims. Finally, the only significant main effects were for victim race on both severity and sentence-crimes were perceived as more severe and longer sentences were given when victims were African-American.

Overall, the researchers concluded that perceptions of bias crime and mock jury decisions are influenced by extra-legal variables. They felt that inter-group relation theories could account for their findings. Of particular interest was the failure of Caucasians to demonstrate in-group favoritism when judging guilt and sentencing. It was conjectured that perhaps this demonstrates the belief in the loss of social benefit for Caucasians who misuse advantages of their status. The finding that Caucasians also failed to base their severity ratings at all on victim race but sentenced more severely when a Caucasian was encouraged to attack an African American was offered as a possible example of aversive racism theory, by which Caucasians are expected to appear non-prejudiced in the face of salient racial issues. On the contrary, some findings for minority respondents, particularly their higher severity ratings for crimes against African-Americans, was offered as an example of in-group favoritism and/or an attempt to "preserve the status of minority groups...by protecting them from negative or unsympathetic evaluations of hate crimes" (Marcus-Newhall et al. 2002, 129).

Influence of Attitudes on Opinions of Bias Crime
Cowan, Heiple, Marquez, Khatchadourian and McNevin (2005) surveyed college students to assess the influence of heterosexism on approval of hate crime and hate speech. In terms of hate crime, the researchers focused on a "measure of approval of violence against gay men and lesbians" measured by the Anti-Gay Violence Attitudes Scale (73). Students also completed the Kite Homosexuality Attitude Scale - for which a high score indicates greater old-fashioned heterosexism - as well as the Modern Heterosexism Scale, and multiple measures designed to tap their views regarding the harm of hate speech, the benefits of freedom of speech and costs of censorship, and their responses to hate speech scenarios. The findings revealed a strong positive correlation between old fashioned heterosexism and approval of hate crime against gays and lesbians as well as a negative association between such heterosexism and the "perceived harm of hate speech and the ratings of offensiveness and harmfulness" of hate speech scenarios. Similar associations with modern heterosexism were found to be based on their "overlap with old-fashioned heterosexism," except for its negative association with the harm of hate speech (78).

As reported in 2004, Dunbar and Molina explored students' feelings towards hate crime laws with a particular interest in factors that might influence such views. Not surprisingly based on prior polls and research, statements supporting hate crime laws were favored by the majority of students. However, the study also revealed that "individuals may oppose these laws as an extension of their opposition to inter-group equity and social justice in general," as the researchers found that agreement with arguments against hate crime laws were associated with higher scores on measures of prejudice, machismo, and anti-semitism as well as negative feelings towards hate crime laws (107). Greater agreement with libertarianism and the arguments that "hate crime laws unfairly cater to special interest political groups" (identity politics) or that the media distorts the hate crime problem to seem a more serious issue than it is were significantly correlated with all three attitudinal measures, and identity politics also was associated with negative feelings towards hate crime laws. Identity politics and media distortion were also the two most strongly agreed with anti-hate crime law arguments. Men received higher scores for all three attitudinal measures and support for the identity politics measure, although overall age, gender, and political orientation did not significantly influence hate crime affect. Positive feelings toward hate crime laws were associated with more accurate knowledge of anti-discrimination laws and agreement with the argument that "hate crime laws help to solve the problems our society faces" (civil society). The greatest agreement for pro-hate crime law arguments were the civil society argument and that such laws are needed to "discourage the escalation of inter-group violence (social engineering)" and because they help protect vulnerable groups (104).

That said, the research suggests that citizen's views on bias crime may be influenced by social background characteristics of the respondents, perpetrators and/or victims, and contextual factors of the crime, all of which may affect perceptions of the severity of the crime and the guilt and/or sentencing of bias crime perpetrators. In addition, citizens' heterosexism as well as their views on "inter-group equity and social justice" may further influence their stand on bias crime and bias crime legislation.

That said, overall the current public opinion research on bias crime tends to focus on the views of college students or those actively involved with the bias crime issue and thus may not reflect the views of the general public. Also, the narrow approaches taken by the available studies do not allow for a comprehensive view of individuals' thoughts on bias crime, what motivates them and how they impact their specific views on legally addressing bias crime.

CHAPTER 5

Public Opinion Research on Crime and Punishment and Its Relevance to Bias Crime

Legally, a bias crime occurs when an individual commits a crime against another in some part because of that victim's race, religion, sexual orientation or some other personal trait or status. Thus, citizens' views on legal responses to bias crime are likely to reflect their perceptions about such crime. However, while providing hints as to the nature and dimensions of such views, the available public opinion research on bias crime simply does not offer a strong model to explore them. However, research on public opinion on crime and public support for other punitive criminal policies suggests that citizens' direct crime concerns and more abstract social concerns may influence their punitiveness. As such, it offers insight for understanding citizens' views on bias crime and bias crime legislation. However, research on public punitiveness also suggests that citizens' views may be less punitive and more complex than previously assessed and that methodological issues may help explain the discrepancy between support for punitive legislation, such as bias crime legislation, and support for its actual application.

The Punitive American Public

Since the late 1970's, polls and research studies have generally depicted a punitive American public, highly supportive of more severe sentences for criminals in either type or duration. In fact, since then the American public has generally viewed the criminal justice system's treatment of crime and criminals as insufficiently harsh, particularly in terms of punishment, and generally been supportive of tougher anti-crime legislation (Flanagan and Longmire 1996; Roberts and Stalans 1997). Based on an extensive review of the research on public opinion on crime and punishment, scholars have acknowledged that the "public harbors punitive attitudes toward offenders, favors the use of prison sentences as a response to crime, and is generally supportive of get-tough initiatives" (Cullen et al. 2000, 26). Thus, citizens' views on bias crime and their support for bias crime legislation may reflect their general feelings towards crime and their general desire for greater punitiveness. However, Cullen and his colleagues concluded that general survey questions may not measure the complexity of the public's views on such issues, and there is growing evidence that the extent of American public punitiveness may not fully capture such views (Hutton 2005). That said, punitiveness is clearly a documented component of citizen views, and thus research has been conducted to explore what influences it.

Instrumental Crime Concerns and Punitiveness

In *Crime in the Public Mind*, Kathryn Taylor Gaubatz explores and confirms the American consensus that "harsh policies must be pursued" (1995, 6). She concludes that public support for greater punitiveness is primarily a result of people's instrumental crime concerns and the influence those concerns have on their beliefs about the appropriate function of the criminal justice system. In particular, people who are concerned primarily with issues of security and desert are more likely to support punishment for purposes of deterrence and/or retribution and to believe in the need for greater criminal punitiveness. In contrast, people who oppose, or are less willing to support, greater criminal punitiveness support harsh policies primarily for the purpose of incapacitation. While they are concerned with security, their social compassion for offenders and recognition of social causes of crime temper their need for criminal retribution and thus their desire to be harsher on criminals.

Given the influence of security – "the basic human desire for protection from loss or harm to self, family or community" (Gaubatz 1995, 45) – on punishment objectives regardless of people's punitiveness, identifying factors that influence people's sense of security may be pivotal to understanding their opinions on crime policy. These factors are likely to include their perceptions of current crime and punishment, the harm crime poses, their personal vulnerability to crime, and the vulnerability of others and their desire to protect them. However, research also indicates that perceptions of the threat posed by crime, as well as people's support for different sentencing goals, vary based on type of crime (Roberts and Stalans

1997). Thus, exploring these factors in terms of people's perceptions of bias crime, as well as crime in general, may help to explain opinions about bias crime legislation.

Perception of Crime and Punishment

People's security concerns about crime, and thus their opinions on punishment objectives and crime policy, are likely to be influenced by their perceptions of crime and punishment. While research documents that most Americans are interested in crime and justice, it also indicates that most are ill-informed as to the nature or prevalence of crime, the content of specific laws, or the functioning of the criminal justice system. The public generally holds pessimistic misperceptions of the crime rate and its general direction; overestimates the proportion of violent to non-violent crimes; is generally unaware of even the most well publicized legal reforms; and underestimates the sentences given for different crimes and offenders. It is this general lack of knowledge that appears to drive the general consensus that the criminal justice system needs to be harsher. Research also indicates that when people are asked about crime in general, the leniency of the courts, or sentencing, the majority imagine a violent, recidivist offender, a violent crime, and a worst-case scenario (Roberts and Stalans 1997). Thus in general, people's perceptions of crime are likely to be relatively negative and extreme, raise security concerns, and support the need for harsher legislation.

Large minorities of the public report following news about bias crime (44%) and hearing much about bias crime legislation (33%) (Center for Survey Research and Analysis-University of Connecticut). However, more in-depth public opinion research on bias crime and the findings on the public's general knowledge of crime suggest that people's perceptions of the nature and dimensions of the typical bias crime may be far from accurate, perhaps for some in part because of the atypical nature of the bias crimes presented by the media. In particular, people tend to describe bias crime in terms of a level of violence atypical of such crime, and they may perceive the most violent and hate-motivated crimes and offenders when asked about bias crime legislation. Thus, people's perceptions of bias crime may mirror those of crime in general absent knowledge of, or familiarity with, bias crime. Their opinions about bias crime legislation are likely influenced by those perceptions, regardless of their accuracy, and the security concerns they raise. This also suggests that people's willingness to apply a sentence enhancement to a specific bias crime may reflect how well their perceptions of bias crime match a specific incident rather than how representative an incident is of a typical bias crime.

<u>Greater Harm</u>

People's security concerns also are likely to be affected by their perceptions of crime seriousness. Research suggests that assessments of the harm of crime influence people's perceptions of crime seriousness and their punitiveness (Roberts and Stalans 1997). In general, the greater the harm perceived, the more serious the crime will be assessed and the harsher it will be punished. Much academic debate on bias crime concerns its potential "greater harm." The greater harm principle claims that bias crime is more physically and psychologically harmful because of its biased motivation, and that its harms extend beyond its immediate victims to their communities and society. Thus, people's opinion of bias crime legislation may reflect their perceptions of its greater harm. Their willingness to apply a bias crime sentence enhancement to a hypothetical bias crime may depend on how the harm of a specific incident compares to their perceptions of bias crime's greater harm.

The importance of physical injury to assessments of harm is well documented. People tend to rate crimes they perceive to involve threat of or actual physical injury as more serious and respond to them with greater punitiveness (Roberts and Stalans 1997). Thus, people's support for bias crime legislation may depend on the physical harm or injury they associate with what they perceive to be bias crime's underlying crime. Their beliefs as to whether bias crime generally involves personal or property crime, as well as the level of violence, number of assailants, amount of physical damage and recovery time, and possibility of violent acts of retaliation may be of particular importance. Initial public opinion research on bias crime suggests that people tend to perceive bias crimes as violent personal crimes involving potential physical harms beyond those to their immediate victims.

However, research also indicates that people's opinions on the seriousness of bias crime and the need for bias crime legislation may be influenced by their perception of bias crime's psychological harms (Vogel 2000). Academic debate and elite opinion on the issue suggest that people's assessments of bias crime's psychological harms may include evaluation of harm to victims, their communities, and society. People may perceive that victims suffer feelings of powerlessness, fear and intimidation leading to a host of deleterious conditions including anger, anxiety and depression. They may believe that biased victimization and its resulting psychological harms will be vicariously suffered by people in the community or society, particularly those who share the victim's status. Or they may perceive that bias crime leads to greater community and social unrest because of its inherent discrimination. According to public opinion research on bias crime, people perceive these possible psychological harms of bias crime and use them to justify their belief in the greater harm and seriousness of bias crime and their support for harsher penalties for such crime. Thus people's willingness to apply a bias crime sentence enhancement may depend on the extent to which the bias crime in question evokes the harms they expect from such crimes.

Vulnerability
People's security-based concerns also may be influenced by their perceptions of their own vulnerability to crime, a factor often equated with fear of crime. While research findings are somewhat inconsistent, there is weak evidence that people who fear becoming the victim of crime tend to be more punitive (Langworthy and Whitehead 1986). Forty to fifty percent of Americans consistently report "that they are afraid to walk alone at night near their home, and more than half say that becoming a victim of crime is something that they personally worry about" (Maguire and Pastore 1997; Warr 1995, 2000). In addition, people's fear of crime varies by offense type. According to Warr and Stafford (1983), people's fear of a particular offense is a result of not only the perceived seriousness of the offense but the perceived risk of it occurring. It follows that a person's sense of personal vulnerability to crime–their perceived risk of personal victimization–is likely to influence their punitiveness, and their support for bias crime legislation may depend on their perceived risk of becoming a bias crime victim.

People's perceptions of their vulnerability to bias crime are likely to be contingent on their perception of bias crime and how closely it crosses dimensions of their lives. Their perceptions of bias crime's prevalence, causes, victims, locations, and contexts may be particularly relevant. For example, if a person believes he does not fit the typical profile of a bias crime victim, does not live in or frequent an area where such crime occurs, or does not engage in behavior that motivates such crime, his concern for his safety is likely to be low, lessening the need for protective measures such as more punitive legislation. However, a gay man living in San Francisco and publicly advocating for gay rights may perceive himself as a more probable target of a bias crime, be more concerned with safety, and more supportive of bias crime legislation. Thus, people's perception of the danger bias crime poses to them is likely to influence their desire for protection and their receptiveness to punitive legislation. It follows that their willingness to apply a bias crime sentence enhancement may depend on the extent to which a hypothetical bias crime reflects an incident to which they feel vulnerable.

Who might feel vulnerable to bias crime has not been studied. However, given the groups protected under bias crime legislation, racial, ethnic, religious and sex-based minorities may feel most vulnerable. In addition, research indicates that women, the elderly, persons with low incomes or levels of education, and racial and ethnic minorities tend to be more fearful of crime. Thus, within the groups typically targeted for bias crime, people in these categories may feel particularly vulnerable-not because they are hated but because they perceive themselves to be easy or available targets for crime in general. Research also suggests that fear of crime is also shaped by the mass media because of its consistent distortion of the true nature of crime through its emphasis on, and exaggeration of, violent and sensational crimes (Flanagan and Longmire 1996). Therefore people's perceptions and fear of bias crime are likely to be influenced by their exposure to national coverage of the most violent and heinous bias crimes, such as the Matthew Shepard and James Byrd Jr. cases, as well as more local, and perhaps less severe cases, that may be used as a gauge of local conditions.

Finally, although findings are inconsistent, personal and/or secondary (vicarious) victimization may influence fear of crime (Skogan and Maxfield 1981; Stafford and Galle 1984). Bias crime victimization may be especially important to views on bias crime as it provides an additional source of information on, and perhaps a more intense feeling on and response to, such crime. Secondary bias crime victimization may be particularly relevant to views on the issue given the greater vicarious harm potentially posed by bias crime.

<u>Vulnerability and Protection of Others</u>
People's security concerns also may be contingent on their perceptions of the vulnerability of others to crime and their desire to protect those people. Research indicates that altruistic fear of crime may be "more common and frequently more intense than personal fear" and that "many of the protective measures historically assumed to be self-

protective are in fact intended primarily to protect significant others" (Warr and Ellison 2000, 556). While this research has focused only on immediate family and has not explored the impact of altruistic fear on legislative punitiveness, it suggests that even if one does not feel personally vulnerable to crime, he may still recognize the danger to, and the need to take measures to protect, those he does view as vulnerable.

Although it is unclear how far altruistic concern spreads, people's responses to bias crime legislation may be affected by it. People's assessment of the vulnerability of others to bias crime is likely to depend on the criteria they use for determining their own vulnerability. Thus, depending on what those factors are, an entire family or only particular members may be deemed in potential danger of bias crime. For instance, a mother may feel that her family is relatively safe except her son who is openly gay. Beyond the family, people's altruistic concerns are likely to turn to those emotionally and physically closest to them. For example, a person may consider the vulnerability of an African-American co-worker who lives in a racist part of town. Finally, people's concern for potential victims beyond their family, friends and acquaintances may depend on their awareness of, and/or feelings for, such persons or groups.

Although research has not explored it, people's personal tolerance may affect their altruistic fear of crime and bias crime specifically. Given that bias crime focuses so strongly on the status of the parties involved, the extent of people's altruistic concerns may reflect their feelings about the particular groups they perceive to be involved.[15] For example, a person who is intolerant of homosexuality may not be as concerned with the safety of gays and lesbians, and depending on the level of his dislike for them, may avoid supporting any law perceived as providing them with special protection or that might be seen as condoning their behavior. On the other hand, a person who advocates for the civil rights of gays and lesbians is likely to be not only familiar with the potential vulnerability of those groups but concerned for their safety and supportive of measures that will protect them. Thus, people's altruistic concerns in the face of bias crime are likely to depend on the extent to which they accept, tolerate or hate those they perceive to be its victims and conversely their tolerance for its offenders. As such, their support for bias crime legislation may depend on who they believe to be vulnerable to bias crime and whether they desire to protect them, and their willingness to apply sentence enhancements may be based on who is victimized.

In all, people's opinions about bias crime legislation may be influenced by their general perceptions of crime and punishment, the harm crime poses, their personal vulnerability to crime, and the vulnerability of others and their desire to protect them. In the context of Gaubatz's research, these factors likely affect the nature and intensity of people's security concerns and in turn may influence their demands for punitive retribution or the perceived need for incapacitation and thus their support for more punitive crime legislation, such as bias crime legislation. In addition, to the extent that people perceive bias crime as more of a security concern than crime in general the more likely that concern is to drive support for bias crime legislation. People's social compassion for offenders or consideration of society's flaws may influence their relative punitiveness but are less likely to affect the need to punish or incapacitate when people perceive bias crime to raise serious security concerns that demand strong measures of social protection. Whether or not people's general support for bias crime legislation translates into their willingness to apply penalty enhancements to a specific bias crime may depend on how their perceptions of bias crime, the harm it poses, and their own and others' vulnerability to such crime is highlighted by that offense.

Symbolic Crime Concerns and Punitiveness

While support for bias crime legislation may reflect people's concerns related to instrumental concerns regarding crime and punishment, it also may be influenced by symbolic crime concerns, particularly their perceptions of the social condition of society.[16] In their study on public opinion about three-strikes legislation, Tyler and Boeckmann (1997) found people's perceptions of the social and moral cohesion of society to be predictive of their general punitiveness and support for punitive legislation. Of particular importance to those perceptions are people's assessments of the quality and strength of social bonds and moral consensus. People who believe that social ties are breaking down or that a shared set of moral values is being diluted are pessimistic about society's cohesion and stability. The authors concluded that for such people criminal behavior, as a direct violation of society's norms and values, is symbolic of society's social and moral deterioration. They also found that such people are more likely to believe that responses to crime that rely on strong social ties and shared moral values such as rehabilitative measures or shaming are too difficult or ineffective and thus are generally supportive of more punitive sanctions, which they perceive as more effective for reasserting social control and reaffirming the social and moral values they believe necessary for society's cohesion and stability.

Tyler and his colleagues also report that people's socio-political values–their beliefs about, or philosophies of, the appropriate relationship between people and their government–are strong predictors of their perceptions of society's cohesion and in turn their general punitiveness and support for punitive legislation. Authoritarians, people who favor concentration of power and absolute submission to elites and the government, generally are more inclined to view society as morally less cohesive than liberals, who favor individual autonomy and authority restricted by constitutional protections. As a result, authoritarians tend to be more punitive and supportive of the death penalty and three-strikes legislation (Tyler and Weber 1982; Tyler and Boeckmann 1997). Additional research also suggests that people's criminal justice opinions may be grounded in their values regarding freedom (people's opinions on the appropriate limits on governmental social control and individual liberty) as well as equality (application of uniform treatment and outcomes and justice) and equity (administration and evaluation of fairness) (Gaubatz 1995). In all, people's values–the principles they believe should direct interaction among people and between people and their government– may play an important role in their opinions of punitive legislation, potentially because of how they define a cohesive and stable society and the factors they believe support strong social bonds and an appropriate moral consensus.

People's opinions on bias crime legislation may reflect symbolic concerns based solely on what crime, rather than bias crime, suggests about society's cohesion. As a violation of society's codified norms and values, crime may be perceived by definition as a threat to social stability requiring punishment to reassert social control and reaffirm proper behavior. However, opinions on bias crime may be especially subject to concerns of social cohesion based on its biased nature. Because of the emphasis on the biased motivation of such crimes, people's attention may be drawn to the bias involved and the status, norms and values that evoke it. In turn, they may be inclined to consider social diversity-society being comprised of persons differing in their status, norms and values–and its ramifications for a stable and cohesive society.

According to Tyler and Boeckmann (1997), people's perceptions of social cohesion and stability do appear to reflect concerns with social diversity. In particular, people who believe that social diversity weakens the social bonds and moral consensus that hold society together tend to perceive a less stable and cohesive society as that diversity increases. In turn they tend to be more punitive. So people who view social diversity as problematic may view bias crime as but a symptom of increased social diversity and its negative impact on society and thus see society as less cohesive and more in need of punitive crime legislation such as bias crime legislation. However, in the context of bias crime, the connection between social diversity, social cohesion and punitiveness may be more complex.

People who perceive social diversity to be highly beneficial to society may be more likely to view bias crime as a threat to a cohesive society because of the intolerance on which it is based and in response support more punitive measures to address it. Thus, the more tolerant people are and the more concerned they are with the current level of tolerance in society, the more inclined they may be to support bias crime legislation to counter a threat to social diversity and cohesion. Therefore, bias crime legislation may receive support from both those who are intolerant because they believe diversity threatens social cohesion and stability and those who are highly tolerant and believe that bias crime threatens that cohesion and stability. At the same time, those who are highly intolerant of the groups protected by bias crime legislation may perceive bias crime legislation as either sending a dangerous message of tolerance or inappropriately providing equal or special treatment for groups that threaten society, and they may even sympathize with a bias offender's motivation, if not his crime. Therefore, such people may be less likely to support bias crime legislation that might reaffirm tolerance for bias crime victims.

Research suggests that people with less commitment to libertarian notions of freedom and equality-whose values are narrowly defined or highly conditioned in principle or application-are likely to be less tolerant than those whose interpretations of such values are more absolute (McClosky and Brill 1983).[17] For example, a person who is committed to equal treatment as an essential component to a cohesive society but believes it does not apply to homosexuals because their sexual orientation is immoral is likely to be less tolerant of gays and lesbians. His perception of the size and growth of gay and lesbian populations and the nature and severity of the threat they pose thus may influence his perception of the vulnerability of society's cohesion to its acceptance or tolerance of homosexuals. The greater the perceived vulnerability, the more likely he may be concerned with the message of tolerance that bias crime legislation might convey rather than bias crime's message of intolerance.

On the other hand, a person who is strongly committed to equal treatment and believes that social cohesion depends on its stringent application to all is likely to tolerate, if not accept, people with non-traditional sexual orientations. His response to bias crime against gays and lesbians is likely to reflect his perception of society's vulnerability to the message of intolerance such crime conveys. The greater the perceived vulnerability, the more likely he is to perceive the offender's biased motivation, in addition to his crime, as threatening to social cohesion and feel the need to send a message that condemns the offender's intolerance and reaffirms the appropriateness of equal, if not special, protection for gays and lesbians, thereby strengthening social cohesion. Thus, his support for bias crime legislation is likely to depend on whether he perceives it to send the appropriate message of equal or special protection.

Thus, people's opinions on bias crime legislation may depend on their own tolerance for others and its influence on whether they believe that to maintain society's cohesion a message needs to be sent that reaffirms tolerance and, if so, whether bias crime legislation sends the right message. The appropriate message is likely to vary based on their perceptions of the victims of bias crime and the degree of prejudice involved. Thus, people's willingness to apply bias crime sentence enhancements to hypothetical bias crimes may not reflect perfectly their general support for such legislation but rather how their perceptions of bias crime and the tolerance issues involved match any specific incident. For example, a person who bases their general support on society's vulnerability to the intolerance demonstrated by hate groups' violent attacks on minorities may be unwilling to apply a sentence enhancement to a crime involving a youth who spray paints a swastika on an overpass because he thinks it is a cool design. The differences in the victim or the threat to social cohesion involved may not similarly demand reaffirmation of social tolerance through more severe punishment. However, research suggests that tolerance is a rather consistent value, meaning people who tend to be tolerant toward one group are more likely to be tolerant across the board (Glynn et al.

1999; McClosky and Brill 1983). Thus, people's responses may be influenced more by the degree of bias involved rather than victim status, barring extreme emotions towards a particular group(s).

In all, people may view bias crime as symbolic of the state of tolerance in society. Therefore, their general opinions of bias crime legislation may reflect whether or not, and if so how, they perceive tolerance to impact the social and moral cohesion and stability of society. Specifically, people who perceive the intolerance of bias crime as more threatening to social cohesion are more likely to reaffirm tolerance through support for bias crime legislation. Their assessment as to the threat and need for punishment are likely to depend primarily on their own values and tolerance and how they influence their definition of a cohesive society. People whose values promote greater tolerance generally may be more likely to support bias crime legislation based on tolerance concerns more than others. However, their support also may depend on their perception of the appropriate message of tolerance requiring reaffirmation and whether bias crime legislation conveys it. Finally, people's willingness to apply sentence enhancements may be influenced not only by their general support for bias crime legislation but the extent to which a specific incident matches their perception of the threat of intolerance presented by bias crime.

Instrumental Versus Symbolic Crime Concerns and Punishment

People's opinions on bias crime legislation thus may depend on either instrumental and/or symbolic concerns related to crime, bias crime, or both. Given the minimal public opinion research on bias crime, those concerns may take different forms than those theorized. However, the available research does offer preliminary support for the potential importance of both greater harm and perceptions of the appropriate treatment of those whose status, norms and values are different on opinions of bias crime. Such findings suggest that concerns based on perceptions of security and social cohesion may be particularly relevant to opinions on bias crime legislation.

The relative influence of instrumental and symbolic concerns may be particularly contingent on people's perceptions of the immediate danger bias crime poses, especially if its potential victims include themselves or those closest to them. Given that people tend to overestimate the amount of violent crime in society, picture violent crimes when asked about crime in general, and perceive bias crime to involve greater harm than other crimes, their first thoughts on bias crime may be to its physical and psychological dangers and the need to punish its offenders for security-based purposes. Whether people's support for punitive bias crime legislation reflects a need for safety for themselves or others from crime in general or bias crime in particular, the greater that perceived need the more likely instrumental concerns are to trump more symbolic concerns.

On the other hand, some people's opinions on bias crime legislation may be influenced primarily by their perceptions of the symbolic messages crime or bias crime send regarding social cohesion and stability. These people may be less concerned about the direct harms of crime or bias crime potentially because of their greater knowledge of the issues, such as familiarity with the infrequency and low-level nature of most bias crimes. Or they may be concerned about direct harms but believe that the symbolic implications of crime and bias crime demand greater attention. Those whose opinions on bias crime reflect their views on crime in general may consider what crime says about social and moral cohesion, while those whose opinions depend more on the bias of such crime may be drawn to issues of social diversity and tolerance and its perceived impact on social and moral cohesion. Either way, people's support for bias crime legislation will depend on how well they perceive it to address their symbolic concerns.

While people's opinions on bias crime legislation may be influenced by their concerns with either instrumental or symbolic concerns related to crime and/or bias crime, they perhaps are more likely to reflect both. For many people both types of concerns are likely to be influential, the more critical controlling their immediate and general opinions of punitive legislation and the secondary further supporting or potentially tempering their overall punitiveness or willingness to support punitive legislation given particular incidents. For others there may be little distinction between instrumental and symbolic concerns. People's thoughts on the immediate harm of crime or bias crime may be intertwined with their perception of how it reflects society's social and moral cohesion. Their preferred method for responding to crime or bias crime may be tied to how well it addresses all of these concerns.

Beyond the Public's Punitiveness

Although instrumental and more symbolic concerns may influence public support for punitive criminal justice policies, a growing body of research supports the contention that beyond the public's often cited punitiveness lies much more complex, nuanced and moderate views. However, such views generally have been untapped because of the nature of popular survey methodology. The problem lies in the reliance on global or general, rather than specific, questioning, which leads to different considerations by the public and seemingly more punitive views. This distinction could help explain the growing body of research that finds the public less willing to apply punitive policies that in general they strongly support, including bias crime legislation.

Global Versus Specific Questioning
While global questioning seeks respondents' views on a general criminal policy, specific questioning asks for a response to a concrete case related to a particular policy. In the case of bias crime legislation, a global question would ask citizens whether they would support legislation that authorized more severe punishment for offenders who committed their crime because of prejudice against their victim. Specific questioning might involve asking them more in-depth questions regarding a policy that offer them additional information including alternative policies or asking them to respond to a specific crime and criminal based on a hypothetical bias crime vignette. In other words, specific questioning places the object of general questioning in a less abstract, more concrete, context. It also tends to result in less punitive views towards crime and criminals.

This phenomenon is evident in the findings of polls and research on the death penalty, three strikes legislation and mandatory sentencing. In the 1990's as majority support existed for the death penalty, sharp declines in such support were found when respondents were asked to support or oppose the death penalty under particular crime and criminal circumstances (Princeton Survey Research Associates/Newsweek 1996). Similar findings were reported by Durham, Elrod and Kinkade (1996) when they provided citizens with death-eligible cases. Although the majority of cases across the board were given the death penalty, only 13 percent of the respondents gave the death penalty across the board. In the case of three strikes legislation, Applegate et al. (1996b) documented only 17 percent approval for applying such legislation to specific eligible offenders even when 88 percent of the sample supported the legislation in the abstract. Finally, with regard to mandatory sentencing, Russonello and Stewart (2001), asking multiple questions that included offender category, arguments for and against such sentencing, and hypotheticals found majority opposition to mandatory sentencing, a policy that in general received majority support.

Different Focal Points Based on Questioning
The distinction between responses to global and specific questioning may be a result of the type of considerations the two are likely to provoke. Cullen and his colleagues (2000) propose, in accord with Finkel's 1996 work, that global questions prompt concerns with general societal protection whereas specific questions provoke assessments of individual fairness in sentencing. Since research suggests that when presented with generic crime questions the public considers the question in the context of the most serious violent crime and criminal thus likely increasing considerations of dangerousness (Roberts 2003, 499), it seems reasonable that their views may be highly punitive but perhaps deemed inappropriate for many hypothetical cases. Hutton (2005) offers a similar suggestion noting Garland's distinction between individualist and structuralist accounts of criminal actions, the former concerned with assessing individual blame and appropriate punishment for the criminal, the latter with the greater social conditions that foster such crime and their impact on society, somewhat similar to Tyler and Boeckmann's (1997) concern with the symbolic concerns of crime. In essence, public views based on general/global questioning may be more likely to give rise to structuralist considerations of the need to protect society both from the general danger of crime and what it symbolizes, which may give rise to greater punitiveness that citizen's are not willing to deem fair or just in the more specific context of an individual crime and criminal. In fact Roberts and Hough conclude from their analyses of public attitudes on criminal justice that "a bedrock of support exists for the principle of proportionality in sentencing" (2005, 150). By not providing the information or opportunity for respondents to assess individual responsibility and punishment, global questioning more likely captures views related to general protection of society. Given the public's lack of familiarity with crime and punishment and their propensity to conceptualize crime and criminals in their extremes, it is perhaps not surprising that such questioning results in highly punitive views. On the other hand, specific questioning, by providing a basis for an

individualist account, provides citizens an opportunity to demonstrate the depth of their commitment to those policies in terms of their proportionality to specific crimes and criminals. In fact, Roberts concludes from a review of international findings that public support for mandatory sentencing "is strongest when a general question is posed...but when confronted with specific cases, the public rejects mandatory sentences" in large part it seems because of their concern with proportionality in sentencing (2003, 505). And, Steen and Cohen offer the public's proportionality concerns with their own recent findings of "minimal public support for harsher penalties" for hate crimes compared to similar ambiguously motivated crimes (2004, 118) in light of strong majority support for hate crime sentence enhancements.

As concluded by Roberts and Hough, although there are many instances in which the public will respond to crime punitively, "when questions are put to the public in a more appropriate manner (specific questioning), people are very interested in less punitive responses to crime, particularly when [they] generate some tangible benefit, such as reparation for the crime victim" (2005, 151). In all, such research seems to suggest that citizens' views of bias crime legislation could be more punitive in the abstract than in the context of being asked to apply such legislation to specific bias crime incidents. This difference would likely be based on a shift in their primary focus from the dangerousness of hate crimes and what they symbolize to society to concern with the proportionality of sentences for specific offenders and perhaps how a given sentence might be beneficial to the victim. If such research holds in the context of bias crime, as Steen and Cohen's research suggests, then the factors that make bias crime worse in the abstract must either not be perceived as existing in more specific criminal cases or not be deemed appropriate to determinations of proportionate sentencing.

CHAPTER 6

The Current Study – Design to Analysis

The available public opinion research on crime and bias crime offers insights into potentially relevant factors for studying citizens' opinions on bias crime legislation. However, the theoretical connections suggested by such research were not strong enough to support a hypothesis-driven model on which to base the current study. In light of the relatively scant research on bias crime, such a structured approach could result in an examination of researcher-driven expectations rather than providing an opportunity to fully explore citizens' views. Current bias crime research simply does not provide assurance that the public's thoughts reflect researchers' or academics' and thus leading them down too structured a path might serve to shape rather than examine their opinions, especially if bias crime is not a topic to which the public has given extensive thought. Thus the current research is an exploratory study of citizens' views on bias crime. Such an approach can facilitate the identification of potentially-relevant constructs and hypotheses for a topic without comprehensive theory and research while allowing the perspectives offered as well as unexpected issues to be investigated. While not testing a specific model of potentially predictive variables obviously limits my ability to speak directly to the relevance of many of the variables and perspectives suggested by prior research, allowing for a broader exploration of opinions provides a comprehensive and open-minded approach more appropriate for such a relatively new area of research.

Methodology

To that end, the study data was collected using a qualitative design relying on in-person interviews (Appendix A) and supported by personal background questionnaires (Appendix B). While qualitative interviews can be "time consuming, privacy endangering, and

77

intellectually and emotionally demanding in ways that quantitative interviews rarely are" (McCracken 1988, 27), these potential risks are generally considered offset by their benefits. Qualitative interviews provide respondents with "the opportunity to engage in an unusual form of sociality" in which they and their ideas are given a full and private hearing (Cannell and Axelrod 1956 and Caplow 1956 cited in McCracken 1988, 27). This opportunity may offer further benefits by allowing participants to be the center of attention, present an unheard case, undergo a process of self-scrutiny, and in some instances experience a catharsis effect.

An interview protocol was used to guide the interviews. Such a pre-planned questionnaire "establishes channels for the direction and scope of discourse" while maintaining distance and preserving the least amount of distraction possible for the investigator (McCracken 1988, 24). For the current study, it facilitated an interview process that provided some sense of order to the data collection, decreased the opportunity for unintended bias that might have resulted from unscripted questions, and allowed my full attention to be on participant responses rather than the dimensions of the interview.

The development of the protocol was guided by McCracken's method of qualitative inquiry, which first calls for a review of analytic and cultural constructs related to the research topic. According to McCracken, the literature review (review of analytic constructs) plays a key role in the quality of a qualitative research design because of its importance for the "manufacturing of distance" and questionnaire construction. Manufacturing distance allows the investigator to "see familiar data in unfamiliar ways" (1988, 24). "It is necessary to create a critical awareness of matters with which we have a deep and blinding familiarity" so as to allow us to truly capture what respondents have to offer (23). In preparing the project's literature review, I absorbed the data, concepts, and issues of previous researchers on a range of topics, including formulation of views, personal values, opinion on crime and punishment, and opinion on bias crime and bias crime legislation, while carefully assessing the conscious and unconscious assumptions of each work. As a result, I familiarized myself with the expected and allowed for the possibility of the unexpected – in this case that which simply had not been tapped by prior research. This process helped me to develop the theoretical constructs and enhanced my ability to design an interview questionnaire that could tap them without shaping or distorting participants' views.

The review of cultural constructs addresses concerns related to what McCracken refers to as "investigator as instrument." This concept acknowledges that researchers' own experiences and imaginations influence their ability to make sense of and analyze the wide and seemingly disordered assortment of data from qualitative interviews. Even when individuals' views match the researchers', it is necessary for those views to be substantiated within the context of individuals' comments and data analysis. The researchers' acknowledgment of their own views provides awareness of potential personal biases as well as positions against which to recognize and develop potential alternative views. This process is particularly important with topics, like public opinion on bias crime, for which scant and narrowly-focused research is available. Considering and acknowledging my own opinions on bias crime legislation not only familiarized me with some potential areas of inquiry but more importantly allowed me to explore a host of potentially varying or opposing views that provided further insight into potentially-relevant constructs for investigation. It also allowed me to collect and analyze the data outside the context and confines of my own beliefs and cultural assumptions and with an eye toward avoiding my own potential biases.

My initial interest in bias crime stemmed from my own somewhat conflicted views on bias crime legislation. While recognizing the seriousness of the issue and the need to address it, I was generally concerned about the legality and potentially negative impact of authorizing longer sentences for hate or bias without some corresponding physical difference between bias and non-bias crime not otherwise addressed by criminal law and sanctioning. At the same time, I was intrigued by the poll findings of majority support for bias crime legislation and what arguments might support that view and how they might impact my own thinking on the issue. As such, I wanted to ensure that the current study provided both the minority and majority positions on bias crime legislation an opportunity to share and explain their views while also offering participants the freedom to sit on the fence if their views placed them there.

Based on both the analytic and cultural reviews, broad research domains capable of capturing the constructs deemed potentially relevant to citizens' views on bias crime were identified. Those domains included people's thoughts on crime and punishment in general, bias crime and punishment (including bias crime legislation), bias and non-bias crime vignettes, and social cohesion, diversity and tolerance. The goal of the qualitative interview is to allow participants to tell their own stories, in their own words and with their own explanations. Thus, the questionnaire was designed to be as unobtrusive as possible to respondents' sharing of their views. To that end, it included primarily general, open-ended questions designed to elicit conversation rather than solicit particular answers. Floating and planned prompts were used as necessary to sustain conversation and explore particular areas raised by participants' comments.

Floating prompts involve "careful exploitation of several features of everyday speech," (McCracken 1988, 35) including facial expressions such as a raised eyebrow or the repeating of a respondent's word(s) in a particular tone, to denote the need for further explanation. While floating prompts are reactive and relatively unobtrusive, planned prompts are proactive and range in their obtrusiveness. Planned prompts are necessary when general questions and floating prompts fail to elicit respondent comments on constructs of interest. McCracken identifies four varieties, which include "contrast" prompts, in which respondents are asked to compare self-defined concepts, or in the most extreme situations those provided by the interviewer; "category questions," which address respondents' thoughts on formal characteristics or properties of particular categories or constructs; "special incident" prompts, through which respondents are asked to reflect on any instances in which their own expectations were not met; and "auto-driving" strategies, which involve requesting the respondent to comment on a presented stimulus. Because of their highly obtrusive nature, planned prompts were used only to the extent that general questions and floating prompts were ineffective at, or incapable of, acquiring a full understanding of participants' views.

It should be noted that while the intent was always for the research to be exploratory, the originally pre-tested interview protocol made much greater use of planned prompts than the final protocol. Practice interviews were conducted to evaluate the interview protocol's form, substance, and thoroughness as well as the overall effectiveness of the interview process. Attention was paid to how well questions and prompts were understood and initiated and sustained relevant conversation; whether or not relevant but unanticipated constructs arose; and the comfort and trust levels between participants and interviewer. Initially numerous prompts were planned following each general question within each domain to request information concerning specific variables that prior research suggested might impact people's views. While after-interview comments from practice interviewees suggested they did not feel questioned but rather that they had been involved in a dialogue, I found the interviews to be somewhat lopsided in that I was doing too much prompting to raise issues that might have not been deemed relevant by the participants if left to their own opinions. While participants were clearly willing to provide answers, based on their expressions and the manner of their responses to prompts that did not follow directly from their comments, I felt their answers were just answers to my questions rather than expressions of their own thoughts on bias crime. Thus, the final interview protocol was skimmed back to include very general questions within each domain, and any additionally prompted questions were based solely on the need to follow up on the content of participants' previous answers rather than an attempt to obtain answers regarding constructs in no way raised by participants. While obviously this limits my ability to speak to specific variables that participants did not choose to address, it provides a clearer image of their direction of thought on the issue rather than that of prior research. The pre-test results also reinforced my decision not to rely on a more structured overall approach to the topic that would rely too strongly on prepackaged constructs.

The final interview protocol was comprised of five general sections based on the broad domains identified through the review of analytic and cultural constructs: thoughts on crime and punishment, bias crime and punishment, bias crime vignettes, bias crime legislation, and social diversity, coherence and tolerance. Each section was comprised of a few general questions that were followed up with floating and planned prompts, although only when solicited by participants' comments or when absolutely necessary to acquire views on a key area of the study. Within each domain general questions were asked in an order and manner designed to avoid process-based biases with the exception of situations in which participants' comments made order changes necessary for a more smoothly flowing interview. Order across domain also was maintained and designed to best avoid shaping participants' responses.

Interview sections were organized from the general to the specific for the most part. Section one was on crime and punishment and included questions about participants' familiarity or experience with crime, how they would describe it, and their thoughts on appropriate policy for addressing crime and convicted offenders. These questions were meant to tap possible influences on views regarding bias crime but also to provide a base on which to compare views on crime and bias crime. Section two broached similar questions related to bias crime. The only questions not initially planned but that seemed to flow naturally from participants' responses in the first two sections tapped their thoughts on the causes of crime and bias crime and their fear of becoming victims of either. Section three was comprised of questions that solicited participants' views on comparable bias and non-bias crime vignettes.

Although exploratory in nature, the study's focus on people's preferred policy for addressing bias crime and offenders seemed to demand an examination of their commitment to whatever approach they supported, especially in light of the poll data that suggests greater support for bias crime legislation than willingness to apply it. Questioning their willingness to apply their approach to vignettes provided an opportunity to explore that commitment as well as capture a fuller understanding of their approach. It was possible that people's views on bias crime legislation might be based on some amalgam of considerations and perceived situations that may or may not be similarly triggered by specific bias crimes. There are a number of dimensions relevant to bias crime that may differentially influence people's views about whether a crime is a bias crime and/or how it should be handled even if in general they support bias crime legislation. Those dimensions include the status of the victim, the perceived motivation of the perpetrator, the nature of the underlying crime, and the nature of the damage/harm done. Therefore, the vignettes used in the study ranged from vandalism to battery, with both financial and physical harm, included victims based on race, religion and sexual orientation, and both non-biased and biased motivations. They were designed to provide participants with enough of a specific picture to base a solid response on while allowing them to discuss variations that might change their preferred response to the incidents. The inclusion of vignettes on crime in general, in addition to bias crimes, was based on the need for a sense of how participants would respond to the underlying crimes involved in the bias crime vignettes in order to determine the presence and nature of any differences in views between crime and bias crime.

Section four of the interview focused on bias crime legislation, specifically sentence enhancements. The issue was not raised until after the vignette section, unless directly raised by participants themselves, because it was feared that the mention of official responses to bias crime before participants had an opportunity to share their own views might serve to limit participants' angles on the questions and/or willingness to provide their own views that might contradict any official approach to the issue thus shaping rather than exploring their views. Bias crime legislation questions tapped participants' familiarity with and support or opposition to it, the reasons for their views, as well as how such legislation should be operationalized in terms of victims/prejudices included and penalties authorized.

The final section of the interview was comprised of questions concerning social diversity, how well people generally get along, the level of tolerance in society, and the role, if any, of the government in promoting tolerance. While it was assumed that these issues might arise unsolicited in early sections of the interview, they were added at the end so as not to potentially skew earlier comments if that was not the case. They were deemed important for exploring the potential symbolic issues related to support for bias crime legislation. Unfortunately, procedural and substantive issues led to this section of the interview being dropped from the final analysis. Substantively it became clear early on that participants were not responding to this section's questions with a mind free from the bias crime issue and therefore their responses were very narrowly focused and thus would not permit a clear assessment of their views on the more general social values of interest. In addition, participants' extensive responses to the previous sections of the interview frequently led to time constraints and taken with the aforementioned issue I determined that the time would be best used for completion of the personal background questionnaire. As such, section five responses were often missing, incomplete and, to the extent available, not relevant to their original purpose.

According to McCracken (1988), the interview is the investigator's third source for identifying and exploring constructs and their relationships. However, the nature of the qualitative method makes it the most difficult to conquer. While a pre-planned questionnaire serves as a road map through relatively undiscovered lands, it is the investigator's job to interpret any "signs" along the way in order to maintain an effective and informative interview. To that end, I 1) paid attention to respondents' words and their personal meanings as well as their facial expressions and demeanor, question avoidance, deliberate distortion, misunderstanding and/or incomprehension; 2) was alert to the implications and assumptions of their comments and the best approaches for broaching them; and 3) tried to keep the interview on track while allowing respondents to tell their stories and not bypassing unanticipated but relevant topics.

The final component of the interview process involved a two-page, self-completed personal background questionnaire that asked respondents about a number of socio-demographic factors including age, race, income, sexual orientation and political and religious affiliation.

Sample Choice and Recruitment

A purposive sample of 40 residents recruited from a college town in rural, western Pennsylvania was chosen for this study. While the location was a decision of convenience, the choice of a purposive sample was in an attempt to increase the likelihood of capturing a range of potential views on the issue. Unfortunately, the scarcity of public opinion data regarding bias crime made it difficult to identify what, if any, sub-samples might provide the most comprehensive glimpse of such views and whether patterns of thinking on the issue track across very broad categories of people or complex sets of characteristics and/or ideals. While the theoretical perspectives and constructs proposed could have been used to define very detailed sub-samples, the lack of knowledge in the area and the exploratory nature and scale of the current research suggested the selection of broader, perhaps more simplified, sampling categories. With these thoughts in mind, five sub-samples were included in the study: self-identified African-Americans, Jews, gays and lesbians, Caucasians with college degrees, and Caucasians without college degrees.

The choice of the first three sub-samples is perhaps the most obvious. As the top three groups from which victims of bias crime are selected, these sub-samples' knowledge and perceptions of bias crime may be similarly or differentially influenced by their status and its link to bias crime. Their status could influence not only their perceptions of what is or should be a bias crime but its harm and their own vulnerability as well as that of others for whom they care about. In addition, their life experiences, including any victimization, to the extent that they are linked to their status, could influence their values and views. It has been theorized that each of these factors may influence how people think about and choose to respond to bias crime. Individual status also may influence views through its impact on participants' social characteristics such as their level of education, political affiliation or lean, or income–all characteristics that polls suggest influence the extent to which people worry about becoming the victim of bias crime, their support for hate crime sentence enhancements, and/or their willingness to protect certain status groups via such legislation.

The highly educated sub-sample was chosen based on its potential to capture people with less punitive views and generally less likely to be victims of the most common form of bias crime – racially motivated bias crime. In general, the more educated people are the less punitive they are likely to be in terms of crime and justice whether liberal or conservative, democrat or republican. In addition, they tend to have greater exposure to more libertarian ideas and concepts, which have been shown to correspond with greater tolerance (Roberts and Stalans 1997). Both general punitiveness and tolerance are theorized as influences on how people perceive and respond to bias crime. At the same time, education is often associated with greater wealth and higher occupational status both of which could influence the nature and level of people's fear of, and exposure to, crime further impacting their perceptions of criminal justice policy.

The final sub-sample was chosen with the expectation that it might capture more punitive but more common views on crime and justice in general and bias crime in particular. Based on research on public opinion in general, it is expected to include people with less education; perhaps greater exposure to, experience with, or fear of crime; more conservative than liberal views as a result of education levels; and likely less tolerant attitudes in general. In addition, by focusing on whites only it offered an opportunity to explore how those statistically less likely to be the victim of a bias crime perceive and react to bias crime and legislative attempts potentially perceived as designed to protect "others."

Attempts also were made in sample recruitment to maintain diversity across participant background characteristics including sex and age. Sex has been shown to be an important factor in views on crime and justice. In general women have been found to be more fearful of crime although more supportive of rehabilitation for violent crime than men (Gaubatz 1995). In addition, women tend to worry about becoming the victim of a hate crime, support hate crime legislation, and demonstrate greater willingness to protect certain groups-particularly homosexuals than men. While age or generation often have been shown to influence views of crime, justice and tolerance, polls indicate that age-based differences regarding bias crime issues only become relevant for those over 70 years of age, who also tend to be less supportive of bias crime legislation. The only restrictions on study participation were that participants had to be at least 18-years of age, to avoid consent complications, and speak English fluently, because of my own language limitations.

As previously indicated, all study participants were recruited from rural Pennsylvania, specifically a combined area of 45 square miles including a county seat borough and surrounding township located approximately an hour-and-a half from the nearest metropolitan center and home to a State university, the largest employer of the area. According to Census data, in 2000 the combined population of the borough and township was just under 29,000. Comparable to the U.S. overall, 46 percent of the population was male. However, somewhat unusual, the racial makeup of the area was predominately white (93%). Black and Asian were the only other racial categories accounting for one or more percent of the population, 4 and 2 percent respectively. The average median age of the region was 32 just under the U.S. average of 35, and 39 percent of the population over 15 years old was married. Both these figures were substantially higher (10% or more) in the township as compared with the borough statistics, likely explained by the fact that the University is situated within the borough and much of the area is home to students. Economic statistics showed a median household income of $28,000, substantially lower than the nation ($42,000) even in the township, which alone posted a median income of $24,000. The median family income for the population was just over $48,000, consistent with the national average of $50,000. In terms of education, nearly 90 percent of citizens over 25 held at least high school degrees and 35 percent at least a Bachelor's degree, both 10 percent higher than national figures (Indiana County Statistical Demographics 2004; American Fact Finder, 2006). No overall figures could be located regarding specific religious affiliation for the study area, although figures for the relevant county indicated a total of 171 religious congregations as of 2000 claiming over 38,000 adherents, 90 percent of the total population of the county. The religious congregations included mainline and evangelical protestant faiths (49%, 43%), Catholics (7%), orthodox faiths (4%) and other, which included Latter Day Saints, Judaism, and Unitarian Universalists (2%). It is known that the Jewish and Unitarian Universalist congregation are located in the study area and account for just a little over one percent of the religious adherents in the county (Association of American Religious Bodies, 2002).

Study participants were recruited using a snowball methodology once initial participants were identified. Initial participants were recruited with the assistance of personal and occupational acquaintances in the study region familiar with the sample needs of the project. These acquaintances included University contacts from a number of departments (religious and African American studies, criminology) and other offices on campus (religious, race and sexual orientation based organizations) with possible connections to the populations from which I wished to recruit. They were able to recommend and provide contact information for communities and/or organizations as well as additional individual contacts, primarily local religious, social, and organizational leaders, within the region that could offer the greatest opportunity to recruit a diverse sample within the specified categories and were of immense assistance given my lack of familiarity with the region. Initial contacts were not included as participants in the sample because the need to provide them detailed information on the study and its purpose would likely have served to bias their responses, and also to avoid interviewing individuals who in some instances could have been labeled informed activists, whose answers I believed would not reflect those of the general public. Although the first few recruits were identified primarily through University contacts, efforts were made thereafter to identify participants not directly affiliated with the University. However, given the size of the community and the fact that the University is the primary employer, it was difficult to identify people without at least an indirect affiliation with the University. In addition, while the final sample included both University and non-University participants, it was found that non-University potential participants who authorized others to provide me with their contact information were more difficult to enlist in the study, although only one directly refused and only a handful of others failed to return phone messages or emails.

Based on contact recommendations and my own study of the area, recruitment cards were distributed throughout the study region via community centers, social and religious organizations, local businesses, and individuals. These cards identified the general nature, purpose and requirements of the study along with my contact information. Acquaintances and local leaders in addition to distributing recruitment cards through their venues also provided recruitment cards directly to those they felt might be interested in participating, the approach that seemed most successful at enlisting additional participants. At no time were potential participants names or contact information given to me without those individuals' consent (See Recruitment Card in Appendix C).

Upon contact, interested parties were familiarized via phone or email as to the nature, purpose and requirements of the study, the voluntary and confidential nature of participation, and the need to recruit a diverse sample. To that end they were asked a few filtering questions to ensure that the sub-sample requirements were met. No interested parties refused to answer these questions or had to be turned away because of sample restrictions (See Invitation Email and Filtering Questions in Appendices D and E).

Data Collection

All interviews were conducted between November 2004 and September 2005, the extended collection time primarily being the result of researcher availability and the desire to rely on a snowball sample rather than any significant difficulty in recruiting participants. Interview times and locations were set to fit participants' convenience and comfort, and covered a range of times from early morning to late evening and varied locations including my office, their home or office, and in a few instances a public venue (participants were reminded of the inability to ensure confidentiality in such locations). Each interview began with a brief introduction to the general subject and purpose of the study–understanding of public opinion on crime and punishment in America. The voluntary and confidential nature of the interview and the benefits and potential risks were also reiterated, and participants were notified that they could refuse to answer any question or end the interview at any time. They also were reminded that the interview was being taped, which they had been notified of when they initially volunteered, but that it could be turned off at any time upon their request. All participants were required to sign consent forms which restated these points and indicated their agreement to participate before any interview questions were broached (See Consent Form in Appendix F).

The decision to tape the interviews was based on the belief that it would enhance the quality of the data collection. While tape recording can be a bit unnerving-especially at first, research suggests that it generally does not substantially affect participation or candor unless a respondent's comments could somehow discredit them or have serious ramifications for their lives (Weiss 1994). However, it does offer numerous benefits for the interview and analysis. Weiss suggests that tape recording makes it easier to maintain focus on the respondent and their comments; capture tones and speech patterns as well as gaps in responses, shifts in topics, and stray thoughts; capture more and fuller data than note taking; and avoid losing data because of poor short-term memory. Tape recording also benefits analysis, in terms of substantiating and confirming patterns, and reporting, through more vivid descriptions of respondents and their opinions. As a researcher new to the qualitative interview, tape recordings were expected to and did help me to evaluate and improve my interviewing skills throughout the study and engage in more effective data collection. Given the research topic, the voluntary nature of participation, and the confidential nature of the data, tape-recording was not expected to impede participant solicitation or influence respondent comments. Respondents were notified about the taping when they initially volunteered for the study, and only one potential participant refused to participate owing in part to taping. However, when given the opportunity to participate without taping, he refused for other reasons.

Research suggests that pre-interview steps provide a prime opportunity to reassure respondents and establish an appropriate relationship with them, keys to a comfortable and successful interview. While professionalism was always maintained to establish the seriousness and importance of the study, a sense of general connectedness with respondents in terms of humanity and understanding is necessary to produce an environment in which they will feel comfortable sharing their personal thoughts and experiences. To that end, through information provision, demeanor, appearance and speech, I attempted to "strike a balance between formality and informality" (McCracken 1988, 26) with participants that matched their own state. Pre-interview steps were not rushed, and participants were prompted for any questions, concerns or comments they had regarding any of the information presented or the interview in general. Time also was taken to engage in non-interview related small talk to help create a more comfortable interview environment.

Interviews, all personally conducted, lasted from 35 minutes to, in two instances, over 2 hours, the average being 45 minutes to an hour. In no instance did any participant ask to skip a question, turn off the tape recorder or end the interview. After completing the interview, every participant upon request agreed to self-complete a personal background questionnaire. Before leaving, participants also were asked their thoughts on the interview and their experience, which were overwhelmingly positive and in many instances unsolicited, and were asked if they would be comfortable distributing recruitment cards to others they thought might be interested. To avoid the singularity of views that can sometimes result from a snowball sample, participants were reminded of the need for a diverse sample and my desire to speak with people of all different backgrounds and views. Toward the end of data collection, as it became necessary to recruit participants to fit key sub-samples, participants were carefully steered in the direction of the groups I still needed. Participants also were informed of the importance of not sharing the exact nature of the questions to those to whom they distributed the cards. Unsolicited comments from participant-referred participants suggested they were complying with that request.

Data Transcription and Analysis

In order to improve data collection throughout the process, interviews were transcribed as they were completed, usually within a few days of collection and whenever possible before the next interview. This approach provided the opportunity to 1) record thoughts and impressions on a particular interview before they were forgotten or confused with other interviews; 2) learn from particularly beneficial or disadvantageous means of acquiring data or missed opportunities to explore expected or potentially relevant issues; and 3) add any new and relevant issues to later interviews. By allowing me to recognize my own speech patterns and become more familiar with the types of responses offered by participants, constant transcription of the interviews allowed for constant improvement of the process, which improved the quality of the overall data set. Early transcription also allowed for a more comprehensive sense of the data when it was time to prepare to begin analysis. To help improve the reliability of the transcriptions, and since time and funding did not allow for two transcribers for each interview, all interviews were first listened to fully, then during a second listening transcribed, and then listened to a third time while following along with the transcription to correct errors. To help address the validity of transcriptions, which inherently lose the context of the language, interviews were transcribed verbatim including pauses and were completed with a mind toward the actual interview and the general demeanor, mannerisms and context of participants' answers, a process that was made easier by the fact that transcriptions were completed soon after each interview.

McCracken vividly describes the objective and nature of qualitative data analysis.

> The object of analysis is to determine the categories, relationships, and assumptions that inform the respondent's view of the world in general and the topic in particular. The investigator comes to this undertaking with a sense of what the literature says ought to be there, a sense of how the topic at issue is constituted in his or her own experience, and a glancing sense of what took place in the interview itself. The investigator must be prepared to use all of this material as a guide to what exists there, but he or she must also be prepared to ignore all of this material to see what none of it anticipates. If the full power of discovery inherent in the qualitative interview is to be fully exploited, the investigator must be prepared to glimpse and systematically reconstruct a view of the world that bears no relation to his or her own view or the one evident in the literature (1988, 42).

The importance of his comments became clear from the beginning of data analysis. Given the exploratory nature of the study but the organized structure of the interview protocol, analysis of the interview data involved both deductive and inductive coding processes. An initial set of codes was identified based on the general questions used to guide the interviews and the nature of the expected responses to such questions based on prior research and theorized perspectives. During a preliminary coding, it became clear that because of the general nature of the interview questions and the many different directions that participants' comments took, new codes and modification of some of the original codes was necessary to capture the content and meaning of the ideas suggested by the comments. In order to stay true to the interviews, codes were labeled and defined to fit the data rather than squeezing that data into similar codes that might more directly reflect literature or prior research. Such inductive/open coding was then used within each interview question, interview section, and the interview as a whole. Numerous readings of all the interviews resulted in a number of seemingly relevant variables and values by which the interviews were then coded. As coding of interviews was conducted, themes and patterns of consistency and contradiction were identified within individual interviews. After full coding of the individual interviews, the whole set of interviews was analyzed with an eye towards overall themes and patterns. In all, the data was analyzed from the specific to the ever more general to examine the possibility of general academic conclusions concerning the participants' views.

All data coding and analysis was primarily conducted by hand. While it was my original intent to rely on a computer-assisted qualitative analysis package for backup, the nature of the data, along with time and technical constraints and a personal preference for working with hard rather than electric copy, led me to bypass this option. However, a word-processing program was used for searching transcripts for words and phrases to serve as a backup of manual coding of the data as well as for organizing the transcripts and maintaining computer backups of coded comments. In addition, SPSS was used as a repository for general interview coding to allow for quick referral to relevant interviews and comments as well as retrieval of descriptive statistics. While relying on a qualitative analysis package can provide a second set of eyes on the data, my personal data collection and detailed transcription and coding processes allow me to feel comfortable that key issues were not overlooked.

The Final Sample

In the end, the current analysis cannot be generalized beyond the current sample as a result of its size and non-random selection. However, it does provide a glimpse into the views on bias crime of 40 citizens of rural, western Pennsylvania, and the overall patterns and themes reflected in those views, providing additional information on which to base more structured future research on the topic and perhaps other punitive criminal justice policies.

The final sample matched the original sample requirements, including eight members of each of the five sub-sample communities and, based on participant responses to the personal background questionnaire, was more diverse on some measures than others. Although women were slightly over sampled, both sexes were adequately represented – 23 and 17 respectively, and not for lack of trying. Participants of both sexes were more likely to successfully recruit female participants. Participants ranged in age from 19 to 85, the average age being 42 and the rest creating a nice distribution across 10-year ranges (19-29 = 10; 30-39 = 11; 40-49 = 7; 50+ = 12). They had lived in rural PA an average of 25 years (range 2-60). Three-quarters of the sample were or had been married and a little over half had an average of 2 kids. Aside from the African-American sub-sample, all participants identified their race as white, Caucasian, Anglo or Semitic. This is not surprising given the general lack of diversity in the study region, the fact that two sub-samples were limited to Caucasians, and the limited number of African-American Jews. Three quarters of the sample identified themselves as heterosexual, the rest self identifying as non-heterosexual (homosexual, bisexual, queer and gradations) except one participant who chose to skip the question. The vast majority of participants (31) identified themselves as religious (22) or spiritual (9). Eight identified their religion as Judaism however the religious identification of the rest of the sample was very diverse including: Agnostic, Catholic, Baptist, Pagan, Protestant, Christian, Methodist, Lutheran, United Universalist, and Shamanism.

The three sample characteristics showing the least amount of diversity were politics, education, and income. Respondents were fairly split in their self-defining as political (29 yes, 19 no), however in the sample overall and for those identifying themselves as political, the vast majority were democrats and/or identified themselves as moderate or liberal. This perhaps is not surprising given the overall sample was 63 percent minority because of the sub-samples and minorities tend toward democratic affiliation. Also participants were recruited from a college town and over half (24) had a college degree or post graduate degree, 11 had some college and only four had a high school degree or less, and education tends to correlate with more democratic and/or liberal views. This skewed education also likely explains the highly skewed incomes of the sample. Half earned over $60,000, and the rest somewhat evenly split between $20-30,000 and less than 20,000. This lack of diversity most likely stems from three sources: the nature of my initial contacts, most of whom where in some way connected to the local university; the choice of sub-samples–since two samples were highly correlated with education (highly educated and Jewish-as I was told by almost every Jewish participant it would be almost impossible to find local Jews without a college degree who were over 18); and the lack of response from recruitment cards left at working class businesses and establishments for workers and customers-self exclusion. These skewed numbers do serve to limit the findings and, based on research, likely skewed the results toward less punitive approaches to crime and punishment and perhaps more tolerant views and greater support for the need for bias crime legislation. However, at the same time, it might serve to better reflect the views of those most willing to share their views on social issues and those in a financial, educational or occupational position to influence policy in the area of bias crime. Findings that demonstrate variation in their views or discrepancies between their views and the government's response to bias crime could have far ranging implications.

Overall, the sampling strategy, although resulting in a final sample somewhat skewed demographically, did not seem to produce a sample ripe with extreme views on the issue either for those participants who represented groups more vulnerable to bias crimes or not. In addition, although members of the former category were more likely to have experienced hate-based incidents, for the most part their experiences did not seem to have had such an intensive impact on their lives as to warrant ample reflection on the bias crime issue or extreme views on it. That is not to say many did not feel strongly about the issue only that their views did not seem extreme in the sense of their falling on either end of a continuum of views toward bias crime. Their views reflected neither Archie Bunker-style bigotry nor a desire for treatment of biased offenders beyond that logically justified by the nature of the crime. Finally, although a few participants raised local bias-related experiences or events, for the most part these factors seemed to serve as examples of a more general awareness held by such participants of their potential targeting for bias crimes rather than a factor driving their current views. The succeeding chapters provide descriptions and analyses of those 40 citizens' views.

CHAPTER 7

Citizens' Views on Bias Crime

This chapter sets the stage for participants' views on the appropriate approaches to bias crime by serving three functions. First, it places their views in a general context by providing a brief statistical introduction to bias crime and bias crime legislation in Pennsylvania and when possible the sample region. Second, it provides a detailed outline of participants' general views on bias crime. It explores their general familiarity with and perceptions of bias crime; how they would explain it and what they think are its causes; their personal experience with and fear of such crime; and whether they perceive of it as a problem and how it makes them feel. Finally, the chapter offers a comparison of participants' views of bias crime compared to those of crime in general.

Bias Crime Legislation in Pennsylvania

Pennsylvania has substantive hate crime legislation known as the Ethnic Intimidation Act. Passed in December 2002, Pa. C.S. 2710(a), defines ethnic intimidation as "any crime against a person, arson, criminal mischief, or any other type of property destruction, criminal trespass or harassment by communication or address that is committed" "...with malicious intent toward the actual or perceived race, color, religion, national origin, ancestry, mental or physical disability, sexual orientation, gender or gender identity of another individual or group of individuals." If it can be proven beyond a reasonable doubt that the offender is guilty of an underlying crime and it was committed with malicious intent based on "hatred or anger toward one of the specified characteristics of the victim," then the defendant can be convicted of ethnic intimidation and receive a punishment harsher than would have been possible for just the underlying crime. The State also has an Institutional Vandalism statute, which under 18 Pa. C.S. 3307 a person commits "if he knowingly desecrates a venerated object, vandalizes, defaces or otherwise damages..." places of worship, schools, community centers and other institutions or personal property of those institutions. Though not directly a hate crime statute, the institutions it covers are often the targets of hate-based offenders. Pennsylvania sentencing statutes also allow offenders of institutional vandalism to be sentenced to supervised community service "including repairing or restoring damaged property" if the sentencing court feels the offender would "benefit" from such activity (*Sentencing for Criminal Mischief* 42 Pa.C.S 9720). The State also allows for civil rights redress for personal injury as a result of ethnic intimidation or institutional vandalism (*Civil Rights Violations* 42 Pa. C.S. 8309). Finally, the Ethnic Intimidation Statistics Collection Act (71 P.S. 250) mandates the Pennsylvania State Police to collect information on crimes motivated by bias. Although Pennsylvania's Ethnic Intimidation Act was passed within the last few years, only 30 percent of participants believed that the State had such legislation, perhaps not surprising given that only about one-third even mentioned hate crime legislation in any general or specific form before being asked about such legislation directly.

It also should be noted that Pennsylvania's laws surrounding bias crime are fairly typical. According to the Anti-Defamation League's (2007) comparison of state hate crime laws, Pennsylvania is with the majority of states in its recognition and authorization of criminal penalties for bias-motivated violence and intimidation and institutional vandalism; its authorization of civil actions for such incidents; and its legislation requiring data collection on bias crimes. In addition, its laws recognize bias based on race, religion, ethnicity, sexual orientation, gender and disability as do the laws of the majority of states. However, Pennsylvania is also one of only eleven states that recognize bias based on transgender/gender identity.

Bias Crime in Pennsylvania

In 2004, the last year for which national and PA State data were available at the time of the current study, 7,649 biased incidents (9,035 offenses) were reported nationwide. According to the PA Uniform Crime Report (2004), 136 hate crime incidents (143 offenses), involving 171 victims and 172 offenders, were reported in Pennsylvania, down three incidents since 2003. Forty-five percent of those offenses were crimes against persons (compared to the national 63%), 32 percent against property, and the rest were incidents of disorderly conduct. Similar to national statistics, the majority of offenses (66%) were motivated by race; anti-black motivation accounting for 47.8 percent. Another 18 percent of the State's bias crimes were motivated by sexual orientation, primarily against men, and 12 percent by religion, almost entirely against Jews. No hate crimes were reported for the study region during 2004 or the previous year. From an analysis of hate crime incidents reported to the Human Relations Commission in Pennsylvania from 1984 to 1999, Wilson and Ruback concluded that "hate offenses tended to be relatively minor acts" with "the most commonly reported incidents involving noncriminal behavior and minor property offenses" (2003, 385).

Overall, nothing in the official bias crime, or general crime, statistics suggests a high rate of crime or bias crime in the State or sample region or any significant change in either that might be expected to influence participants' views or relative views on the issues.

Perceptions of Bias Crime

Although only 33 percent of study participants mentioned bias crime legislation and no bias crimes were actually reported in the sample region, the sample as a whole demonstrated fairly concise familiarity with the concept of bias crime. In fact, when asked whether familiar with "crimes committed against other people because of who they are or what they believe" every participant answered affirmatively and many went so far as to label such crime as hate or bias crime. Further, when asked to explain or describe bias crime, all but three participants did so in a way that confirmed their general understanding of the concept - a crime committed because of some type of prejudice/bias/hate toward the victim because of their status.

Initial comments made by the remaining three participants left it unclear whether they understood bias crime in its fullest context or could truly distinguish it from non-bias crime. A Jewish, female, college student demonstrated her "familiarity" by raising the Rodney King incident. While certainly this incident could be labeled a hate crime, her follow-up comments suggested that her perception of bias crime was geared more towards discriminatory acts, particularly those by people in a position of some type of authority rather than crimes in general committed because of bias or prejudice. A college-educated, retired woman, while labeling such crime hate crime went on to actually describe and discuss her views on "violent" or anger-based crime rather than bias or hate crime. An elderly, high-school educated, African-American woman seemed to similarly think of violent crime when initially asked about bias crime. Although when asked how she felt about such crime she indicated, "It's different for me because I am black and they have no right. We are all humans and...our blood is the same regardless of what nationality or color people are," (12) the rest of her comments did not reflect a clear distinction between what is generally thought of as bias and non-bias crime. Because of the difficulties in determining whether these women's comments were reflecting their thoughts on "bias crime" as it is legally defined, they were left out of the analysis. Their perceptions of bias crime do offer insight into how some citizens may misperceive legal concepts and suggest that their thoughts on and responses to such crimes may be misinterpreted if such perceptions are not collected or taken into consideration by researchers. However, given the study's interest in how citizens specifically view and prefer to respond to what the law recognizes as bias crime, including their remarks in analysis would disregard the fact that their comments do not actually reflect their views on "bias crime". In addition, two of these participants' interviews were fairly confusing making clear understanding or interpretation of many of their comments impossible.

Aside from those few, the study participants, as they claimed, seemed quite familiar with the general concept of bias crime. According to the Federal government, "a hate crime, also often referred to as bias crime, is a criminal offense committed against a person, property or society that is motivated, in whole or in part, by the offender's bias against a race, religion, disability, sexual orientation, or ethnicity/national origin" (U.S. Dept. of Justice 2006). While no study participant defined such crime verbatim many offered their own definitions or descriptions that coherently identified the main elements of bias crime – a crime motivated by prejudice against some particular group because they are somehow different. Also interesting is the fact that the majority of participants' definitions focused on the act, its victim(s), or its consequences rather than characteristics of the offenders. This could reflect participants' familiarity with actual bias crime legislation, which rarely defines bias crime in terms of offender characteristics, or their focus on the crime itself, which at its core includes an act and particular victim regardless of who commits it.

> 3-It's like any sort of crime...like beating someone up, like defacing their property...that's committed solely because that person is you know black or gay or Arabic or you know something like that that makes them different.

16-I would say it was a crime committed against somebody because of who they are...because of their color, because of their race...anybody that is different from the norm of the area.

17-I think it's something that is a crime that is committed against another person because of the color of their skin, because of their sexual orientation, because of their religion, because of race, and I think it is not always physical.

19-Crimes against people for their religious beliefs or their sexual preferences or their color or race.

13-Crime an individual commits against another because of who they are – how they are different.

21-I would say that a person, an individual or a group of individuals in some way hurts or violates another individual on the basis of usually their race or their religious belief or their sexual orientation.

Some participants chose to explain bias crime through examples or added examples to clarify their own definitions or descriptions. Their examples ranged from very general depictions of bias crime to actual local or national incidents.

7-There are all different kinds from the Ku Klux Klan burning people's homes, hanging people...even putting like a cross up. I think in some ways sexual harassment can be a bias crime in a way...To the abortion clinic, people burning abortion clinics because they don't believe in that...Bombing anything because it has to do with someone who's a Jew.

34-...hate crime is usually racially motivated. It could be racially or sexual preference someone of a group disliking someone of another group or another practice...A Christian radical like a fundamentalist Christian you know burning down a Muslim mosque something like that that's a hate crime...I see a bunch of jocks beating on a homosexual in the

locker room as a hate crime...some guys out in Texas I think
it was skinheads that dragged the black dude with the truck.

31-I think hate crime is a violent crime against a person that's
a member of a group in order to attack that group. One that
affected me the most was the Matthew Shepard case and just
them attacking him because he was gay and it sent this thing
through the community. It did affect everybody in the gay
community.

27-We've had someone recently in the nearby city who was
going after Jews and after 9/11 a poor Indian gentleman was
beaten up and actually they thought he was Arabic so they
were actually trying to beat up Arabic people as if every
Arabic person in the world you know had anything to do with
9/11.

9-I guess it would just be a hate crime is where you harm
someone or someone's business, property or do some kind of
harm to them... based solely on an emotional hatred of that
person, a hatred of something they do, believe in, or the color
of their skin...The black church 3 miles down the road got
burned to the ground. That was a hate crime because the three
men who were doing it were white supremacists who were
expressing their anger at the fact that blacks are allowed off
the plantation.

40-There was a hate crime where there was a black family
who moved in and they burned a cross in their yard and that
just horrified this town...I think it's just wrong whether it's
their color or their nationality, or sexual preference, whatever.

Finally, a few provided more personal examples/experiences with bias
crime or similarly indicated that the best way to describe such crime to
another was to offer examples that would touch people either by
sharing the most extreme/shocking examples of bias crimes or
examples that would hit them close to home.

2-Oh, I'm familiar with hate crimes. Look at my window.
That's because I am the only black in this area and we can
only assume that it was a hate crime. They shot at it.

14-You have to give them something that is personal. I would try to explain it in a way that was personal to them. Somebody didn't like your sister because she is a woman. A guy is going around killing women because they are women. Getting beat up for being black or white or Hispanic.

18-Six million Jews and the gas chambers in Germany during the war. That is a big hate crime. Imprisoned African slaves...and how they could be killed, beaten or torn away from their families. That is a hate crime. Anybody with a Hispanic sound to their name or with an accent...people putting them down as greasers. Any Asian...they call them slant eyes. To me that is a hate crime. That is how I would explain it to somebody.

Another interesting note regarding participants' general explanations of bias crime was the mix of minority and non-minority participants who were able to offer clear definitions and examples of bias crime. While minorities were more likely to provide personal examples or experiences of bias crime, the depictions of bias crime shared above are not those of only minority participants, who it might be thought would be more familiar with such crime given their status and greater likelihood of victimization.

To follow-up on their general explanations of bias crime, most participants were asked to describe a typical bias crime. The majority responded by commenting on the nature of the underlying crime (47%) or both the underlying crime and the typical victim (40%). Of the remaining participants, two commented solely on the victims of bias crime and two answered that they simply did not know. Only three participants ever mentioned anything about the perpetrators of bias crimes, other than in terms of their bias. Two particularly mentioned crime committed by hate groups (KKK and white supremacists), and one indicated that most bias crimes are committed by white males-a statement consistent with national data. However, in general, participants' responses suggested that for most bias crime is not viewed as a static incident involving one particular type of crime or victim but rather they "run the gamut" (30) ranging from "property crime to you know physical violence and beyond" (25). In fact, their comments might best be described as suggesting that for them there is not a "typical" bias crime.

Over half of participants asked indicated that the typical bias crime, in terms of the nature or seriousness of the underlying crime, varies from rather low-level crimes against persons or property crimes, such as harassment, intimidation and vandalism, to simple and aggravated assaults, to murder.

> 36-You can get something just as basic as someone throwing a mud ball at your window, to something as severe as killing a man because he's gay.

> 16-When I think of hate crime, I think of it being as bad as a murder or a theft or that kind of thing but I also feel like hate crime can be as simple as slandering or saying something negative or beating them down with words.

> 39-Sometimes it could be physical, sometimes…they can say mean things against someone…I mean we've used examples of if someone's black to say mean things you know, with us being Jewish we've talked about the holocaust. I think they go all across the gamut. I mean not to long ago there was something in the south where there was someone black I think was dragged behind a car or something and there I forgot how long ago but a young man was a homosexual and you know so I mean there's that level of murder too. Gays are still beaten up. There's a whole gamut.

However, of those who said it varied, a third indicated that they believed most were rather low-level person or property crimes. Only two suggested that serious crimes, such as aggravated assault, robbery or murder accounted for most bias crimes. It is unclear whether the remaining felt their truly was no "typical" type of bias crime or perhaps simply were not sure what that might be.

> 28-It seems like there's more low level kind of stuff like jeering and calling people names and pushing them around but I think there are some serious crimes but I don't think there are as many serious as there are simple ones.

24-There's murder, there's lesser ones, there's slander and people who get beaten up on the street for no reason or for their lifestyle reason. I would guess that murder or robbery would be one of the top two.

Only nine participants pointed to a specific type of underlying crime as typical, six indicating that the typical bias crime involved serious crimes such as aggravated assaults, violent beatings and murder, three the lower level offenses of harassment or arson. In all, less than a quarter of participants viewed bias crime as a crime primarily involving serious predicate offenses, namely aggravated assaults, robberies and murders-a view inconsistent with official statistics. According to the FBI (U.S. Dept. of Justice 2006), the majority of hate crimes are in fact low-level crimes against persons (primarily intimidation and simple assaults) and property crimes. In fact, in 2004 less than 20 percent of hate crimes involved serious violent crimes against persons. Thus, the majority of participants' perceptions of the underlying nature of bias crimes are very much in line with statistics or at least not in opposition to them.

In terms of victims of bias crime, fourteen participants specifically mentioned victim and/or prejudice type when asked about the typical bias crime. Three felt that the typical victim varied across the primary categories of potential victims-victims based on race, religion, ethnicity, and sexual orientation. Of the 12 who identified a typical group(s) as the most common victim(s), they mentioned persons of different races or sexual orientation most frequently (7 each). Religious victims were mentioned by two participants and ethnic victims by one. One participant was rather vague preferring to label "stereotyped groups" as the typical victims.

13-I would say it mostly happens against homosexuals and racial minorities and perpetrated I would say, mostly by white males...

11-An awful lot of it is with regard to race but I think more recently, an awful lot of it tends to be against gays and to give the example of the young man who was tied to the fence and railings. They are more prevalent today.

28-Like the Ku Klux Klan I guess like abusing and torturing black people, gay-bashing and stuff like that.

18-Right now...I think the most typical type of hate crime would be like Matthew Shepard – crimes against gays, lesbians, trans-gendered, bisexual people, because it is things like people don't really care about, they are not important. They say the NAACP can protect Black people, which it tries and other people too, it's not just black people. But there is a small community of gay people here in town and I know they have problems even getting a place to have a party.

According to the latest national statistics, most participants were not far off the mark. Race-based bias crimes accounted for the majority (54 percent) of bias crimes in 2005, sexual orientation and religious-based crimes accounting 16 percent each, and ethnicity-based crimes 14 percent (U.S. Dept. of Justice 2006).

Based on participants' responses to the typical bias crime question as well as their mention of different types of bias crimes and victims throughout the general bias crime section of the interview, the sample appeared to perceive bias crimes in a way that included a range of both crimes and victims. A majority of participants mentioned the possibility of bias crimes involving physical assaults of some sort (87%) or harassment or intimidation (54%). Another 46 percent specifically mentioned bias-based property crimes. In addition, a majority of participants in one way or another mentioned bias based on race (89%), religion (69%), and sexual orientation (76%). Thirty-eight percent mentioned bias based on the ethnic or national origin and another 35 percent mentioned victims of bias crime simply being "different" or "minorities" or "stereotyped groups [that people are] traditionally biased against." And these numbers may be lower than might be expected if participants were asked specifically to identify as fully as they could the potential crimes or victims of bias crime, which they were not asked to do. That and the fact that ethnic/national origin minorities were essentially not represented in the study might explain why ethnicity/national origin, an anchoring victim/prejudice provision of most bias crime legislation, was raised the least. Other potential bases for victimization identified by a minority of participants included gender, politics, disability, and transexuality. In terms of perpetrators of bias crime, aside from three participants who mentioned them in reference to the typical crime, only four additional participants raised the issue during the bias crime section of the interview, referring in some way to the commission of such crimes by hate groups.

Overall, the sample if not versed in the official bias crime statistics, seemed adequately familiar with the concept and the types of crimes and victims that hate crime legislation often serves to address. This familiarity provided a foundation on which to confidently explore participants' experiences with and views on bias crime and to compare them to similar experiences and thoughts on crime in general.

Causes of Bias Crime

Participants were asked to share their views on the causes of bias crime, which they seemed quite quick to identify. Although they offered a range of such causes and most offered more than one, their responses placed emphasis on three: upbringing, ignorance/fear, and society. Nearly 60 percent of participants felt that upbringing was a cause of bias crime. They were clearly of the opinion that hate is generally learned not innate-that children learn from their parents' opinions and the environmental influences in which their parents raise them, and often those children go on to consciously or not teach that hatred or prejudice to their children, and the generational cycle continues.

> 32-I think it's how you are raised you know I mean it all stems from that. And it's all brought down too because I certainly wasn't raised like that but I'm from this town and my parents live deep, deep in the country and their next door neighbors probably every single person around them would look at me and like gasp if they saw me and my husband and my child walking into the room (interracial couple). So it's like my father's mother didn't raise him like that therefore my father didn't raise me like that. But its all brought down it just keeps cycling from generation to generation.

> 18-Depending on how the person is brought up – maybe they were brought up all their life listening to their parents or friends or whoever downgrading other people so this is how they grew up thinking that this is normal for them to feel this way. And then when they raise children, they raise their

children this way. Unless they are very extraordinary children, they are going to grow up the same way.

7-I think, obviously there are certain things, too, that are passed from generation to generation, certain beliefs and that stuff. What parents teach their children and the strong feelings, that is hard to break sometimes.

33-I mean obviously it's the way you're raised you know. How you are influenced. How your opinions are formed things like that.

40-We are not born with hate in our hearts. It is a learned behavior. It is a choice. I can either hate your desk or I can like your desk, it has done nothing to me, but yet I hate it. It is a learned behavior that needs to be stamped out. It's parenting. If your dad says I hate white people and you know over the years all he talked about was white people did this and white people did that, it's something you pick up, maybe subconsciously, you automatically assume all white people are bad.

13-It comes from the parents, family, without a doubt.

Half of the sample placed the origin of bias crime in ignorance and/or fear. In terms of ignorance, participants felt that people often lack understanding or knowledge of, education regarding, and/or exposure to people different from themselves. For many participants this ignorance was thought to breed discomfort or fear of the unknown or change, which it was felt could result in strong emotions and even violence against those who were feared.

17-Personally, ignorance. I think part of it is, especially when you live in a very homogenous society, not having any contact with people who are outside of your race, religion or whatever, your sexual orientation.

3-Ignorance on the part of the people committing the crime, like if you don't know a whole lot about the certain group or certain ethnicity, that kind of thing. If you don't know a whole lot about it you might be more afraid of it. And I think that just leads people, you know, if you're scared of it, that makes you angry and that leads to violence and stuff like that.

6-Fear. Lack of being open-minded about whatever it is. Mostly it is probably fear. I don't want to say uneducated because there are Ph.D. people who hate...So it maybe more fear than anything. And so afraid that if I start saying that it's ok and let those people alone, then others will call me gay or homo.

15-Ignorance. Some people don't understand something fully and therefore they want to eradicate it.

16-I think there is a lot of racist people and when I say racist I don't necessarily mean by color but by everything. I think it is much more common in the world in general, just a lot of people don't like people who are different from them because we have a fear of people we don't know. Fear of the unknown, ignorance and the safety and keeping things the same and fear of change and people that are different coming in.

31-I think it is fear on the part of the person committing the crime – fear of something they just don't understand.

It was clear to a number of participants that upbringing, fear and ignorance were intricately linked, and that upbringing served as a key force in a child's ability and willingness to try to understand if not appreciate differences.

35-Ignorance I think. I think people don't understand the way in which gender or sexual orientation exists from people or they choose not to based on ignorant religious beliefs or adherence to tradition or you know inheriting their families' beliefs or whatever.

19-For some reason people call my husband hermaphrodite or transvestite (actually trans-gendered) which they don't quite know what they are talking about...and that is ignorance. But I also believe that some of the hate crimes and racist crimes is ignorance. They are misinformed or uninformed. It is the way they are raised.

37-Clearly I would say it's just the way people are brought up and the impressions that they are given as they are kids and getting older. For instance, many people around here don't know any Jews, they don't know a whole lot of blacks around here and they'll say things about not wanting to go to Pittsburgh or NYC because of the people who are there and being afraid of them not really understanding what the situation would actually be but just having an impression in their minds. And it would seem like somehow people could be better educated to not be so fearful of the unknown.

30-It has to do with the lack of education, lack of proper upbringing because somebody is not born with a bias of any particular kind, they develop it. And so what makes this developed or why this is appealing to this person is all by their frame of reference be it their parents or their whole social circle that they are part of you know.

Nearly forty percent of participants commented in such a way as to suggest that society actually promotes or at least perpetuates bias crime. For some it was the general nature or culture of our society, while others pointed to some specific aspect of society, including its laws, religion, politics, or media.

35-I think in a lot of ways…legally…or even structurally…we sort of justify it and maybe not vocally like hey its okay to gay bash but there aren't…a lot of penalties in place or there isn't you know a very critical discourse on this behavior or this activity saying this is not okay this is not acceptable. I mean our constitution says you know we exist under one god but yet we're supposed to be a secular nation today and that drives me crazy. So of course when we are dealing with these sort of very traditional perspectives even written into the law and sodomy laws have been in effect you know all over the country for how long and…17 states still have them on the books…the fact that they're on paper I mean that doesn't do a whole lot for my rights.

19-It has been allowed in our country to go on for so long. There is still in the hate crime legal jargon in PA, sexual orientation is not included. It is not okay to fire a gay person for being a gay, but it says nothing about a trans-gendered person.

33-Our country despite the melting pot behind it, I think it's very divisive. I think in our country we're being segregated into small groups.

30-I think that there are narrow-minded people. I think that there are a lot of organizations that you know focus on that or feed on it.

17-Media I think to a certain extent. I think we sensationalize hate crimes a lot...I think the media also in that if there is some hate crime that seems interesting, it somehow peaks the interest of Hollywood then it is all over. We are seeing it in crime dramas and if that is your only exposure to it and you don't understand that people have a different sexual orientation or people are in some way different from you, it can sometimes fuel the fires.

One participant in particular, a middle-aged, college-educated, African-American man, spoke at length about American's ingrained territoriality and its influence on the fear and ignorance that make bias and violence prevalent in the U.S.

34-It's a little bit ingrained in us I think because...we are an anxious nation... I mean we are so anxious so afraid of anybody remotely different from us you know. I don't know, men being afraid of feminists and jocks being afraid of homosexuals, what's all that coming from. It's the insecurities of a person and having those same biases and just not being educated about who it is you're dealing with. There are places in big cities where they practice tolerance of each other, they practice some civility but that doesn't mean that they completely integrate with each other...So people do treat each other with some kind of tolerance but there seems like there is something underneath there...But there are a lot of

areas that are very isolated where places kind of like here I
mean this place is changing a little bit but you step five miles
out of here and its heehaw. So that is changing but this
country has been built on violence and its survived off
violence I mean its really lived off it for a long time...I mean
everybody says it's how we're raised but it seems to be
something special about Americans that they have a fear about
invasion of property or invasion of land. I think Americans
are very possessive about the area around them. You know
they cut out little areas and they really want to keep it that way
and they don't want anybody stepping in. It is cultural it's
like a whole bunch of different countries...that neighborhood
is kind of like a little country, then all the Guatemalans come
in and its like "holy shit what's happening they gonna take our
jobs gonna take our women you know what I mean they're
gonna start bringing the drugs in here and all of this other
stuff...It's anybody you see as being different I mean it's
territoriality. I mean we are ingrained with that.

Some participants, nearly 20 percent, suggested that bias crime
might stem from something beyond a mere cultural characteristic to a
quality of human nature. In particular, they implied that there was
something about human nature that drives people to need to feel better
than, or to have power over, others-to ensure their worth relative to
others.

7-I think some of it is there is this sense among people, there
is kind of this social psychology thing, this idea that I need to
feel power, I need to feel better than somebody, so who can I
target? Who is safe to target. And so it gives people that
sense of power over, that I'm not on the bottom run, that kind
of thing.

18-People have passed somebody that they feel better than.
The poorest person has to, if they are uneducated or illiterate,
feel like they have passed somebody who they are better than
in order to make themselves feel better. So if they can find a
group of people, or several groups of people, depending on
who you are talking about...and thinking that he is better than
them, it makes him feel better and bigger.

11-I think the other thing too is that people get angry when they think other people are getting more than they are, or having more opportunities than they are having and they deserve more. So I think you will find that even if it is universal like with the Shiites and the whatever – the same kinds of things are happening.

Although overall these participants' seem to offer a rather pessimistic prognosis, one participant offered a bit of hope given his perception that learning to deal with differences was a relatively new issue for the country implying perhaps that over time it could get past it.

38-I think it's just human nature something about it is engrained…And encountering differences in this country a lot of time means encountering change. You know the people next door are playing music that is very unusual for you and you don't want to have to hear it and it bothers you. It doesn't, it's not familiar like rain its familiar like acid or something you know. It doesn't feel good, it doesn't suit you. But you know I wonder about that. I think that as a country and just globally looking at it demographically we are maybe the first generation or maybe the second or third generation…very early on in the evolution of human psyche where you have to really deal with different people. I mean it's only been how long since really…you could encounter people of every race in your day. I mean that was impossible probably a hundred years ago accept in a few places…And humanity's not use to that. We haven't grown into that, so maybe it's growing pains.

All of the causes thus far raised seem to suggest an external pressure influencing an individual's likelihood to engage in such crime or at least hold opinions or attitudes that would support such behavior. They suggest an awareness or acknowledgement that either or both a person's home and/or social environment plays a strong role in the creation of the conditions necessary for such crime. However, about a quarter of the sample identified causes of bias crime that could be viewed as focusing on issues internal to the perpetrator, or that were at least discussed from that perspective, rather than somehow a reflection of his external environment, although only a couple of those failed to mention other more social factors that might lead to bias crime. Some participants simply pointed to hateful or prejudiced people as the cause, others to an individual's low self esteem, overly strong ego, or personal insecurity, fears or anger. Only two participants seemed to present the perpetrators as almost evil, one who felt that there are those in society who want power over others and use whatever means available to get it and another who felt that the perpetrators of bias crime were the same as other criminals, violent and/or self righteous.

Two additional findings of note arose from participants' views on the causes of bias crime. It would seem that minority participants who identified ignorance as a cause of bias crime were more likely to fear bias crime than those who did not. In addition, those minorities who indicated human nature as a cause of bias crime were less likely to fear bias crime than those who did not. Unfortunately, the data are not sufficient to explore or explain these findings although they might suggest that perceptions of causes of bias crime might influence participants' preferred approaches to such crime given that fear is often associated with responses to crime.

<u>Causes of Crime</u>
Participants also were asked about their views of crime in general to compare with their views on the causes of bias crime. Based on their responses, social factors were clearly viewed as a main cause of criminal behavior. The only distinctions were how many social factors they recognized and where along a continuum of specific to more abstract social causes of crimes participants' views fell. Upbringing/parenting was a frequently mentioned cause, 45 percent of participants identifying it as either a direct or indirect cause of crime in general. In particular, participants lamented the nonexistence or breaking down of a strong social support structure for kids that they deemed as important for the development of appropriate attitudes and behaviors. They felt parents and the social environments in which they allowed their children to be raised were not providing such a structure leading to crime or other issues they associated with crime including anger, frustration, and/or lack of respect for authority.

However, the most frequently mentioned cause of crime in general was economics. Participants' economic comments covered three general areas. One was the idea of crime as an economic necessity-loss of jobs and poverty require people to simply do what they see as necessary to meet their financial needs. Another was the idea that such economic loss has led to an increase in two-parent working households leading to the parenting issues mentioned above. Finally, participants raised the issue of the stratified nature of U.S. society. They shared the belief that America puts forth a dream of economic possibility but then generates social and class inequality including a permanent underclass of have nots who because of their relative position may come to view crime as a feasible response to their predicament.

Finally, only about a quarter of participants discussed causes of crime in a way that focused more on the individual criminal than his environment-mentioning biological factors, lack of impulse control, the thrill of crime for the individual, or the criminals' inability to just live their own lives. Only two of those discussed such factors absent from comments concerning more social issues external the individual criminal.

Comparing Causes of Crime and Bias Crime
Whether it be parenting, economics, or other societal factors raised by participants including American norms and values, American politics and government, and/or problems with social priorities, participants' focus on social causes of crime was a theme that carried through their thinking on, and perceptions of, both crime in general and bias crime by a rough three to one margin. While participants were not asked about the type of crime they considered when discussing crime in general, their primary emphasis on economics might suggest that their thoughts turned more to property offenses or at least financially-motivated violent offenses. This would make sense given that most crime in the U.S. is of such a nature. However, prior research has suggested that when asked about crime people tend to consider the most serious crimes and worse case scenarios. That said, it could be that in thinking about causes of crime participants were less focused on the outcome of a crime and more on what motivates it. Although, the different perspectives on the economic basis for crime could serve to explain both financially-motivated offenses where the need for money is the clear motivation and more violent crimes where perhaps the economic social order may be perceived as a motivating factor for the pressures that might lead to such crime.

On the other hand, when asked about the causes of bias crime, participants clearly pictured non-financially-motivated crimes, focusing on low-level intimidation and vandalism and frequently mentioning more violent crimes. Given the very definition of bias crime it is perhaps not surprising that participants would consider the causes of bias and prejudice more so perhaps than the underlying crime. While society's economic social order could be offered as a viable explanation for bias and prejudice and thus motivate bias crime, participants' comments seem to suggest that such a link was not considered or if so it was not viewed as direct or necessary a condition for bias crime as other sources of biased or prejudicial attitudes.

In all, participants were willing to look beyond the criminal for the causes of crime and bias crime, and their willingness to explore what some might perceive as more abstract and/or indirect causes of crime did not, it would seem, owe to their distance from crime and bias crime as many had been its victims. Considerations of the extent to which participants' causes of crime might explain or correlate with their causes of bias crime revealed very little insight. Those mentioning a particular cause of crime in general, such as upbringing or society, were no more likely than others to mention that same factor as a cause of bias crime or vice versa. This of course could be explained by the different perceptions of crime in general and bias crime discussed above. The only patterns that did seem to emerge were that those who mentioned society as a cause of crime seemed more likely to indicate fear as a cause of bias crime, whereas those who mentioned economics were less likely to do so. Though participants' comments do not offer an explanation for this finding, it could be that it is easier for participants to link the nature of society to fear and in turn prejudice than economics. Unfortunately, the available data does not allow such an explanation to be assessed, and the nature of participants' comments on causes of crime and bias crime even when labeled the same (ex. society for both) are different allowing for only cautious comparisons at best.

Bias Crime Victimization or Experiences

Nearly half (46%) of the study participants reported being the victim of a bias crime or having experienced a bias-motivated incident because of their status or connection to a member of a minority group. Women (86%) were twice as likely as men (44%) to report such victimization. Perhaps not surprisingly, traditional "minority" participants were much more likely than non-minorities to claim victimization. Seventy percent of minority participants offered such experiences compared to seven percent of non-minorities. In fact, all but two of the victims fell within the minority groups specifically sampled in the study (African

American, Jewish, Gay/Lesbian). Eighty-six percent of African-American participants reported bias crime victimization compared to 63 percent of gays and lesbians, and 57 percent of Jewish participants. The other participants who reported bias victimization included a Wicca (who from here on out is considered a religious minority for purposes of analysis) and the Caucasian wife/mother of an interracial family. All but one victim shared at least a general description of their experience. Based on their comments, the nature of those experiences was split between verbal incidents and physical (personal or property) incidents. Beyond description, this distinction was deemed necessary to separate experiences that were likely actual bias crimes (physical incidents) from those that likely would not legally be labeled as such (verbal incidents). Given the often sketchy descriptions from obviously potentially biased sources-the victims-this was viewed as the best way to distinguish between likely hate-based incidents and bias crimes. Given that such participants perceived themselves to be victims of these experiences, whether they were crimes or not, the term victimization is used throughout the analysis. However, it should be recognized that those categorized as victims of verbal incidents were most likely not the victims of a crime, which could influence their views. Unfortunately, the current data does not allow for further exploration of that influence beyond analysis of participant views based on the dichotomy presented.

Those who reported a verbal incident reported experiencing name calling and harassment based on their race or membership in an interracial couple, their Jewish faith, or their sexual preference-lesbian, gay or trans-gendered. While most participants simply offered their experiences without directly discussing whether they perceived it as a crime or not, a few did indicate that they were not sure it would be a crime or at least implied that it if it were it was not all that serious and likely would not have been reported. A couple of participants also shared that they did not feel that simple name calling without more should be considered a crime primarily it seemed because they felt the criminal justice system had more important things to address and that such a focus would overburden the system. Although additional information would have been necessary to determine whether such incidents were in fact bias crimes, given the comments available it is likely that most of the incidents reported would not have risen to such a level, the majority being of the nature of religious or racial slurs shouted in passing. However, the line even legally is often blurry providing some explanation for why citizens might not be sure exactly where it is drawn. Even though many of these incidents probably were not crimes, they served as examples and reminders of the bias and hate that can rise to the level of crime.

> 35-I've seen a lot of people give me dirty looks or make comments under their breath or make comments to my face. I was on the bus in town a couple of years ago with my partner and we weren't doing anything in particular that's affectionate, we weren't holding hands, nothing. We were just having a conversation on the bus and this 90 year old dude with an oxygen tank huddles by us and says "You are gonna burn in hell you faggots" and then runs off the bus.

Participants who reported more physical incidents reported property crimes including vandalism or destruction of property as well as personal crimes such as literally being thrown out of stores, chased by persons in vehicles and, for one participant, assaulted by the member of a hate group. Again these individuals apparently were chosen as victims because of their race, or membership in an interracial family, sexual preference or religion, although the majority (5) appeared to have been chosen based on race.

> 2-Look at my window. That's because I am the only black in this area and we can assume that it was a hate crime. They shot it.

> 36-The mud ball on the window... I have my pentagon on my window and I don't know how many mud balls I have had on my window...You know even like the comments when I go to my car, my scratched car [believed to be hate crime], [they yell] "the Satan worshiper" blah blah blah.

> 9-I have been thrown out of stores in another state. They threw me out. And it was all because I was wearing a Wicca pentacle on a chain. And they saw that and tossed me right out of the store and told me they wouldn't serve me and didn't want me back. I had people who saw me and some friends of mine who were Wicca and actually chased us down the street threatening us. They said we should be burned at the stake like they used to do.

34-Yeah I got jumped by some skinheads. I was at a party with a...friend of mine in the military...and I think they had come to the party later and they jumped me [and beat me up] on the way home on the way back...me and my friend, and he's white, so they beat him up too.

Fear of Bias Crime

Participants also were asked whether or not they feared becoming the victim of a bias crime. In total, 15 (38%) of the 32 participants who responded indicated that they held such a fear. While it might be expected that prior victims of such crimes might be more fearful of future victimization, the data did not appear to support this contention. Fifty percent of the victims of bias crime reported fearing future victimization compared to 41 percent of non-victims. Even considering minorities only, bias victimization did not seem to be a good predictor of fear of such victimization. In fact, of those minorities who claimed to have a personal experience, only half indicated that they were in fear of future victimization. In addition, neither the nature of their experience (verbal or physical) nor how they viewed the seriousness of the predicate offense of a "typical" bias crime seemed to influence whether victims were fearful of biased victimization. However, it should be noted that when asked about personal experiences some participants' answers seemed more provoked by a desire to answer the question honestly rather than a clear memory of an incident that provoked a strong emotional response. The general nature of their experiences and/or how they have dealt with them could explain to some extent why victims were not more likely to fear crime. Unfortunately, these observations were based more on the tone and manner of some participants' responses to the experience question, which could not be assessed after the fact for most participants and so were not viable for additional analysis.

Minority participants were more likely than non-minorities to fear bias-related victimization. Fifty percent of minorities in the sample claimed being fearful (60 to 70% within each minority group sampled) compared to only 15 percent of non-minorities. This is perhaps not surprising given that according to reported statistics, the victims of bias crime are more often members of traditional minority groups, and that the participants, in their description of bias crimes and typical bias crimes, clearly were skewed toward viewing bias crimes as perpetrated against minority groups, although bias crime laws by definition include crimes perpetrated against majority groups. Thus, it seems sensible that minorities might perceive themselves as more likely targets and thus perhaps feel more vulnerable to bias victimization. The only two non-traditional minorities who reported being fearful of bias crime victimization identified themselves as potential targets of bias crime based on their occupation or ideology, rather than their racial, religious or ethnic majority status. For one it was his role as a teacher and the other his strongly held and shared republican beliefs. Though this study does not provide any direct data to test the notion, it may be that people who generally perceive of themselves as members of the general majority in terms of the anchoring provisions of bias crime legislation, may not fear bias crime perpetrated against them because of their majority status but because of their membership in some less traditional "minority".

Minorities who feared bias crime victimization provided a few different reasons for such fear. A few discussed their fear in relation to their own victimization or bias-based experiences, which they suggested made them more aware of the potential for such an occurrence and gave them a better perception than others perhaps of how often bias incidents take place.

> 32-(interracial) I had pictures of my daughter at work up on my desk and one day I went into work there were stab holes through her face, one through the middle of her face...So I took these to my immediate supervisor...and she just said it seems like a practical joker to her...One man at work had a swastika flag as a screen saver, a raped woman and several naked women just flashing...And I had gone to the head boss and said I don't care what this man practices outside of work but...I go please have him take it off and then a serious of events happened...the pictures of my child and like I had been working their eight years and I asked I did step down from my supervisory position. I asked them to actually terminate me but they said because there was just a series of things like just silly things. Like my husband has long dreadlocks and so they [people at work] were all going to wear dreadlock wigs to work. And there was just like a series of things that were pelting toward me...I was afraid to get in my car. These people scared me to death....So his way of solving the

problem, he said they were afraid what they might do to me so he has me coming in at a later time so I don't have contact with them.

9-Yes (I fear becoming the victim of a hate crime). I'm probably more aware of it than most people. I am watching out for it. I would say I really fear it a whole lot...I have actually been thrown out of stores...and it was all because I was wearing a Wicca pentacle on a chain...I had people who saw me and some friends of mine who were Wicca and actually chased us down the street, threatening us. They said we should be burned at the stake like they used to do.

Other minorities, whether previous victims or not, seemed fearful based on a combination of their status and surroundings. Some recognized that something about them made them standout in their particularly homogenous community, whether it was their decision to present an atypical appearance, their membership in a distinct religious minority, or their interracial relationship. In addition, a few mentioned incidents in their communities that made them particularly concerned.

37-Yes. It's not foremost in my thoughts again but there are sometimes when it has crossed my mind being at the synagogue and we're certainly a minority in town. Generally, I think we get along fine with people but for some reason some people who've never met us don't necessarily like us. And there have been times when I've been concerned that we were having some kind of big gathering at the synagogue and I have asked the police to just keep any eye on the area, just drop by. And we've had some graffiti placed on the building and just things in the news that might trigger events that concern us.

27-Yes I do. Periodically anti-Semitism goes up and down and there have been more incidents of anti-Semitism at Universities...And there use to be this guy in a nearby town and he'd come from another state and basically they were saying we won't put you in prison if you leave the state and he came here. And he was a white supremacist and he built under his house this huge underground thing...and he hadn't committed any crimes but he was collecting weapons and collecting followers and he really hated Jews. And our synagogue in town we stopped publicizing when our services were. We didn't want people to know where we were because we were afraid that they would do something against the synagogue. He's gone know and it has only been in like the last 3 or 4 years we've begun when we're having an event publicizing it.

25-Yes because here we are a distinct minority. There have been issues that I know of in the past with kids in high school being harassed and beat up and just that fact that this area does have a little history of anti-Semitism. I mean there was a Klan march years ago, one of my first years here and so, I think it is a potential. Now the synagogue hasn't been targeted that I know of, although there's been some recent graffiti.

35-Oh yeah, very much more so [than other crime]. I feel like specifically the last couple of years the way I choose to express my gender is very much not normal since I'm a woman wearing my long shorts and having a buzzed head and having piercings...And people always double take...and children stare...I think yeah I'm queering up the norm so I'm doing my job my part to throw a wrench in the system and that's good and that makes me feel good. But it's definitely threatening and scary at the same time...And so I think that it's tangled up with you know feeling empowered but also feeling threatened and feeling that I at any point in time could be a victim of a crime because I look different. I stand out and people will look at me – the little filing cabinet in their head doesn't know where to put me and so they freak out...I've seen a lot of people give me dirty looks or make comments under their breath or make comments to my face.

34-I'm more afraid of it-a hate crime-than anything else. I'm even afraid more of a bias crime because I do think they can happen a lot more than what people let on to even-we're a very, very bias people I mean that's what we are and it's what this country's been built on...It's always in the back of my mind...Like I know if I'd be walking my wife home (interracial) from a bar late at night most likely a cop's going to follow you...it has happened before. It can come from those who enforce the law...and I think that's my biggest, my bigger fear the kind of ambiguity about it. You know what I mean, it can really come from anybody...Not everybody would kill, not everybody is extremely violent...but I think everybody has a bias you know anybody can be pushed to do things that are a result of bias. And that's dangerous man, that's very dangerous. That's scary to me.

Minorities who indicated that they did not fear bias crime victimization discussed that lack of fear in a few different ways including that their experiences had not been life threatening, that they lived in a safe area, or that they recognized that their was a potential for such an occurrence but just lived prudently.

16-Around here, no. Down in the south, I definitely felt more fear. I felt sticking out more being Yankee, being Jewish and everybody asking me what church you go to. Around here, I have heard about that, I haven't experienced any of that. I feel like it is pretty safe.

39-Well I think there's always the potential [to become a victim]. Do I worry about it no. I have a son who a couple of years ago went off to college and I worry about all sorts of things. No I don't fear but would I encourage my son to go to school in Iowa where I thought there were Neo Nazis – no. So I mean it's not part of my everyday life but it's in the back of my head...There are prudent things that you do in your life but I don't worry about it day to day.

30-No, not really. Personally I'm not familiar with anyone [who has been a victim] other than what's on the news. I mean I think there's racial prejudice or different types of prejudice in any community and it's you know I may have experienced it on a very, very low level name calling but you know certainly nothing that was life threatening.

And a few participants indicated that they had worked past their fear or found a sense of security in other sources such as religion. These included both the elderly African-American women who had her picture window shot and the woman who had been the victim of much property damage and verbal harassment because of her Wicca faith.

2-No and I'll be very honest and I'll tell you this. First you gotta fight Jesus and you don't want any part of that. So I'm not afraid. I stay in this house with my granddaughter. I am not afraid.

36-No. That's one of the major things that I've really tried to deal with in my life because I grew up with a lot of fear [in general]. That was one of the things that made a major transition in my life. But I expected every worse case scenario and dealt with it and ultimately what's the worse thing that can happen, I could die. I'm fine with that.

Although most non-minorities did not feel it necessary to discuss their lack of fear, two did. One indicated that she was not afraid because she "felt comfortable with most people" (5). The other indicated that he was not afraid even in light of his own acknowledgement that as a member of a minority advocacy group he could become a target.

13-I though of it...I'm straight but I am a member of Safe Zone...Sometimes I have seen...how white people who aided in the cause of Civil Rights...got treated. So it's not like I walk down the street looking around my shoulder. But I understand that something like that may happen...but I can't say I'm afraid of it.

One participant, a female reverend of the Unitarian Universalist faith-a highly inclusive faith-simply was not willing to give in to the pessimism of fear even though she knew people who had fallen victim to bias crimes. "There have been times in my life when I've thought boy you
better be careful you could get hurt but I believe so much in political change and the just and equitable world that I usually keep fighting" (21).

In all, participants fear or lack of fear of becoming the victim of a bias crime appeared first and foremost to be a factor of their status. Those who were more apt to perceive of themselves as a potential victim (predominantly traditional minorities) seemed more likely to fear such victimization. However, beyond that initial perception of potential, two other issues seemed to influence participants' fear. First, many seemed to consider the likelihood of such victimization in regard to the extent to which their surroundings might serve to highlight their different status or hold a specific bias-based danger. Second, more from their tone and overall thoughts than their actual words, a few participants seemed unwilling to let the potential of victimization place them in fear; their personalities or their strong convictions seemed to help them get past it.

Other factors raised that appeared to have some influence on participants' fear of bias crime included religion, politics, sex and education. All but sex were assessed based on participants' responses to specific questions on their personal background questionnaires. Participants were asked, "Do you consider yourself a religious person?" "Do you consider yourself a political person?" and "What is the highest level of education you have obtained?" Participants who self labeled as "religious" seemed less likely to fear bias victimization than those who did not. The difference was specifically strong for non-minorities, however even for minorities, those who considered themselves to be religious were less likely to fear bias victimization than those who were not. In fact those who were religious were evenly split on their fear whereas 75 percent of those who were not religious were fearful. Although participants were not asked to directly discuss their religions or religious beliefs, a couple of participants did mention how their faith gave them strength, and perhaps it is such strength that allows those who are religious to not fear or to overcome fear.

In terms of politics, those who considered themselves to be political seemed more likely to fear bias victimization than those who did not, and political minorities were the most likely to fear bias victimization. Although participants' comments do not shine light on these findings, it may be that political minorities are more vocal and/or active in their communities and as such perceive themselves and their differences to be more in the spotlight and thus a more obvious target for those who would be biased against them.

Regarding participant sex, although for the sample overall it did not appear to influence fear of bias victimization, for minority participants, men were more fearful than woman. They also were more likely than woman to have been the victims of physical bias crimes, although overall for minorities those with more serious victimizations were no more fearful than those with verbal experiences.

Finally, minority participants with a college degree (especially those with just a bachelor's degree) were more fearful of bias victimization than those with just some college even though the latter were more likely than the other two to claim bias victimization. Unfortunately, the sample size and the nature of the questions asked make analysis beyond these basic findings difficult.

Comparison of Fear of Crime and Bias Crime
That said, the current study was not designed to tap more than a self-admission of fear or lack of fear and general thoughts surrounding it. However, participants' fear of bias crime did seem for the most part consistent (or at least not obviously inconsistent) with their fear of crime in general. In all, 80 percent of participants who provided clear responses to both questions (30) feared both or neither crime or bias crime or feared crime in general but not bias crime specifically, and 60 percent of those who feared bias crime also indicated fear of crime in general. This would seem logical assuming people's assessment of fear of crime in general is based on their fear of any specific type of crime, including bias crime-although it should be noted that no participants specifically mentioned their bias victimization during the general crime portion of the interview.

Six participants offered seemingly inconsistent fear of crime and bias crime answers, indicating a fear of bias crime but not crime in general. This suggests that either their answers were cognitively inconsistent or that their assessment of fear of crime in general was not as simple as their fear of any particular type of crime or at least bias crime. Four of the six were of minority status and three had been the victims of bias crime (one extensive name calling and family discrimination and harassment, the others property or physical crimes against their person), making them particularly aware of the potential for such victimization and one would think might lead them to think of bias crime when asked about fear of crime. The two non-minority participants who feared bias crime only indicated concern that because they were a teacher or shared their strongly-held republican beliefs they might be targeted for such crime. Unfortunately, the data does not provide the information necessary to determine why these participants' fear of bias crime does not lead to a fear of crime although it does suggest an interesting avenue for future research on fear of crime.

There were also several participants (6) who feared crime but not bias crime. Perhaps not surprising, three were non-minorities, two who failed to comment on their lack of fear and one who indicated that although he was aware of the possibility of victimization because of his membership in a gay-advocacy group (although he was straight) he was not afraid of becoming the victim of a bias crime. The other three participants who feared crime but not bias crime were members of racial or religious minorities. Although they each reported being victims of bias name calling or minor harassment, they seemed to have the sense that they were safe in their current environment. One older African-American woman whose husband was white indicated that she'd been the victim of "nasty remarks...[but] they aren't going to do something – they would have done it by now" (11). The other, a middle aged Jewish mom, although acknowledging the presence of the KKK in the area, had not had any real experience with bias since she was a kid and felt much safer in her current surroundings than she did when she lived in the South during her college years (16). The final participant who feared crime only was a gay man who, while claiming he could not say he was afraid, went on at length about the precautions and daily considerations and decisions he had to make in every aspect of his life based on his sexual preference and being in and staying safe in his environment, which he indicated might be viewed by others as paranoia, but apparently provided him with a sense of control and safety rather than a sense of fear (or perhaps a denial of his fear) (38).

Bias Crime as a Problem

Though not quite half the sample had been the victim of a bias crime and/or feared bias crime, there was still an overall sense that bias crime in the U.S. is a problem, for most a moderate to serious problem. Although a few failed to elaborate on their overall assessment that it was "absolutely" a problem or a "serious" problem, many shared their general thoughts on the notion, which covered a number of different issues including the presence of prejudice people, differences between crime and bias crime, variation in the bias crime problem over time and place, and comments related to the reporting of, and response to, bias crime. For a few, their assessment of bias crime as a problem seemed linked to their consideration of peoples' inability to be open minded or comfortable enough with those who are different to, as one participant put it, "live and let live." And for a couple of those participants, the

problem seemed exacerbated by their perception that it might not be
possible to change such people's thinking.

5-I thinks it is a problem in this country. I wish people would
just let people live and let live. That's my theory in life. It is
sad. I don't know how you control it. I don't think you can
actually change a person's way of thinking but I think that is a
problem.

20-Yeah it's a problem. I still think most people can't see
somebody for who they are whenever their situation is the
race or their gender or their look, their sexual preference.
People only see whatever they believe fits into their belief
system. But I do think it is a problem because people can't
just let people do what they want in their own home or to
them...Whatever someone does or chooses to do is their
business as long as it doesn't hurt somebody.

22-It's a problem because it's illegal and in the United States
everyone is suppose to have equal rights and that is not always
the case. So I mean I think it's a problem because everyone
deserves a chance and deserves to be equal.

33-I do think it is a problem but I mean once again going back
to the root of it it's just people are uncomfortable with what
they don't know. So obviously you know like I think it's a
problem but you can't change people's opinions and if you
could change people's opinions it wouldn't be such an issue.

A few participants' perceptions of bias crime as a problem seemed
specifically related to their belief that bias crime was some how
different than non-bias crime. They seemed to suggest that for them
bias crime was worse and more problematic because it was a crime
against humanity, because of its special target, or because of the greater
number of people it was perceived to affect.

13-Yeah, definitely [a problem]...I think this is a different
type of crime. This is a crime against humanity. So I think
when you have one instance it becomes a problem.

25-Yeah [it is a problem]. I think it's emotionally-it produces a more visceral response [than other crime] because again it does have a target. Again being part of an ethnic group, my being Jewish, it does I think in that sense it's more of an emotional worry.

31-I would probably say it's a medium problem but I think it's more important than a lot of other crimes just because it affects so many people when it is done.

Some participants' comments concerned how the problem of bias crime varies depending on region, area and/or time and the extent to which the nature of an area some how provides optimal conditions for such crime or some how promotes the views that lead to it or against it. For a few, it seemed that their region was spared the problem.

24-In particular areas [it's a problem]. You won't see it in small towns like here, at least I don't think you do. But I think where you have more diverse cultures clashing maybe in other cities that are more diverse yeah I think it's a big problem.

39-I think that it's there in the U.S. and I think that it's maybe probably more in certain areas and certain times. I think that in the south you're more apt [to have it]-the KKK is there. Although we have some Klan around here I understand you're more apt see that down there.

In addition, a few participants indicated some sense that things were perhaps generally getting a little better, at least was less likely to be swept under the rug, or no worse than in other countries. However, it was not clear that they all felt that real progress had been made.

14-I think so. I think a lot of people hate. As far as racism in America, I think it is just there. It is not as blatant as it used to be, but it is there...a couple of years ago somebody said racism was dead...so why are we classified as dark green and light green in the military?

15-I don't know if it is as big of a crime as it was in the 60's but it is definitely a problem.

21-Yes...I think there may have been more hate crimes a hundred years ago. When I think of race I mean there were certainly more in that people could get away with very violent crimes against African American or Hispanic individuals where now they're called to the carpet or to the courtroom...And I think the whole glbt issues have benefited from that 100 years of work from that minority they fairly quickly became an issue where there has been some isolated crimes but I don't know that we can get away with this sort of stuff the way I think we use to be able to.

26-I think it probably is [a problem]. I don't know if it's as big or worse than in other countries because I really do think we're trying to create an atmosphere of tolerance. I think we've come an awful long way in terms of how tolerant we are...I think that's because teachers have done good work in teaching a level of tolerance. I think we in the states do that very well...I know we've got more work to do but I think there is definite, definite progress made.

A few participants referred in some way to the current reporting of, or response to, bias crime.

3-I don't know anything about the rate of it or anything like that but I do think it's a problem and you know, they keep trying to get hate crime legislation passed and I think that is important.

17-I think it is a moderate sized problem...I think it often goes unpunished and unnoticed or we don't react to it as quickly as we do a crime that actually physically hurt somebody...I think that when you are talking about some kind of violence or physical scar that somebody may carry with them it is just something that as a human I think it makes your skin crawl...I think that there are probably not enough people who have ever had a hate crime committed against them to actually have a strong feeling about it.

28-I think it's more of a problem looking at the smaller scale because there's a lot of stuff that goes on that isn't reported that happens and I think that's a bigger problem.

Only a few participants, while still acknowledging bias crime as a problem, commented in such a way as to suggest that the issue might be to some extent overblown or at least that it was just part of life.

10-I think it is and it isn't. I don't think it is as big a problem as some people think it is but it is a problem...I would say some of these radical groups think that every crime that's against another person is a hate crime, and I don't really think that is what it is.

29-Not a serious problem. I think it's overblown because they, the media outlet, they see one thing they like to cover and they cover it like crazy...One incident such as when the policeman shoved the black kid's head into the car, which was excessive in that case and hopefully the police officer was disciplined, but I think they take things out of proportion. And America as a society, we see one thing we go nuts.

40-I suppose it is a problem in different states maybe down south because of what we're hearing with the hurricane – they're all feeling that because they were low income poverty level, women just having babies and they have no education and they felt that they were targeted. I don't know that I agree with that...I get upset when I hear them cry out you're picking on us because we're African Americans or poor.

16-In the scheme of things, it probably isn't a huge problem or at least the government doesn't seem to think it is... they have many more issues to deal with...so I think it has to be more at a local level...If there is a big problem, I think the local people should deal with it more so than the U.S. just because there are so many bigger problems.

8-I don't think it is a moot thing. I think that we have always had hate crimes. I think it is just part of being a human being. Again, I think it is kind of interesting that we are looking at it as hate crime. It seems to me that most crimes is hate anyway or at least frustration.

Neither fear of bias crime nor prior bias-based victimization seemed to explain the direction of participants' comments. In fact, even those who seemed less committed to the "problem" label, specifically those who felt it was sometimes overblown or had gotten better in some ways, included those who feared and/or had been the victims of bias crime.

Feelings on Bias Crime

Finally, in an attempt to capture more general thoughts on the issue besides a researcher-imposed notion of bias crime as a problem, participants were asked about their feelings on bias crime. Specifically, they were asked, "How would you say you feel about bias crime, if at all?" Perhaps more than any other, their responses to this question seemed to somewhat capture the shift in many participants' tone and demeanor that was noticed when the interview topic changed from crime to bias crime. When discussing crime, participants seemed to take the interview seriously, answered intently, and for the most part seemed involved with the content. However, when discussing bias crime, they seemed to take on a more serious or perhaps heavier manner.   While participants shared many of the same emotions regarding both crime and bias crime, their tone seemed to suggest they were somehow more moved by bias crime.   Unfortunately, this observation was not really captured in participants' language and only became obvious to this researcher upon later reflection and after numerous interviews, making more careful assessment difficult. Therefore, this conclusion is offered with caution as it can really only be supported by researcher gut feeling. That said, participants' feelings on bias crime did vary from those on crime in general and did offer some indications of what about bias crime might provoke more intense responses.

Compared to their feelings on crime in general, many fewer participants' responses to bias crime related to their own fear of crime or general safety. In fact, only two participants' comments vaguely addressed these issues; one who used the question to discuss his own personal experiences with discrimination and one who mentioned being scared because of his perception that biased perpetrators might not stop but rather go on to hate and victimize other groups. Instead participants seemed overwhelming angered and/or saddened by bias crime. "It makes me mad. It makes me real mad. It makes me sad too for the people who it is against, also for just everybody in general, spurts of anger, spurts of sorrow" (13). In most instances, participants' feelings seemed motivated by the nature of bias crime, their inability to understand it, and/or concerns regarding whether and/or how it could, is or has been addressed.

In fact, a large number of participants held feelings that seemed driven by the unique nature of bias crime-namely its biased motivation. For them, its nature and its manifestations distinguished it from other crime in such a way that seemed to evoke stronger emotions. While many spoke directly about bias crime being different than other crime, others seemed to imply such a difference, which resulted in a host of emotions including sadness, irritation, frustration and anger. On the other hand, a few participants indicated that bias crime was not really different than non-bias crime. Descriptive excerpts for these participants will be discussed in chapter 7 in which the issue of whether bias crime is different than non-bias crimes is of particular focus.

Other participants felt shock or disbelief that such crimes would occur. Again, their emotions seemed linked to the nature of bias crime rather than just the criminal act itself. Although it is certainly possible that they felt this way about other specific crimes, clearly the inability to put themselves in the shoes of someone who could commit such a crime-who could hate to such an extreme that they might act to injure another-seemed to distinguish their feelings on bias crime from their thoughts on just the underlying crime.

9-The reason I went into criminal justice was because of James Byrd and Matthew Shepard. I keep pictures of them on the wall by my desk...Those crimes were so baseless. It was based completely on hate and that is...I don't know, they way I grew up I never hated anyone and I never met anyone who hated that vehemently. I completely cannot conceive of what that must be like. Despite the fact that I know it's out there, it still shocks me every single time I hear about it.

20-I think it is ridiculous myself. I grew up in this town and even in this town there is a mainly African-American section of town. And when I grew up I had friends there. I played basketball, I knew black families and didn't have a

problem...I never saw that as a difference...my dad had some
opinions that I can vividly remember disagreeing with since
the beginning...and my cousins had the same opinion of them
[African Americans]...I just remember thinking there are
good kids and bad kids, it doesn't matter [what race they
are]...I know we do all have our biases...but to actually take
it to a level where they want to hurt somebody or infringe on
that person's right to be here, I find that really difficult to
understand.

32-I feel disgusted because I just don't understand. There's
nothing about me that can understand it.

17-It is one of the things that irks me more than anything
when it comes to crime, probably because it touches me more
greatly too. It is the type of crime that I don't think I will ever
understand ever.

Others' feelings seemed tied to their thoughts on whether or how
bias crime has or could be handled. Some wondered whether the
perpetrators of such crime could change, others how exactly that might
happen-mentioning factors both social and legal in nature. A couple of
participants were clearly disturbed by society's role in potentially
promoting bias crime through the legitimization of prejudice or its
failure to care enough about the victims of bias crime to demand or
provide an adequate response. Finally, a couple of participants were
saddened because of what little overall progress on the relevant issues
has been made over the years.

37-I hate bias crime (laugh). It's another type of crime but it's
one that you would think could be cured maybe with some
different upbringing.

15-I think it is horrible. Sometimes you wonder if education
is really the answer....I think it would take longer to educate
[hate crime perpetrators] but it should be educated when they
start grade school instead of waiting until they are locked up,
which is more prevention than anything. The whole thing is
for someone to get reelected for another term, they want to see
results in 4 years or 2 years instead of waiting for 20 years to
see the results of the things that they did. They shovel all the

money into corrections instead of education. We need both, but education is definitely going to be more effective, I think.

19-[I feel] sick. There was a trans-gendered woman...she was 17. She was killed out in California. She went to a party with 4 men and they thought she was a woman and they were trying to do sex acts and found out she was a man and they killed her violently and the jury came back hung...I don't think they care enough about this victim because she was trans-gendered.

35-I think it's outrageous, it makes me angry. I mean I think perpetuating violence against anyone is horrible and wrong...but it makes me angry, it's like we legitimize sexism, we legitimize heterosexism through these institutions and through our laws.

11-It makes me feel really sad. I think about the fact that I've been in education all these years and started my studying of multi-cultural and diversity issues some 35 or 40 years ago and then to be at this stage now, it is so disappointing.

16-I think it is sad. I think that it is unfair and we have come a long way, and yet we really haven't come a long way. Yes we have given the right to women...And before then it was blacks. And now we have problems because of people who are afraid of Arabs, that kind of thing. So pick the new flavor of the month. So yes we have come a long way, but yet we haven't. We just picked new people to say bad things about.

But overall, participants' feelings seemed to reflect emotional responses provoked by more than the fact that bias crime was a crime. The nature of bias crime, both for minorities and non-minorities alike, seemed to strike a nerve concerned with something beyond personal safety. Even though participants were asked how they felt about bias crime before their fear of such crime was broached, and nearly a majority of participants feared such crime and nearly a majority had been the victims of bias crime, only one participant discussed feelings of bias crime in relation to personal fear or experience. Participants' comments regarding their feelings of bias crime and bias crime as a problem together seem to reflect an intense response to the targeting of people for differential treatment based on who someone is or what they believe and society's promotion of or failure to address such treatment, especially when it takes criminal form. Perhaps one participant was just more succinct in his comments when he said bias crime is, "...a different type of crime...a crime against humanity" (13). Perhaps it is that perceived difference that takes bias crime beyond crime to another more intense level for many.

Summary of Citizens' Views on Bias Crime

Overall, the vast majority of study participants seemed more than eager to discuss their thoughts on bias crime. Regardless of whether or not they were a member of a minority, the victim of a bias crime, or in fear of becoming such a victim, they seemed aware of not only the existence and general nature of bias crimes but also in agreement that it was a problem, a problem that for most seemed to provoke rather intense emotions in tone and language. While participants' comments regarding various bias-crime related issues often overlapped in theme, they also offered variation including in the area of causes of crime and reasons for perceptions of bias crime as a problem and the feelings it evoked. Somewhat unexpectedly, there did not seem to be any distinction across or within general views regarding bias crime across the different subgroups sampled. Each group seemed fairly well represented by the different categories and views presented except for those few instances that already have been mentioned.

CHAPTER 8

Citizens' Bias Crime Policy Preferences

To explore the overall phenomenon of support for bias crime legislation but seeming lack of willingness to apply it, participants were questioned about their policy preferences towards bias crime from three different perspectives: their abstract policy preferences for handling bias crime; their specific responses to bias crime vignettes; and their support for bias crime legislation. This chapter focuses on participants' abstract policy preferences, which were explored through questions on their familiarity with U.S. bias crime policy, how they would like to see such crime handled, whether they felt that a judge or jury in a case should be informed that a crime is motivated by bias, and how society should be dealing with people who commit bias crimes. In addition, participants' earlier comments regarding bias crime in general are reported to the extent that they address these issues.

Perhaps not surprising given responses to national polls on bias crime legislation, 75 percent of participants viewed bias crime as different from non-bias crime and advocated for a different response to such crime. However, their support for a different response was not an automatic vote for a more punitive sentence. Participants' responses to bias crime were divided between those more punitive, different in terms of rehabilitation, or a combination of both. That said, the nature of their responses to bias crime were overwhelmingly consistent with the type of approach they advocated for crime in general, just of a different magnitude or method.

Citizens' Perceptions of Current U.S. Bias Crime Policy

Participants were fairly evenly split in their reporting of whether they were familiar with how bias crimes are handled in the U.S. Of the fifty percent who implied some familiarity, 67 percent (a third of the overall sample) directly mentioned state or federal bias/hate crime legislation or their belief that bias crimes could be prosecuted or punished differently than non-bias crimes. Although it is questionable how familiar participants were with bias crime legislation as they were not asked to describe or explain it, several did note that that they were not particularly familiar with its details and only one discussed it beyond indicating that it allowed different punishment for bias crimes. Over half of the participants who implied familiarity went on to discuss how bias crimes are not handled as seriously as non-bias crimes in terms of enforcement, prosecution or sentencing because of a lack of training and/or sensitivity or outright bigotry and discrimination. These participants were frustrated by their own and others' experiences with police responses to harassment and other low-level bias offenses. While it is not possible to determine the extent to which they were familiar with how seriously such incidents would be taken if not based on bias, there was certainly a general perception that it would be handled even less seriously if the incident were bias motivated. In all, nearly 20 percent of the sample directly indicated concern that such crimes were not treated as seriously as other crimes, and 28 percent indicated a problem concerning the lax enforcement of hate crime laws.

19-They are not doing enough and they aren't doing it fast enough, but at least they are attempting. They have some hate crimes law on the books now. I don't think they take them quite as seriously. We are a low priority...the hate crimes don't get the same attention...The police don't have enough training...I have actually called the police on neighbors for harassment, had them come to the house and told them what was said and this person actually threatened to slash my tires. And the cop said to me, "well people can call me a pig all day long and I can't arrest them...sticks and stones can break your bones."

35-I think there's a lot of debate with it [hate crime] but in terms of how it gets played out in the legal system my assumption is that it's not really taken seriously if we still have sodomy laws on the book, if we still do not allow gay marriage if you know all of these sort of things are in place. I think it should be taken more seriously. How that gets translated into actual action or policy I don't know...but I would like to see more radical and more liberal people at least help set the agenda for the laws around hate crimes.

38-If your criminal investigation team has absolutely no sense of crimes being motivated by hatred for some group of people for whatever it might be then that's just a blind spot in their investigative powers...[Black and gays] are two groups where there's a huge blind spot because they're not represented on the criminal investigation side...gays are certainly systematically not gonna make it as a policeman or they're kept in office jobs or they're waving cars by at construction sites...That's the way that it is, the government no one discriminates against you accept the people you have to actually work with and put up with everyday...And policeman are very, very anti-gay...But there's another thing about the hate crimes which is that if you look at the way crimes are investigated...you get a sense that if there isn't a procedure for investigating a certain type of crime then I would call it a blind spot...It gets ignored. I can give you an example of a domestic dispute...and it was basically a [gay] couple one was beating the other one up to the point of hospitalization. The police came and laughed because they were fags fighting and did nothing...So you know you don't have gay guys willing to really investigate or deal with these things on the police squad.

36-I know how this town handles it – they don't. I'm always the one that's wrong...A man physically came after me and I was frightened to the point where I got in my car and went to the police station. When they found out I had a pentagram in my window, they didn't pay any attention to me...When I call for help or assistance they don't come anymore. That's why I go out of town a lot...When I go outside my apartment and I get hit in the head with a ball; I don't go outside. But I don't fear it, I just avoid it because if I go outside it's more of avoiding the legal system cause when I go outside and report it they right away say "what did you do to bring it on?" Well I don't know I was talking on my cell phone and I went out and locked my door and I get slammed with a ball.

31-In my own experience I've had friends that have been victims of harassment and the attitude of the officials the police and a lot of it's the law-basically they can't do anything until this level of harassment has occurred...A lot of it was the attitude of the police officer. One that I'm familiar with is that they called the police, the police came out and he says "well you know you are being this open [gay] you've got to expect stuff like this" and he made it pretty blatant that he didn't agree with this lifestyle.

Other participants indicating a familiarity with the U.S. approach commented on factors that they felt influenced the handling of bias crime including where the crime/incident took place – what community, school, workplace; who was in charge, especially in terms of workplace incidents; and whether or not the media got involved.

14-It the media gets a hold of it...the government is going to do anything and everything in their power to set an example. But if not...this is a crime, but not an actual crime...But it is still serious but the media doesn't get hold of it and blow it out of proportion or bring it the public's attention, there won't be an outcry. It's probably even more the case for hate and bias crimes.

7-They are not as serious in the ranking for some reason. I don't know why because I think they should be more serious and so I think that maybe they are not in terms of how they are punished. I'm glad to hear that more is being done so I think we are moving in the right direction. Of course there are many communities where I'm sure it can be easily looked over...and some of the crimes are committed by policemen themselves.

22-I think...in schools when hate crimes go on or even in colleges I think that schools tend to take that pretty seriously because they have to. And in the workplace, I don't know that it's always enforced because I think it probably depends on who is in charge.

Finally, only one participant mentioned the sentencing approach to bias crimes, indicating the lack of effectiveness of the lock 'em up approach. "Yeah throw them in jail that's all they do. They throw them in jail with other people just like them and those people form their clicks and they do the same shit in jail that they were doing out on the street. It's not very effective" (34).

It was not expected that this initial question would explore in-depth measures, legal or otherwise, taken by the U.S to deal with bias crime. However, it was deemed important to get a sense of participants' general awareness and understanding of how the issue is being addressed as it might in turn influence their views on how bias crime should be handled. To tap their own views, participants first were asked how, if at all, they thought society should deal with bias crime. Both that question and the familiarity question, by not mentioning the criminal justice system, were designed in such a way as to provide participants with the option of discussing either legal and/or non-legal approaches to bias crime. However, the vast majority of participants' comments primarily focused on the criminal justice system's approach (current or preferred) to bias crime rather than social (non-legal) approaches to such crime regardless of the specific question, even in light of the fact that participants' perceptions of the causes of and thoughts regarding bias crime emphasized social conditions. In addition, although the initial approach question was designed to tap participants' approaches to bias crime in general and the final two questions to specifically explore participants' thoughts on the criminal justice system's approach concerning sanctioning convicted bias offenders, most participants used the questions somewhat interchangeably to discuss their thoughts on bias crime and criminals, and so they are analyzed together to assess participants' preferred policies for addressing bias crime.

It should be noted that an analysis of similar questions designed to explore participants' preferred approaches to crime and criminals in general led to a similar phenomenon. Participants' focus on the criminal justice system and criminal sanctions when discussing both crime and bias crime could be the result of interviewees expecting that criminal justice-related answers would be the desired or appropriate responses to a crime and punishment interview. However, other factors that may have influenced their responses include 1) a social emphasis on crime as the purview of the criminal justice system, 2) the need to focus first or foremost on what might be assessed as the more immediate problem or even danger-the crime and/or criminal, and/or 3) a focus on the quick fix rather than the often perceived or actually more complex, expensive, more difficult and long-term problems leading to crime and solutions to them.

Bias Crime – Same or Different Than Non-Bias Crime

Based on comments to the combined bias "approach" questions, the simple pattern that emerged distinguished participants based on whether they felt that bias crime/criminals should be handled the similarly to, or differently than, non-bias crimes/criminals. As expected given the relatively stable findings of national opinion polls, the majority of participants suggested that they would treat bias crimes differently (56%). Of the remaining participants, twenty-five percent preferred similar treatment for bias crime, nine percent was unsure, and 8 percent did not make their thoughts clear.

An overriding influence on their general preferences was how participants perceived bias crimes compared to non-bias crimes. Three quarters of the sample clearly commented on this issue with the majority (75%) noting how bias crime was somehow different/distinct. Perhaps not surprisingly, seventy-five percent of those participants felt that bias crimes/criminals should be handled differently, the other 25 percent not knowing or being unclear as to how they would handle such offenders. Eighty-six percent of those who spoke to the similarity of the two types of crimes felt that they should be treated similarly. Only one such participant claimed they should be treated differently. However, he indicated that he did not believe bias and non bias crimes could be differentiated but went on to say that if a bias crime could be proven 100 percent-which he doubted was possible-he would support a harsher penalty for its possible deterrent effect. The other twenty-five percent of participants who did not directly address whether bias crimes were the same as or different than non-bias crimes or whose views of this issue could not be assessed were fairly evenly split on the decision whether to treat bias crimes similarly or differently.

Similar Crime, Similar Sanction
The theme that seemed to hold the "similar treatment" group together was their overarching sense that a hate crime is not a crime distinct from other crime, at least for the purposes of sanctioning, and thus should receive the same treatment as comparable non-bias crimes. This belief seemed to be supported by two trains of thought. The first, and most frequently voiced, was summed up by the phrase "a crime is a crime." These participants seemed to view bias crime, for purposes of the criminal justice response, primarily in terms of its underlying crime. For them, the motive for that action was not deemed an

appropriate, nor for some a legal, basis for differential sentencing. Crime is the act not the intent behind it.

40-I don't think it should be different. I think it should be straight across the board. A crime is a crime no matter what. And I mean obviously it'll come up like a hate crime...but I think the punishment for the crime shouldn't matter.

8-I don't think a bias motive is more serious than a non-bias motive. I think the person was harmed regardless of what the cause is of the situation, whether you are Jewish or you have more money than I do. The person was harmed. So the transgression is the thing that I think we have to be punished for not the motive for it. I don't think the penalty should be any greater for people that commit hate crimes.

24-I think it [bias crime] is horrible [but] I think a crime is a crime...I think it should be treated as the same kind of crime as someone who murders someone arbitrarily. I think the punishment should fit the crime whether it's a hate crime or whether it's murder or just something else.

30-[It is probably not necessary for judge or jury to know it was a hate crime] probably just that it was an assault or whatever...I'm not a lawyer but...in order to get a person convicted it has to be what fits within the framework of the laws and I don't think it's illegal to think in a certain way, it's illegal to act a certain way...treat them similarly because its by the act as opposed to the reason for the act.

5-I think it should be dealt with like any other crime...I think the crime that is committed should be dealt with. It doesn't really matter if it was a hate crime, they should still get the punishment that they deserve whether it be they murdered someone or beat someone up, it shouldn't really matter...I think they do judge people on their opinions but I think it should be based on the crime.

The second, though not mutually exclusive, conception of the notion that bias crime is not a distinct crime was based on the view that all or most crimes are "hate" crimes because they involve hate or at least anger to some extent or degree, and/or even if different types or degrees of hate could be assessed, they would be inappropriate factors on which to base punishment. As indicated by one participant's comments above, apparently a "hate-based" motive as conceptualized in hate crime legislation is not perceived by all as a more serious motive than other hate based motives, or at least a basis for differential treatment. A related issue, raised by one participant, is the difficulty in actually proving when a crime is hate-based for the purpose of hate crime legislation as opposed to hateful in some other way.

> 33-I think that like a crime is a crime…but its unfortunate I mean I understand where people are coming from with the whole hate crime thing…It's unfortunate but I don't think they should be punished any more or less…I'm gay but I don't really know that I believe in hate crime legislation per se. You know any crime committed against another person is obviously influenced by some sort of anger or hate regardless of why, what or how. Like you know you are angry at the world, you're robbing a store, you shoot the counter clerk and kill him. Like any kind of crime really has some kind of hate or anger behind it. So I think it would be really difficult to decide if someone would shoot and kill me like did they do it because you know I just happened to be unlucky to be standing there or they shot me because of my sexuality even if they attacked me verbally with slander.

> 29-What I've got from it [bias crime] is if you commit a crime against a minority, they consider that a hate crime which I feel a hate crime is something premeditated. If you don't like a person I would consider that doing it because you hate them too. I don't see the difference between the two. It all seems to go under a hate crime to me…I think bias crime should be treated the same as non-bias crimes just because a crime is a crime…most crimes if you are doing it because of anger it's a hate crime to me.

A final issue raised by a sole participant supporting similar treatment for bias crime offenders was concern that hate crime legislation might have consequences unproductive to its goal.

33-If anything I mean I think that it (hate crime legislation) hurts the situation...I think people sort of cop an attitude about that sort of thing and think oh why should they be treated any differently than me, why should this crime be worse than what happened to my son just because he was not black or Jewish or whatever.

These participants' preference to treat bias crime the same as non-bias crime did not necessarily equate with a belief that the judge or jury should not know that a crime might be hate based. However, some did indicate that bias-related evidence was not necessary information for the court to have because they felt strongly that it should not influence an offender's sanction or they feared that it might cause the judge/jury to act on emotion rather than facts of the case.

20-No, I don't think [it is necessary for judge/jury to know that it is a bias crime]. I think if someone gets killed or murdered, that is the crime itself...I think if they go by the crime and the punishment fits the crime, then it's ok. That person is still going to, no matter what the punishment is, is going to hate. I think if a punishment is what a punishment is supposed to be [for the underlying crime] that is ok.

8-You know, no, I don't think they need to know. I think it is a peripheral detail. I think that you have to deal with the data of the crime itself...What I'm thinking is that when you look at something as a hate crime, you present that particular issue, I think it is very, very difficult for most individuals to separate their emotions from their cognitive process.

Others felt that hate-based evidence should be included for reasons other than punishment. Some participants indicated that it might be relevant to determining a criminal's repeat offender status, which they felt would be as relevant to sentencing biased offenders as it would for other criminals. Others felt such information was important for a full understanding of the crime or perhaps to prove the crime, in terms of it demonstrating the offender in fact had a motive for committing the underlying crime. For one participant, the information was necessary simply as an avenue for reminding people, in this case court actors and participants, of the continued presence of the attitudes that such crimes highlight.

> 29-I don't think they [judge/jury] need to know unless there was a previous history of behavior like that but if it's a first offense or something like that I don't think it is relevant. Because they [repeat offenders] in that case would be a danger to society and if you keep them in jail not as long as they should they might get out and commit another crime if they've done it on previous occasions.

> 40-I think it's probably important for them [judge or jury] to know but I don't think it should make up their mind as to the punishment. I mean whatever is wrong is still wrong. It's still a murder, it's still endangerment, or ruining property...I don't think they should be treated any differently.

> 8-I think it [hate-based evidence] is valid to show the response to emotion as evidence in terms of the reasons, motive for committing a crime. I see it as evidence but I don't think a bias motive is more serious than a non-bias motive.

> 19-Yes [the judge and jury should know]. It should make them aware that prejudice and ignorance still exist. I think we have to have tougher laws against hate crimes [because we currently do not take them as serious as similar non-bias crimes] but the same as any other crime.

In all, these participants simply did not view the hateful nature of legally-defined bias crime as a factor reserved solely for bias crime and/or a factor relevant to the determination of criminal sanctions.

Different Crime, Different Sanction
However, the majority of study participants did not seem to agree that a "crime is a crime" or that all crimes are hate crimes. Instead, they viewed bias crime as a different crime, somehow more serious than non-bias crime. For this reason, a vast majority of such participants

(75%) felt such crime deserved a different criminal sanction. They provided a number of very general to specific rationales for their overall perception of bias crime as distinct. However, they each seemed to fall into one of three mutually inclusive categories: nature/motive, victim selection or premeditation, and/or greater harm.

Several participants were seemingly unable or perhaps thought it unnecessary to explain what it was beyond the general nature of bias crime-its biased or hate-based motivation-that distinguished it from other crimes as to justify differential treatment. For them, the underlying bias or hate of such crime simply made it a worse, more serious crime. The one participant who seemed to express the feelings these participants conveyed in the angst and emotion behind their words and their search for more specific language that would explain what made hate worthy of greater distain or treatment put it this way, "I think this is a different type of crime. This is a crime against humanity" (13).

> 21-...this is different than someone going out and someone murdering someone out of revenge or some sort of tit for tat...That's different to me than something that stems from fear and hatred rather than from a need or belief... I would say yes, definitely [it is something a judge/jury would need to know about] because it is a significant factor...an important piece of information to know and that it might possibly influence the sentence.

> 9-If that is the motive [hate/bias], it's a different crime. What makes it different is the motivation behind the crime and how those people should be treated as a form of punishment.

> 38-They're [bias crimes] pervasive and they're a certain kind of crime. They aren't the same kind of crime as other crimes and...also just morally and ethnically it makes sense to do something special for a special type of crime. And I do recognize it as different even though it looks like a beating or a murder or a serial killer...and really I don't think the same punishments fit the bill.

Other participants were a bit more specific in their explanations of the more troubling and distinct nature of bias crimes, pointing to the specificity of victim selection in such crimes, and/or what they perceived as the greater premeditation of bias crime-seemingly because of the hate that must exist before committing a crime against a specific individual based on their status. Although premeditation is a legal factor in criminal law and relevant to crime seriousness and culpability, it is unclear whether participants were suggesting that any bias crime is legally premeditated solely because the perpetrator held a bias against a certain type of victim.

> 18-Of all the types of crime, I think hate crimes are different because of the specificity of it. A junkie needing a fix would try to knock anybody on the head to get their money or something that they can pawn to get their fix. A person hanging out specifically targeting one group or another, that just seems colder, more planned out than just a spur of the moment street crime or bank robbery or something...a hate crime has to be somebody who hates or really dislikes a black, a Jew, a Catholic, a gay person. I think it is colder. Hate crime is colder.

> 39-I think it's a conscious decision on someone's part to do something like that, those aren't crimes of passion. I came in and found my husband in bed with another woman and you know picked up the lamp and hit them both with it...You know an Episcopalian family moved in next door and I've spent my life not liking people who eat white bread and mayonnaise you know so I smear their house with mayonnaise and light it on fire. I'm being facetious you know but that takes thought, premeditation and I'm sorry that's malicious. And that obviously makes me angry. So somebody ought to pay for that. I personally think that's a whole different level of something and I think you treat that differently.

> 7-In my opinion they [bias crimes] are different. One of them is very much more premeditated, it's planned out, it's thought out, it is based on hate. The other one seems more based on an emotional reaction, something that might not be premeditated...I think there is a different level...It's not like this crime, regardless of the situation, somebody is dead, everybody gets the same punishment. I don't agree with that.

I think it depends on the situation, and I do think that hate crime should be punished more severely.

25-Yeah I mean I believe there's a special distinction that comes with you know larger penalties for hate crimes. I think it's appropriate. It's a good thing. It doesn't change the event, it doesn't change the likelihood of it happening again. I don't think it's enough of a deterrent. I guess it's more of a visceral response than that it would actually be helpful [to have bias crime legislation]. It's a more serious crime....because it's maliciously targeting a person or group rather than meeting a need for money or something like that.

16-My gut feeling says to me that if somebody legitimately chose this person because they were different or something like that, then yeah, I think there should be a harsher response because that means that it was premeditated in a way because they picked out somebody specifically because of what they were, their creed or whatever, as opposed to picking up the stranger, just anybody. In a way that's premeditated because you wanted to do it but it's not as much as specifically picking this person because of that [creed].

A final group of participants' comments seemed to emphasize some manner of greater harm presented by bias crime, harm either to the immediate victim, the victim's greater community, or society as a whole. These participants felt that bias crime could be more painful for immediate victims, impact the lives of other members of the victim's group, and more likely than other crimes lead to recidivism and potential retaliation.

31-It should be punished more severely because it is a crime against more people. Just like when you punish somebody more severely if they kill fifteen people rather than one person who did it in the act of passion or whatever. When someone does a hate crime, they're not just doing the crime against the person, they are doing the violence against...the whole group and trying to silence or terrorize that group.

37-If you are on the receiving end of the threat [bias crime] it really could control the way you live the way you think, your thoughts about your family.

3-Obviously it's wrong if people are going to steal something out of someone's car...but I think it's worse if you are doing it just because they are Jewish or something. Well, I'm gay...it would suck if someone broke into my house or beat me up for my wallet...but in my mind, it would hurt personally...if it was because I am gay. Like I would be angry if a crime was committed against me, but it would hurt emotionally if it was because of who I am.

17-I feel differently about it than other crimes. It is one of those things that irks me more than anything when it comes to crime probably because it touches me more greatly too. It is the type of crime that I don't think I will ever understand. Ever...If you have had a hate crime committed against you, whether you are Jewish or black, or whatever...I think it would make some people shy away from their religion...I think it probably affects the way you bring your kids up too because you are either going to bring them up being proud to be who they are, or in some ways to kind of skulk around and not have them be as they are. I think it probably affects the way you put your foot out-the way you represent yourself.

34-It [bias crime] can lead to other crimes and that's what makes it dangerous and that's why it should be punished more. Racism and cultural differences and xenophobia those are very hostile issues.

15-I think that [hate] makes it worse because it seems like something they would be more apt to do again because they are of that train of thought. Instead of just going up and robbing somebody and saying I probably shouldn't have five years later...a hate crime person is going to see these people for the rest of their life and they might even, in their twisted mind, blame those people for their problems.

27-Well I think it's different because I think with a lot of like our majority property crimes I really think if people were getting a decent enough education and their was enough job opportunities...for those kinds of property crimes...we could take care of that by better education, universal healthcare, and job opportunity. But for hate crimes, no.

In the end, participants who felt that bias crime was somehow different, more serious, more dangerous, or more harmful were more likely than those who did not to believe they should be treated differently and most provided a sense of the nature of that difference. Based on their responses to the general and more specific "approach" questions, participants were grouped by how they suggested convicted biased offenders should be sanctioned "differently". Aside from two participants who wanted to treat such offenders differently but were not at all sure how, the rest were fairly evenly divided on whether they felt that bias crime should be treated more punitively than non-bias crimes (6), with more or different rehabilitation (5), or with a combination of the two (7).[18]

Participants described as more punitive in some way indicated that they wanted the punishment or sentence to be harsher, heavier or more severe for biased offenders and supported that statement with comments suggesting longer sentences, support for hate crime legislation, or harsher conditions, or failed to explain such statements in terms of rehabilitative measures. Of course, this categorization is not meant to suggest that these participants would not necessarily support rehabilitation, only that they failed to mention it. Though participants' explanatory comments primarily concerned how bias crime was different, as indicated above, the two additional justifications for a more punitive approach to such offenders appeared to be retribution and deterrence. However, these concerns were not held across the board, and some participants directly indicated or demonstrated through their words that emotion was clearly a factor in their decisions.

25-I think a judge or jury should be provided with the evidence that it might be [a bias crime]...Yeah I mean there's a special distinction that comes with you know larger penalties for hate crimes. I think it's appropriate. It's a good thing...I guess that's more of a visceral response than that it would actually be helpful because I don't think it functions as a deterrent...It's a more serious crime and should have a more serious punishment... I think it should come with a heavier punishment because it's maliciously targeting a person or group rather than meeting a need for money or something like that.

14-Bias crime is different...Like the guy in Wisconsin, they should have taken them out back, lined them up, and just with baseball bats, knives, forks, spoons, just beat the crap out of them. I'm pretty much an eye for an eye guy...It was clearly a hate crime. That is one of those crimes they should put them in jail because it was hate-based...For sentencing, yes [judge/jury should know], definitely for sentencing. If it was greed, you hear about it. But you killed some man because of his color, his weight, his height, whatever those are hate crimes, they should get a stiffer penalty...much more severe. I would like to see a uniform guideline that says you killed somebody, hate crime, and they're gonna strap you in this chair next week. If it is biased, strap 'em down...[For a less serious bias crime] like vandalism, strap 'em down-no that's a little too harsh but give them some water and a squeegee, clean it off, whatever. Not just this one but that building over there, this one over here. After three or four buildings, they're going to be mad, but they are going to think about it.

31-...it should be punished more severely because it is a crime against more people...I'd like to see hate crime legislation on the national level for all the states.

2-Number 1, they would have to find out if it is a hate crime. And if it's a hate crime, we have to deal with it...Ok, if you shot into my window then there is a punishment for that. Ok, now if it's a hate crime, there's a punishment for a hate crime and for shooting at the window. That is an effective way.

32-The judge/jury should know cause...say nobody ever spoke up and said anything about that then they wouldn't know the initial problem that was behind it...Yes it should affect their sentence. I don't know, perhaps they should be punished more, perhaps it would send a message out there to other people that obviously you cannot do this and this is why.

10-If you can prove it beyond a shadow of a doubt then I think they should know [j/j]...A stiffer penalty, maybe. More time or whatever, more jail time or however they do it, possibly as a deterrent to other people who are going to go and try to do the same thing. Not so much to the person that did the crime...but to maybe make somebody think twice before they go out and pick on a different race or whatever.

Participants described as supporting a combination of measures indicated support for some form of more punitive approach, as explained above, but also referenced more or different rehabilitation as being necessary for biased offenders, or at least for those who commit lower level offenses. For most the rehabilitation deemed appropriate directly related to the biased nature of the crime as opposed to the underlying crime itself. Participants wanted offenders to recognize why the hate behind their behavior was problematic and many indicated the importance of somehow integrating offenders into their victims' worlds either by requiring them to learn about their victims' cultures (maybe through language) or to get to know members of their victims' status groups. Only a couple or participants open to rehabilitation mentioned concern that hate-based offenders might not be able or willing to change. Although this group of participants often suggested that "more" rehabilitation might be necessary, they did not give the impression that their desire for more severe punishment was solely a basis for providing the time necessary for such rehabilitation. Instead, their call for greater punishment seemed to be a direct response to the perceived more serious nature of the crime based on the various reasons participants felt that bias crime was distinct from non-bias crime.

7-I think they should be treated differently...I think that people who do a hate crime probably I mean they should be punished. I think, in that instance, more severely than the guy or women or whoever that just reacted to something. It's not like this crime, regardless of this situation, somebody is dead, everybody gets the same punishment. I don't agree with that. I think it depends on the situation and I do think that hate crime should be punished more severely. I also think that in some way, some kind of learning should take place. I thing it would be great if somebody who has just killed someone who is gay, would have to work with people who are gay or lesbian

and get to know them-do some kind of a rehabilitation in that
way.

16-My gut feeling says that if somebody legitimately chose
this person just because they were different or something like
that then yeah I think there should be a harsher punishment
because that means it was premeditated in a way because they
picked out somebody specifically because of what they were-
their creed or whatever-as opposed to picking up the stranger,
just anybody. So I would say yeah, there should be a little
harsher penalty somehow. These criminals also need some
type...some more education for people that do have that type
of crime-they do need to be educated on the ignorant thing
they did, just because of who they chose.

3-I think we are making strikes towards, you know having a
good hate crime bill, it's important...if they [judge/jury] know
like this crime is not just a random robbery, it was committed
because the person who committed the crime did not like it
because the victim was such and such, I think that it makes it
more serious and that should be taken into consideration when
looking at punishment...I would think that like education is
also crucial while they are in prison or doing their probation.
I think they should be required to learn more about different
groups, like diversity, that kind of thing maybe. You know if
they knew more about the group they targeted, the people they
had targeted, they would feel less like they were a threat to
them or that kind of thing.

34-Yeah [judge/jury should know] because that fuels the
person's intention. I think hate is a very strong motivator. I
think that should bring sentencing down a little bit heavier you
know because of that. I just say give them more punishment
because of the hate, the hate is primarily the reason.
Whenever you're compromising the life of somebody else
than you should probably get life especially when it's hate
motivated. For less serious crimes rehabilitation and the
opportunity for a second chance is important because it is an
opportunity for a very adequate education-forced education
force them to learn something. Dude got a problem with
Spanish people, throw him in a class and make him learn how

to speak freakin' Spanish. You know what I mean that would be a lot more punishing to him than you think, honestly it really would.

Participants described as rehabilitative gave no clear impression that they would support more punitive approaches to bias offenders in the form of longer or more severe sentences, although it was clear from many that rehabilitation might in some instances have to take place in a correctional facility. Instead, their comments focused on the need to provide biased offenders with more or different rehabilitation. While it is possible that those who suggested more rehabilitation might support a longer, more punitive sentence, they did not indicate this need. Given their failure to mention the importance of a more punitive sentence, it would seem that if that were the case it might be based more on the demands of rehabilitation rather than a need for punishment. As with the "combo" group, these participants felt a strong need for hate-based rehabilitation to provide offenders with a better understanding of their victims and reduce their feelings of being threatened by, or fearful of, their victims through some form of integration either directly with the victims themselves or other members of their status group or through more traditional education. Although a couple of these participants made direct reference to specific deterrence, most seemed more concerned with combating the hate.

27-Well the way our prisons are now I really don't know what would be different. My view is there should be different types of rehabilitation available. This is a person who if they didn't get education about differences and learning to express their anger differently, they would be at a high risk once they got out of doing it again.

17-Yes I do think that the judge or jury should know because I think it should change the way we actually sentence the criminal. I think that there should be education. I think there should maybe be some community service involved if we are not talking about someone who is going to be a threat to society, and interaction with whomever he or she has committed the hate crime against.

21-There again I'll go back to my rehabilitation word. To really fix that person is more than just a justice issue. You killed someone so now you have to spend the rest of your life in jail. To really change that person where he or she might be able to, from a jail cell, influence the larger culture you would have to do some intensive interventive training of what or where did this come from, from why do you hate, what's it about. And I would guess on an individual level there are different reasons people take this path. I would think it would be an important piece of information to know and that it might possibly influence the sentence, not the longevity of the sentence necessarily but what happens to that person-how much intervention they get.

9-If hate is the motive, yeah, it's a different crime. What makes it different is the motivation behind the crime and how those people should be treated as a form of punishment. First, I think everyone in the world needs therapy but some need it more than others. I think people who commit hate crimes do need some work. They need some sensitivity or something...They probably need a combination of a few things depending on the particular situation. I mean if they were vehemently threatening to do it again the second they walk out the door, you better lock them up while you're at it.

11-I still have hope that we have alternative ways of helping people get past their hate and their biases against others, and I don't think that is always the same kind of thing you do when you just kill or whatever. One of the things, which I have always felt, is that people that wanted to engage in bias kinds of crimes or hate crimes if given the opportunity to be involved in interacting with other groups, they find a different kind of understanding. The judge or jury should know if a crime is hate-based because I think that you would create a different kind of punishment for that particular person or individuals. And it doesn't have to punishment but rather educational kinds of things.

6-Part of me says yeah it should be handled differently-some extra kind of counseling-that doesn't mean it will change. Doesn't mean that will help them at all. So yes, they may need to be treated differently...They better receive some counseling regarding that type of behavior because that is what put them there and that is what we don't accept in our society.

Same or Different Sanction

The remaining participants represented two groups. The first was made up of three participants who did not make it clear whether they would treat criminals similarly or differently before going on to discuss rehabilitation and/or punishment in a way that still did not make it clear. Although a couple of participants discussed hate-specific rehabilitation similar to the comments noted above, I did not judge this to be sufficient on its own to imply they thought bias crime/criminals should be handled "differently" as for some people it could simply mean they thought it should be handled the same as other crime, which always involved appropriate rehabilitative measures.

The second group included four participants whose comments directly indicated they had not clearly decided whether or not bias crimes should be treated differently. While they spoke mostly of rehabilitation and mentioned punishment, whether they would treat bias crimes differently than non-bias crimes or not was left unsettled, although the content of their "approach" comments did not seem to distinguish them from participants who gave more definitive responses on the issue. Three of the four indicated that bias crime was a different crime for reasons similar to those provided by other participants, and generally they raised the same issues regarding differential treatment, such as the ability to distinguish and/or prove hate crime, deterrence, emotional impact on the sentencing decision, or the possibility of rehabilitating biased offenders. However, more so than others, they did not seem to have reached a point where they were comfortable taking a stance on those issues or side stepping them to make a decision anyway. While some seemed to lean toward either similar or different treatment for biased offenders, they were willing to admit that they were "stuck" or simply "hadn't worked this out."

35-I guess if it were taken more seriously in that the penalties were more severe than any kind of normal crime I guess perhaps I don't know I get really stuck on this because I'd like to say perhaps it would be more of a deterrent. But then we go back to the issue of rehabilitation. You know if I give you a really strict sentence and penalty does that mean you're going to change your beliefs and attitudes and really undermine the ignorance that existed behind that. Certainly you will know as an individual committing the crime that it won't get swept under the rug by the legal system you will be taken seriously and you will be looked at specifically with a bias toward the race or sexual orientation or whatever and that it's wrong that it's ignorant and your targeting a very specific group for a very particular reason. And I think that should be taken seriously. And at the same time I wonder how much of that would really create real change in people attitudes and beliefs.

36-I think personally it should be given as much weight as any other crime that infringes on another person's rights. It should be handled just like any other kind of crime. I think in my opinion to think that change cannot occur is wrong. I think it's good to have it documented that it was a hate crime to possibly be aware…It if was a hate crime the majority of time it's going to happen again it's just a matter of getting caught. But there's so much that it takes in because now if you're child sees you committing a hate crime or sees you doing whatever they're more apt to do the same thing. And it just breeds the discontent. I think if they teach more of how it's wrong in school instead of just worrying about shoving the kids through…A crime is done but just with the evil mind and I forget what it is but if it's there it's going to happen again and if it happens again the punishment gets worse. In my opinion the punishment should get worse as the progression goes. To say something needs to be punished worse because it's a hate crime I don't know. I sit on the fence on that.

26-I'm afraid if people knew [it might be a hate crime] it might bias them toward the alleged criminal…and therefore I don't know that that should be brought in. Having said that, I would have a second caveat about it. How do you know? How do you ascertain that it's a hate crime? Who's to say that? Who makes that determination? That's a slippery slope…because what would appear to be a hate crime to someone else may in point of fact not been that at all. How do you know what was going on inside the heart of the person who perpetrated the crime? So that's not to say we should not try to see if it is hate crime but...I'm very cognizant of the fact that it's always not going to be easy to ascertain it. I would want a person to have a fair hearing...I don't know if the judge or jury should know. I don't know. I don't know how you would do that. I don't know what else you would do...How is that level of hate [in a "hate" crime] different than a hate I feel for you that made me rob you or rape you or kill you? It is a different species of hate I understand but in my mind I haven't worked this out, I just haven't. I have a little difficulty saying that species of hate is different from another species of hate.

28-I would like to see them handle it just as harshly as any other crime because it's a crime but I also think, I don't know, I think it can get out of hand like groups like neo-Nazis or white supremacist groups...I don't know if the judge or jury should know, I guess I think so. I think it adds a little bit to it and because they assaulted them they also assaulted them because they thought what they were doing was wrong so they were kind of taking the law into their own hands. So I think that should be addressed. I'm not sure it should affect their sentence because then again I guess if I think about it like maybe how easy is that to be proved. I mean the person could just say no I just I didn't do it for any reason not because they were black or not because they were gay but I just did it. So I don't know if it could be proved.

Influences on Citizens' Views of Bias Crime as Different

Although the study's non-random sample makes statistical significance irrelevant and the small sample size makes multi-level cross tabs impossible, basic cross tabs were run to help explore any patterns in terms of who thought bias crime was different than other crime and/or who advocated for a different approach to bias crime. Given that participants' perceptions of bias crime as different and their choice to support a different approach were often influenced by similar factors, as well as the fact that the former view was found to be the strongest predictor of the latter, the relevant findings for both are discussed together. Although for the most part participants' comments did not offer direct explanations for identified patterns, possible interpretations based on the available data and speculation are provided.[19]

<u>Bias Crime-Related Factors</u>
As indicated previously, the most obvious influence on participants' general approaches to bias crime (same or different) was whether they clearly indicated that bias crime was the same or different than non-bias crime. This would seem to be an expected finding and suggest at least some cognitive consistency between participants' views of and response to bias crime. In fact, this was one of only two bias crime-related variables for which the choice to treat bias crimes the same actually surpassed the percentage preferring different treatment for those within a given value of the independent variable.

Not surprisingly, the other variable was whether or not participants believed that the judge or jury should know that a crime might be a bias crime for which 82 percent of those who said yes felt that bias crime should be treated differently, whereas 100 percent of those who said no
felt it should be treated the same, again indicating logical consistency in participants' responses. This makes sense since in order for bias criminals to be treated differently by the criminal justice system the court factfinder would need to be privy to such information. As indicated above, those who said that bias crimes/criminals should be treated the same but wanted the judge or jury to know about the nature of the crime felt it was information important for reasons other than sanctioning biased offenders differently.

The only other bias crime-related factors that seemed relevant to participants' decision to treat bias crime the same as or differently than non-bias crime are whether they mentioned problems with the criminal justice system's handling of bias crimes or that human nature was a cause of bias crime. In terms of enforcement problems, several participants were concerned with how the system, the police in particular, approached bias crimes. These individuals seemed more likely to prefer a different approach to bias crimes. Not surprisingly, the mentioning of enforcement problems was highly correlated with the view that bias crime was not treated as seriously as other crimes, and both factors seemed predictive of the view that bias crime was different than other crime. It would seem to make sense that those who felt that the criminal justice system was not taking substantial enough measures to address such crime might also feel that overall such crime needed a more serious approach, thus advocating a different approach.

In terms of causes of bias crimes, those who mentioned human nature-the individual's need to assess their worth relative to others and find themselves on top-were more likely to say that bias crime should be treated differently than those who did not, in fact none of them were willing to say it should be treated the same and all of them thought bias crime was a "different" crime, although there were only four such participants. While participants' comments make it far from obvious, it could be that those who recognize such crime as to some extent hard wired into human needs might see bias crime as a more threatening and/or perhaps more difficult to address crime making it different and demanding of a different approach.

A host of other bias crime-related variables, including fear of bias crime, familiarity with the U.S. approach, other perceived causes of bias crime, and mention of the need for preventative measures to address such crime, did not seem to influence participants' opinions in these matters. In addition, participants who mentioned potential difficulty in proving bias crime, which would seem legally necessary to treat such crime differently, appeared to be no more or less likely than their counterparts to support a similar or different approach to perpetrators of bias crimes.

Crime and Bias Crime-Related Factors

In addition to strictly bias-crime related variables that seemed to impact the choice of approach toward bias crime, two other mixed crime and bias crime variables seemed to influence views on whether crime was different and how it should be treated. It was expected that both fear of crime and personal victimization might influence participants' perceptions of bias crime perhaps by making them more conscious of crimes and their handling and/or their potential or actual impact on victims, and that participants who feared or experienced bias crime might hold more specialized views towards bias crime and its handling given their more direct connection to the issue. However, the results on these factors were somewhat mixed. Overall, the majority of victims viewed bias crime as different and deserving of a different response. In addition, victims of crime were more likely than those who did not report such victimization to describe bias crime as different. However, they were no more likely to treat it differently than non-bias crime. In exploring differences between different types of victimization, participants who had been victims of crime in general or both bias and non-bias crime seemed more willing than victims of only bias crime to indicate bias crime was different; in fact, victims of bias crime were no more likely to indicate such than those who had not been victimized. In terms of treating bias crime differently, only participants with both types of victimization seemed more likely than others to advocate for this position. Thus, it would appear that victimization does lead to a different pattern of views regarding bias crime. However, that pattern was primarily the result of participants who experienced both bias and non-bias crimes, who perhaps find themselves in a better position to actually compare the two experiences and how they were handled, find them different, and thus determine bias crime worthy of a different response. This is perhaps supported by the fact that such participants also were more likely to identify problems with the enforcement of bias crimes and how seriously such crimes were handled as well as identify flaws in the criminal justice system, all of which led participants to view bias crime as different and/or in need of a different response.

Fear of crime also displayed mixed findings. Participants who reported fearing crime of any kind seemed more likely than those without fear to think bias crime was different and that it needed to be handled differently than non-bias crime. In fact, those who feared either crime in general or bias crime were more likely than those who did not to view bias crime as different. However, those who feared only bias crime were less likely than those who feared crime in general or both crime in general and bias crime to advocate for different treatment for bias crime and no more likely than those who did not fear crime to believe the same. However, this small group of five participants included one individual who feared bias crime for an untraditional reason-being a teacher. Another was a lesbian participant and, as discussed below, gay and lesbian participants were less likely than other categories of minorities to view bias crime as different or treat it differently, potentially as a result of their status and/or education. So, it is difficult to tell whether the findings related to fear of bias crime alone would be at all typical.

In general, however, it appears that fear is an indicator of participants' views of bias crime and approaches to it. These findings could be the result of those who fear crime spending more time considering and maybe comparing crimes, or perhaps their thoughts of potential victimization and the relative impact of different crimes on victims. Given that many participants' views on bias crime were related to the victim and their selection, which was not similarly present in their discussions of crime in general, it could be that these participants' fear makes them feel closer to potential victims and thus influences their views of bias crime towards different and greater action to protect its victims (themselves or others). It also is likely relevant that these participants were more likely to mention enforcement problems related to bias crime, which influenced both views, as well as society as a cause of crime, which as discussed below also impacted participants' views of bias crime and whether it should be handled differently than crime in general.

Crime-Related Factors
Given the impact of the general crime-based victimization and fear on bias crime issues, other crime-based variables were analyzed for their potential influence. Participants who mentioned social structure as a cause of crime in general were more likely than others to say bias crime was different and that its perpetrators required a different sanction. It may be that those who view crime as a particularly strong manifestation of the conditions of the overall structure of society view crime as more problematic and in need of different responses than currently taken that would better address its specific causes. Given that overall the causes of bias crime were geared more toward issues of prejudice and ignorance rather than economics, perhaps this led individuals to view it as different and determine that it needed a different response.

In addition to their views on the causes of crime, participants who had at least one good thing to say about the criminal justice or legal system, regardless of whether they then went on to critique it, were more likely than those who did not to support a different approach to bias offenders. It makes some sense that this sign of some trust or hope in the system may have made such participants more confident that the system was capable of a different approach to bias crime that could possibly make a difference. Also, participants who pointed out specific flaws in the system were more likely to conceive of bias crime as a different crime but were not more supportive of a different approach than those who failed to mention such flaws. These flaws generally concerned bureaucratic factors such as poor wages, understaffing, poor funding, overcrowding and other issues that appeared to affect the ability of the system to do justice for the victim. It is unclear why this factor would lead participants to view bias crime as different, although it perhaps makes sense that if they view the system as ineffective they would not deem its implementation of a different response to bias crime as an appropriate response.

Personal Characteristics

Participants' personal characteristics also were analyzed for any influences they might have on their views of bias crime compared to non-bias crimes and their willingness to treat bias crime/criminals differently. Three characteristics seemed most relevant: minority status, sex, and education, and there also appeared to be interactions between these variables. Perhaps not surprisingly, minorities were more likely than non-minorities to think bias crime different and worthy of a different approach, although these findings seemed to hold primarily for Jewish and African-American participants and in terms of a different approach more for minority men than women. Gay and lesbian participants were less likely than other minorities to make such claims, and seemed on par with non-minority participants with a college education in this regard. Women were more likely than men to perceive bias crime as different regardless of minority status. In terms of education, participants with a college or post-graduate degree were more likely to think bias crime different. This may explain some of the differences between gay and lesbian participants and other minorities as they were least likely to have a degree, and it may explain why their support for such claims are more in line with the non-minority college category of participants, who obviously have such degrees but not the minority status.

Minority status, sex and education also seemed to influence the other crime and bias crime-related variables that affected the two issues in question. Without the possibility of statistical analysis beyond mere percentages, it is difficult to overlay the various findings. However, minority status does appear to influence each of the bias variables (victimization, bias crimes not taken as seriously, enforcement problems, and human nature as a cause of bias crime) overall or at least for particular minority groups or men or women of minority status. Thus, sex and particular minority category may be influential in such matters, though the sub-samples available are too small to consider these issues. In addition, education also appears to influence the likelihood of claiming bias victimization and reporting human nature as a cause of bias crime. But again the education effects seem as though they may be interacting with minority status and/or sex. Similar mixed findings appeared when demographic characteristics were analyzed against crime variables related to bias crime as a different crime and/or requiring a different approach. In particular, minority participants were more likely than non-minorities (across all categories) to indicate some sort of fear and/or victimization. Education did not seem to influence participants' level of fear however it did impact victimization. Participants with a post-graduate degree were more likely than those with just some college or a high school degree to report victimization but this seemed to be a factor of sex, holding for women and not men.

Also of interest, aside from participants' claims of whether bias crime was different or that the judge or jury should know about the biased quality of the crime, having only a high school education was the only other variable that resulted in more participants preferring a similar rather than different response to bias crime. However, this claim for "high school" may be unfair given that the interviews for which there were complete data included only two participants with only a high school education or GED.

Unfortunately, for the most part neither the questions asked nor participants' views on crime or bias crime spoke directly to the issues mentioned above. In addition, in many instances the participants shared several different views that seemed to influence their views of bias crime as different and in need of a different response including victimization and/or views regarding fear, enforcement problems with bias crime, seriousness issues related to bias crime, flaws with the criminal justice system, and society as a cause of crime. Finally, the role of minority status, sex and education seemed to interact and influence a number of the relevant factors and views discussed. Given the nature of the study, particularly its small sample size, it is difficult to determine which of any of these factors might be driving the others and thus whether any of the factors discussed could be spurious. Thus, while the findings above seem worthy of future investigation, their support and explanations are speculative at best.

Influences on Different Bias Crime Approaches

Again, the small sample size and even smaller sub-sample sizes for those choosing to treat bias crime differently make exploring influences on how participants wanted to do so difficult. However, cross tabs were run to identify any differences between participants choosing a more punitive versus more or different rehabilitative approach to bias crime. Participants who were categorized as discussing both punitive and rehabilitation-based differences to bias crime were coded as punitive for the purposes of the analysis. Although nearly three quarters of those who advocated a different approach chose a more punitive response, there were some interesting differences amongst those who failed to do so particularly regarding sex, victimization, fear and causes of crime.[20] In addition, there was somewhat surprising consistency across participants preferred method of addressing crime and bias crime - punishment or rehabilitation - even though they preferred more or a different type of that approach, and again sex, victimization and fear seemed to influence that consistency. However, the findings below should be taken with caution given the generally small numbers involved.

The clearest finding was that all participants focusing solely on rehabilitative changes were women, the vast majority of whom were of minority status, primarily African-American. In fact, 46 percent of women who said bias crime should be treated differently discussed a different rehabilitative option compared to being more punitive (18%) or discussing a combination of approaches (27%). There were also additional factors on which these women were different from those participants opting for a more punitive approach to bias crime, in some instances unexpectedly. First, they were more likely to be victims of bias "crime", although almost entirely the victims of verbal incidents rather than physical or property offenses. As such, legally they may not in fact have been victims of bias crime and given the low-level of their encounter maybe more able to rationally assess the reasons behind the crime and how to address it than more serious victims who may have been more moved by the emotion of their experience. This also might explain why they were no more or less fearful than non-victims of bias crime. However, more rehabilitative participants were less likely to indicate a fear of crime in general, which might explain their less punitive views. Given that U.S. citizens tend to be first and foremost punitive, and given that most of the sample wanted a different approach to bias crime, it is perhaps not surprising that even those who were not victims nor fearful were supportive of a more punitive rather than rehabilitative option. The findings also revealed that those participants who mentioned bias crime legislation always chose the more punitive approach, suggesting either true support for it or perhaps indicating that the more punitive option is the one most familiar to citizens.

Second, the participants who supported a different rehabilitative approach to bias crime shared somewhat unexpected views on the causes of crime. Such participants were less likely than their more punitive counterparts to mention ignorance or upbringing as causes of bias crime. This is surprising since given their rehabilitative focus it was expected they might be more attuned to such factors that might seem particularly amenable to rehabilitation. However, these participants were more likely than punitive participants to mention society and human nature as causes of bias crime. Although these causes might seem less amenable to rehabilitation, it may be that as theoretically suggested, individuals who identify more social causes of crime may demonstrate greater compassion for offenders and thus be less punitive. It also should be noted that these same participants were more likely than those more punitive to identify upbringing as a cause of crime in general and not to mention economics. Thus, they may have been more inclined to view crime in general in a way that more encompassed bias crime and thus in discussing causes of bias crime were adding to their earlier comments rather than disregarding the role of upbringing in bias crime. This could further explain why they are willing to try more rehabilitative measures for such crime.

Another interesting finding, as previously indicated, was that most participants (56%) were quite consistent in their preferred approaches to crime in general and bias crime. The two participants who were only punishment-oriented in their discussion of crime in general (both men) supported greater punitive measures for bias crime. Forty-five percent of those who initially discussed rehabilitation discussed only how it should change for bias crime; the others split between discussing more punitive measures for bias crime or a combination of approaches. Of course, the latter participants include all the men who initially discussed rehabilitative measures only and two women. Those participants, who when discussing crime in general supported both punishment and rehabilitation, by a 2 to 1 margin maintained a similar discussion for biased crime; only one such participant shifted to a fully more punitive approach for bias crime. Because the seven shifts in approach focus were from a sole focus on rehabilitation to more punitive measures or a combination of forces or from a combination of approaches to a solely punitive approach, all of these changes are considered more punitive approaches to bias crime.

Though the numbers involved are extremely small, overall Jewish or male participants appeared more likely to switch to a more punitive focus in their discussion of bias crime compared to crime in general. Not surprisingly, those who switched also were more likely to be victims of physical or property-based bias crimes, fear bias crime, and mention that bias crimes were not treated as seriously as other crimes. Such participants might be expected to react more strongly and perhaps more emotionally and negatively toward such crime given their experiences. Also those who reported any kind of victimization were more likely to be inconsistent, as were those who claimed to be fearful, although in both categories men were more likely to switch than woman, perhaps explaining the male distinction indicated above. Finally, those who mentioned preventive measures for addressing bias crime seemed more likely to be consistent than other participants, perhaps addressing any opposing goals through preventive rather than correctional measures.[21]

Approaches to Bias Crime Beyond the Criminal Justice System

As mentioned earlier, two of the "approach to bias crime" questions were written in such a way as to allow participants to feel comfortable in discussing non-legal or non-criminal justice-based responses. In particular, they were asked, "How well would you say the U.S. handles bias crime?" and "How, if at all, do you think society should be dealing with bias crime?" Although participants' overall responses to these questions and the two additional questions concerning how the convicted perpetrators of bias crime should be handled gravitated toward discussion of the criminal justice system, nearly 40 percent of participants also mentioned the importance of non-criminal justice measures for addressing the issue. Such measures included education-based needs as well as more national social changes. A few participants mentioned the need for general public awareness, discussion and education of the differences in the world generally or the bias crime issue more specifically.

> 8-Well, you know, I think anything that creates public discussion can't - I won't say it can't do anything but have a positive effect - but I don't think it is a bad thing to have public discussion about these particular issues.

> 18-My mission in life is to bring people together…and just get them to know what is going on in the world. Even reading the newspaper, looking at CNN news, just so that they will know that things are going on in the world. I think by doing this, maybe they will be aware of what is outside themselves…And

if you don't do this or encourage people to look outside themselves and their little tight circle of friends, they are going to be ignorant.

3-I think back to being proactive. I think instead of just focusing on once the crime has happened, we should focus on preventing the crimes, you know, educating people that not everyone that wears a turban is a terrorist, things like that.

However, the vast majority or participants acknowledged the need for education for the young, particularly through the school systems. Although, some also recognized the difficulty with such measures namely in the form of parents whose views, religious or otherwise, might clash with the lessons of tolerance the schools might try to offer. They also noted the political ramifications of supporting programs that might be helpful in the long term but show few dividends during the election cycle.

36-I think if they teach more about it [hate/bias] and teach more of how it's wrong in school instead of just worrying about shoving the kids through [that would help].

19-[We need] more awareness, more training for young children. Start sex education when the child is a baby and you continue on through the years and I think you need the same training for racism, right up through the years - you start and you never stop as a parent. It should be from parents and teachers...I think it should be incorporated in the school curriculum.

13-[We need] social programming like in schools. When I was in high school, everybody was racist. Seven years later when I am coaching junior high, everybody is homophobic. Like it's the whole new issue...When these kids don't even know what the heck...when their hormones are slamming every which way and they are trying to figure out what they are, they know they like girls...and someone else is in the locker room and they find out he likes guys, it sends them overboard. You got to have something in school that says this is a tree, this is a plant, they're different but why does that matter. There needs to be something around that age group, but then you are going to run into problems with parents because (I don't want to bash religion) it is an issue for religious people, the majority of religious people. It is an issue of morals and ethics. If you start teaching about everybody, homosexuals in schools, it is going to be an evolution versus creation thing. And so it is going to be very hard to implement a program in school that allows educators to expose children to these differences. It's going to be hard to do that when they need to be exposed to this kind of stuff, these kinds of issues and differences and even the similarities...when they are young, the parents at home are a) teaching them hate and b) it's going to be a moral ethical issue. So it is going to be really hard.

15-I think it would take longer [to educate perpetrators of hate crimes] but it [tolerance] should be educated when they start grade school instead of waiting until they are locked up, which is more prevention than anything. The whole thing is for someone to get elected for another term. They want to see results in four years or two years instead of waiting for 20 years to see the results of the things that they did. They shovel all the money into corrections instead of education. We need both but education is definitely going to be more effective I think.

16-I think it is an education kind of thing starting at the schools. Look at Nancy Reagan with the "Just Say No", and I think that started young, it has gotten up to now where kids really don't smoke and I don't think they do as many drugs, I think-it seems to me at least. I know my kids are just so anti-cigarettes and all that kind of stuff and I just think that if we start young...and it took a while for that young age to get up there, but eventually...so if we can start young even in the schools and really have programs talking about the differences of people and that it is okay. I mean it seems such an obvious thing, but I don't think it is taught, and I think it needs to be discussed and it certainly would be nice to talk to the adults, but the adults are the ones that don't change and all that. I think that their racism gets passed down to their kids so we can work the other way up, maybe.

18-I think one thing that might help is with the textbooks in school...I know there has got to be textbooks out there that might have chapters on all the major ethnicities and I think even in a social studies class, those should be the type of textbooks that are bought because people fear the unknown. I look at some of these little kids coming to the University. They have lived in an all-white suburb all their life. Of course, they are going to be afraid to mix too much with black people. Or you get some of these little kids from an all-black area of the city, and they come here. Of course they want to go and be with people who look like them because they don't know how to react to anybody else. And I think the University could do a better job about doing something about that during orientation.

30-It's a hard thing to handle because for instance if someone is getting it from their parents and it's a young child, calling their parents is not going to accomplish anything. You know schools need to get a handle on this but again if you don't have the parents' cooperation what are you going to do. So, education I think is the key and I think it has to be your public education and your religious education because I think there are religions or religious groups that teach intolerance as part of their program.

Two participants in particular seemed to sum up the frustration that many of the participants' tone seemed to allude to when discussing the issue of tolerance in schools as well as the hope that they thought prevention provided.

16- I don't know if they [schools] feel there isn't a big enough need for it yet or what it is but why do you have to wait for something to happen for the need to be addressed?

17-I think if the rest of the infrastructure of the community worked properly, it [bias crime] wouldn't have to get to the legal system. So whether it's in the schools or it's some other way that we are educating and finding people who are hateful, I think we could probably be proactive about it.

Finally, a few other participants viewed the problem and proactive need as even more complex than simply educating around the obstacles presented by parents, religion and/or politics. As one man put it, "If you can figure out society's mentality, then maybe we could start but I think that you've got to start there" (33). These participants felt that society needs to change including our government's use of its constitutional power and our laws, our major religions' lack of acceptance of certain groups, and/or the country's very white, male Christian view of the world. In all, they suggested that our society, while claiming to be open, acts in ways antithetical to the ideas behind being intolerant of hate crimes and that that needs to change if progress is to be made on the bias crime issue.

> 13-The federal government has got to take it...they are saying that it is bad to do bad things to these people however, lets take some rights away from them and use the Constitution which is used to guarantee rights and take them away from people. It is like saying, "don't kill them even if they are a little less human than we are." Unless that changes, it's not going to... I'll tell you what, it's not going to change for a long time because the whole racism issue is still right in our faces.

> 6-We are moving in slow motion, we need as much as we are supposed to be the United States–welcome to the world and everybody perceives us as we are the cutting edge of everything, whatever. We are at the back door, we are back of the times when it comes to being culturally diverse...and being supportive of that...And the challenge again is probably religion behind it all...the Christian Bible, whatever, that's the problem. And people who want to make that change, they need to have organizations that support these people. Because, you know, people [who are different]... they are on campuses, you need to embrace them. They are in our communities–we need to embrace them. They are in the United States–we need to embrace them. And that means changing our laws. Things like embracing same-sex marriages. We need to move on with this and address all our needs...and when the world as a whole starts embracing and stop making it a fad or something wrong and perceived that way, then more people may be more willing to embrace a

different kind of culture because sometimes we show our resistance when we are not trained to support this.

9-How we view things is so aligned with one particular group of people, those usually being white, male, Christian, heterosexual, it is difficult for us to make the sort of changes I think that need to be made. In that retrospect, I am at a loss as to how to improve the way we do things because we first off have to improve ourselves and the way we think about it. The United States does progressively, slowly move forward but really, the pendulum swings.

Summary of Citizens' Bias Crime Perceptions and Preferences

Overall, the vast majority of study participants seemed confident in their labeling of bias crime as different from non-bias crime in some way-either in terms of its inherent nature or its ramifications-and seemingly as a result they supported a different approach to bias crimes/criminals. In fact, other than those who indicated that bias crime was not a different crime, or possibly those with only high school educations, the majority of study participants in every value of the other independent variables considered claimed support for a different approach to bias crime or their was an even split. That being said, 25 percent of the sample-a for the most part mixed assortment of participants, minority and non-minorities, victims and non-victims etc.-felt that bias crime should be treated, even if perhaps more seriously than they are now, the same as any similar underlying crime. Even if they felt that the judge or jury should be informed as to the bias nature of the crime, they felt it should be irrelevant to sentencing, arguing primarily that "a crime is a crime" and/or that hate is hate regardless of the status of the victim. Although the small sample made more particular distinctions difficult, it did appear that a few variables did seem to distinguish those who viewed bias crime as different and/or deserving of a different approach including minority status, sex, education, victimization and fear. Those who were more likely to believe a different response to bias crime was necessary were fairly evenly divided in terms of the type of "different" approach they discussed, some preferring a more punitive measure while others focused on more or different rehabilitative measures-predominantly women-or a combination of both. In addition, the majority of participants' bias crime preferences were consistent with the focus of their discussion for handling crime in general. With regards to both of these findings, sex, victimization and fear arose as relevant factors. Finally a large minority went beyond the criminal justice system to show favor for preventative measures for addressing bias crime, primarily in the form of school or society-based education and awareness.

CHAPTER 9

Citizens' Responses to Bias Crime Vignettes

Another means of exploring participants' preferred approaches to bias crime involved how they would handle convicted offenders of similar bias and non-bias crime vignettes. Such questioning was designed to provide a more application-based assessment of participants' approaches and examine the consistency of participants' abstract approaches with those they actually were willing to apply to specific instances of bias crime. This chapter reports on a number of relevant issues including the nature of participants' responses to non-bias crime vignettes, their categorizing of similar vignettes designed to be viewed as bias crimes as such, their similar or different approach to the bias vignettes generally and compared to their non-bias counterparts, and the nature of their preferred "different" approaches to bias crimes. In addition, although the sample sizes involved diminish quickly, patterns in who held what views are provided and explanations offered to the extent possible.

Of particular interest are findings regarding cognitive consistency and rehabilitation. The vignette findings demonstrate a surprising level of consistency. In fact, participants' prior abstract views were the best predictors of their vignette responses. In terms of rehabilitation, even though half of participants supported a more punitive response to bias crime, its level and nature were not commensurate with that generally authorized by current bias crime legislation. In addition, participants generally combined more punitive measures with an added or changed rehabilitative component for bias crime, overall making rehabilitation a key focus of participants' responses to such crime. Although the nature of the vignettes might explain some of the findings concerning consistency and rehabilitation, the vignettes were designed to better assess participants' responses to the most common of bias crimes and thus those to which criminal legislation and policy would most commonly apply.

173

Relatively low-level crime vignettes were used given concern that the use of more serious crimes, particularly murder or mass murder, which is often the type of vignette used in national poll vignette questions, might be handled so severely that participants would see no need or possibility for harsher punishments for bias versions of such crime. It also was expected that the punitive seriousness with which such crimes might be approached might mask any possible rehabilitative concerns that participants might have. Finally, given that statistically crime in general, and particularly bias crime, is more likely low level offenses in terms of seriousness and criminal sanction, the use of low-level property and violent/person crimes seemed sensible. Each study participant was asked for their response to a bias and non-bias version of the same three crime vignettes. The vignettes used were: an act of vandalism (graffiti) (V1); a street assault involving only minor bumps and bruises (V2); and a bar assault resulting in a broken nose (V3) (See 8.1 for full bias and non-bias versions of the vignettes). After each version of each vignette, participants were asked how they thought the convicted perpetrators of such crimes should be handled. Their responses were coded as punitive-incarceration, punitive-non-incarceration, or rehabilitation-oriented.

8.1   Hypothetical Bias and Non-Bias Crime Vignettes

V1 – Two 19-year-old boys decide to go on a vandalism spree in their neighborhood causing about $400 in damage to remove the graffiti.
Non-bias: They spray paint the name of their favorite rock ban on a local business.
Bias: They spray pain a swastika on a local Jewish temple.

V2 – A couple of male college students are sitting on a bench watching people go by. Along comes a couple holding hands. The two guys jump up, accost the man and shove him to the ground and then let the couple run off. The man receives only minor scratches and bruises.
Non-Bias: The women in the couple looks like their best friend's girlfriend with another guy.
Bias: The couple walking by is an interracial couple.
Bias: The couple walking by is a gay couple.

V3 – A middle-aged construction worker is fired from his job and goes to a local bar to let off some steam. At the bar...
Non-Bias: He runs into his former boss, picks a fight with him and breaks his nose.
Bias: He notices a guy at the bar who he thinks is gay, figure he can probably take him, and so picks a fight with him and breaks his nose.

Punitive-incarceration included any support for jail or prison time, whereas punitive-non-incarceration included any other punitive measures such as probation, fines and fees, and community service advocated as pure work and/or punishment. Rehabilitation included education, treatment, counseling and community service discussed as an experience designed to change offenders' behavior by changing their understanding and/or appreciation of their crime and its consequences for victims rather than simply deter it. Participants were not asked about sanctioning options they did not directly raise unless their statements were unclear. However, when participants indicated that they would treat bias crime differently in some way if they discussed only the different component (such as rehabilitation) but not other components (such as jail time), they were asked if the rest of their approach would remain the same as for the non-bias version of the crime. Although this may have caused some participants to consider further options that had not initially come to them, given that their responses to bias crime immediately followed their responses to the non-bias version of the same crime, this possibility is likely low. In addition, participants' responses to such questions in terms of tone and time (no great pauses) and language (no voiced consideration of the options) did not seem to suggest they were reconsidering or mulling over the issue but simply clarifying what was obvious to them. Finally, given the seemingly low risk, such questioning was deemed necessary to ensure a complete understanding of their approach to the bias crime rather than just an assessment of the component of the approach on which they chose to focus.

Citizens' Responses to Non-Bias Vignettes

To set the stage for participants' views on the bias crime vignettes and how they compare to those on a similar, non-bias crime, their responses to the non-bias crimes are discussed first in brief. Overall, study participants were generally non-punitive across all three vignettes in terms of their support for pure incarceration (jail or prison time). In fact no one supported only jail for V1 and only two participants did for each of V2 and V3, with one repeater, and these three participants seemed to have less in common than not.[22] Although, it should be noted that it is not being suggested that such participants might not also support rehabilitative measures if directly questioned on the issue but rather only indicated that they did not deem it appropriate or important enough to discuss it in response to the vignettes. However, voiced support for punitive measures across the vignettes increased substantially when non-incarceration-based punitive measures were also considered raising punitive support, with or without rehabilitation, to between 45 and 64 percent of the participants depending on the vignette. It reached its highest for V1, which is perhaps explained by the desire to have the perpetrators clean off their graffiti and/or pay for the damages and/or work off their punishment in the community. Of course this coding may falsely assess participants' punitive inclination if they felt that community service served a rehabilitative rather than deterrent function that they failed to acknowledge. Although, it should be noted that many participants were clear in their perception of the punitive nature of this sanction, and those who clearly discussed a rehabilitative component were coded as such.

As the seriousness of the vignette offense increased so to did the number of participants who included jail along with other miscellaneous punitive measures, such as stiff fines and the paying of medical bills, as did the range of the overall amount of jail/prison time. Jail time for V1 involved sentences of a weekend or a few days, whereas jail time for V2, while sometimes including a couple days or overnight, went as high as a month or two, and V3 included all those as well as sanctions of up to six months. Although participants clearly wanted perpetrators to be punished, they were fairly benign in their overall punitive sanctions.

As much as participants were not solely in favor of just jail or prison terms, they were similarly non-disposed to solely rehabilitative sanctions, which were represented by only two participants. Again the participants who offered such views seem more different than alike. A middle-aged, high-school educated blue-collar female felt that rehabilitation would be appropriate for a first time assault without serious injury (V2), while a Caucasian, lesbian college student felt that alcoholics anonymous and/or anger management type approaches would be an appropriate response to the bar fight (V3). An obvious shared trait was these participants' gender holding with earlier findings suggesting women may be more favorable than men to strictly rehabilitative focuses. However, both these women discussed a combination of punitive and rehabilitative approaches when asked about crime and punishment in general, suggesting that perhaps the nature of the vignettes did not quite rise to the level where the punishment was necessary or at least foremost on their mind; in fact one did mention that had the perpetrator been a repeat offender, she would have supported some jail time for the minor assault scenario.

Not surprisingly given research supporting Americans' punitive approach to crime and punishment as well as their continued support for rehabilitation, most of those who offered rehabilitative measures combined them with more punitive sanctions. In fact, the percentage of respondents espousing such combination responses was a fairly consistent 30 percent across all three vignettes. These responses included the punitive measures, both incarceration and not, and similar rehabilitative measures to those mentioned above. In addition, these participants added such rehabilitative measures as mandatory education, closer perpetrator contact with their victims, counseling/therapy, treatment, job training, and community service involving working with victims. As with the punitive participants' discussed above, participants' espousing a combination-approach generally preferred non-incarceration-based punitive measures or both incarceration and non-incarceration measures rather than just jail or prison time.

Thus, overall participants were predominantly punitively oriented based on the three vignettes offered although that support primarily took the form of non-incarcerative sanctions or a combination of non-incarcerative sanctions with minimal jail time, rather than reflecting a strong incarceration emphasis. However, mention of jail time and other punitive sanctions did increase for the physical rather than property offenses. In addition, close to a third of participants emphasized rehabilitative measures, primarily in combination with punitive measures.

Citizens' Labeling of Vignettes as Bias Crimes

The bias crime vignettes were designed to essentially take the non-bias crime and either add a biased motivation or change the current non-biased motivation to a biased one. In particular, the graffiti vignette was changed from spray painting the name of a band on a public business to spraying a swastika on a synagogue; the minor assault was switched from attacking the male in a couple because of mistaken identity to assaulting him because he was evidently part of an interracial or gay couple; the more serious assault was changed from a fired man breaking the nose of his ex-boss in a bar fight to the same man breaking the nose of a bar patron because he assumed he was gay and figured he could take him. The changed vignettes were stated in such a way as to make the bias motivation of the crime evident and the crimes easily labeled as bias crimes by persons with a general understanding of that concept. Thus, it is not surprising that when asked no participants indicated that they thought any of the vignettes were absolutely not bias crimes.[23] In fact, for each vignette at least three quarters of the participants either responded in the affirmative when asked whether they thought any of the vignettes were bias crimes or indicated that the vignette was a bias/hate crime without prompting.

Interestingly, approximately a quarter of participants for each vignette indicated that whether it was a bias crime or not would depend. While about half of the participants made this claim for at least two, and in one case all three, vignettes, the rest raised the issue for only one vignette and the specific vignette they questioned varied. However, participants' reasons for questioning a possible "bias" labeling of the crimes was quite consistent across participants and vignettes. These participants needed to be convinced that the crime was motivated by bias/hate; they wanted some form of tangible proof that bias prompted the crime, and whether or not they were willing in the abstract to treat bias crime differently or not, they weren't comfortable definitively labeling it as such without that further evidence. For V1, these participants, although recognizing the hateful message of the symbol, wanted to know whether the perpetrators understood the message behind the symbol and/or whether it was intended to have the effect it likely would.

> 8-I think you have to really ask the people that did it and try to determine from their testimony whether it is or not [a bias crime]. We are dealing with a generation that really might not have the same reaction to that particular symbol as a holocaust survivor. So it's an interesting situation...I think we have to investigate to find out exactly if hate is the motivating factor or whether it was just an interesting symbol that they wanted to paint there.

> 9-It depends. They are nineteen. It's going to take a lot to derive their actual motive - whether they are jut trying to be cool or whether they really do hate...the motivation, I think, is the important factor in that.

> 13-That is not clear cut. It is in that gray area. I know people who use the word nigger because their parents do. They don't

know what they are saying and they are my age...I think there needs to be an investigation into whether or not it was [intended to be hateful]...the benefit of the doubt needs to be with the perpetrator.

29-It depends what the motivation was. Like if they were truly, if they were really anti-Semitic then yeah but if they were just being idiots no. You've got to take into account the situation beyond what they did.

39-I think you have to look at it and sort of look at the circumstances...You know you see a symptom but what is the pathology behind it...I think you have to look at what's behind it.

For V2 and V3, participants simply wanted to know whether hatred for an interracial or gay couple could be proven as the motivation for the crime. Many would have wanted to see tangible proof presented such as the context of the crime, the perpetrator's language at the time of the crime including racial slurs, the perpetrators' history etc.

10-That borders the hate crime, and then you are stuck with the problem of proving it again...it's so hard to prove I think.

25-I would say it should be determined whether it was some kind of hate crime issue...[they should consider] the person's past history of behavior, if they acted like that before, and the circumstances of the incident like did they make racial slurs.

26-If there's any evidence at all that it was done because the man was African-American or whatever, that becomes a different thing. But without any proof of that, and how do you introduce that proof, and maybe there are ways of doing that, but if that was not introduced then no, I don't think you can ratchet up what you do...Well there should have been dialogue and the women would have come forth and said they were saying things and because we were together and because it was black and white. There'd be some proof coming that there were comments or statements made before hand that this somehow was perpetrated because of interracial stuff...Is there a history? Was there something that week actually? Is there testimony coming forth that this is an ongoing thing in their psyches. If it is, then this could look like that is partly what's perpetrating this-if you've got something tangible.

13-[You've got to] decide whether or not it's a hate crime. Just because I know someone is gay and I kick the shit out of him isn't the same as me kicking the crap out of him because he is gay. There is obviously a difference...if it was because he was gay, you would probably know from what he was saying to him...I never heard or seen anybody beat the crap out of somebody and remain silent.

26-I don't know how you would be able to ascertain that this was prompted by the fact that they had a different sexual preference.

In all, these participants could see the possible bias/hate-based motive in the vignettes. However, they also could see the possibility of non-bias based reasons for the behavior presented and thus were unwilling to certify all the scenarios as bias crimes. Whether their counterparts also saw such possibilities but failed to voice them or would have demanded similar evidence if actually required by law to determine the perpetrators fate is unclear. It may be that some people require greater proof than others to call a crime a bias crime or simply that some are more hesitant to make definitive claims without confirming their suspicions about the likely context of the crime. However, whatever the case, it seems to be fairly well dispersed across different types of participants in terms of demographics and particular views when examined across all three vignettes. In fact, interestingly, those participants who were reluctant to view and treat bias crime differently because of their belief that the underlying crime rather than its intent should drive criminal sanctions were no more likely to question the bias crime label for the vignettes than others. However, it may be that those participants answered the question based on their view as to how the legal system would have labeled the vignettes rather than whether they thought the idea of labeling crimes bias crimes should be appropriate or relevant to the handling of such crimes.

Although the number of missing respondents and the often small case sizes make comparisons difficult, there were a few differences between those who labeled the crimes as bias crimes and those who said it depended. One of the particularly interesting findings concerned minority status. Although overall minority status versus non-minority status did not appear to influence participants' responses, African-Americans appeared to be less likely than other sub-sample categories to say it "depends" for at least one of the three vignettes. This may be because they were least likely to say depends for V2 (the interracial couple). Although overall this appears to be the only sub-sample category difference, in V3 (with a gay victim) gay and lesbian participants as well as participants with a bachelor's degree seemed more likely to say "depends" than others. These findings suggest that for some minority categories their status may influence when they are willing to define a crime as a bias crime, particularly perhaps if it involves their own status, although not necessarily in the same ways. While African-Americans seemed to not question the vignette with a racist bias, gays and lesbian seemed to be more likely to question one with a bias based potentially on sexual orientation.

Other factors that seemed to influence whether or not participants were willing to label the vignettes as bias crimes were sex, victimization and proof. In particular, men seemed more likely than women in the sample to suggest it "depends." This held true for both V2 and V3. Victims of bias crime were less likely than non-victims overall to question the biased nature of a crime but this may be an issue of sex given that women were more likely than men to be the victims of bias crime. Finally, and perhaps not surprisingly, overall those who mentioned potential problems with proving hate when discussing bias crime in general were more likely to say it depends particularly with regards to V3, suggesting the problem may be with the vignette rather than great reluctance on this group's part to identify crimes as bias crimes without more than general information. Somewhat surprisingly, there appeared to be no difference between those who thought bias crime generally should be treated the same as or differently than non-bias crime, although perhaps this should not be a surprise given that such determinations were not based on issues of proof and as indicated earlier, participants were more likely labeling the crimes based on the perception of what legal bias crimes are rather than their own assessment of whether such labeling is necessary or appropriate.

Again, these findings are highly questionable given the number of participants for which the issue was not directly addressed as well as the small number of cases on which they were based. However, overall the majority of participants addressing the issue did find all of the bias versions of the vignettes to be bias crimes, or at least potentially bias crimes, and provided a response as though they were. The rest, while not addressing the issue clearly, neither indicated that the vignettes were not bias crimes nor responded to them in a way that suggested that their responses, whether treating the bias and non-bias crimes the same or different, were made without awareness of the general difference in the nature of the two vignettes or based on some other non-bias related factor present in the vignette.

Citizens' Responses to Bias Crime Vignettes – Same or Different

Responses to the bias crime vignettes were analyzed individually for each vignette and across vignettes to determine the extent to which participants would treat bias crimes the similarly to, or differently than, non-bias crimes.[24] Given the difficulty in trying to assess whether participants considered their responses to bias crime to be the same or different than those to the non-bias crimes, I decided to make my own assessment based on their responses to the vignettes. If they discussed any change in their approach to the bias crime vignette, whether it was more punitive (punitive), involved more or different rehabilitation (rehabilitative), or both (combination), they were coded as treating bias crime differently, and if not, they were coded as "same." Given they responded to three actual bias crimes, their overall same/different assessments were based on their consistent approach to at least two of the three vignettes, although the vast majority of participants were consistent across all three. Based on those evaluations, 72 percent of the 32 study participants whose comments could be assessed responded to the bias crime vignettes in some way differently than the matched non-bias crimes.

Somewhat surprisingly, for the most part, participants' approaches could have been best predicted by their abstract approach to bias crime voiced earlier in their interviews, suggesting substantial cognitive consistency. Only four of the 23 participants who provided clear abstract views and specific responses to the vignettes failed to maintain a similar approach, and further review of their responses suggested that their "inconsistency" might be more a matter of whether they considered different rehabilitation as treating bias crime differently (or whether all crimes receive different rehabilitation based on the nature of the crime), whether they felt bias crime could actually be proven, or whether a different approach was worth at least a shot.[25] These respondents failed to differ in any obvious way from other respondents.

Although the majority of participants, regardless of other factors measured, advocated and actually applied a different response to bias crimes, some groups did seem to be more likely than not to treat the bias crime vignettes the same as their non-bias crime counterparts. Not surprisingly, participants who indicated that bias crime was not a different crime and those who believed that the judge or jury did not need to be provided with hate-based information concerning a case were more likely to treat the bias and non-bias vignettes the same. In addition, participants who did not report general crime victimization; did not mention that they felt that the criminal justice system was unfair (discriminatory in some way based on race, class, income etc); or who only had a high school diploma (only 2 cases) were more likely than not to treat bias crimes the same.

A few variables seemed to make participants more likely than their counterparts to treat bias crime the same but not more often than not. They included participants who indicated no fear of bias crime; did not mention human nature as a cause of bias crime or that bias crime was not treated as seriously as other crimes or that the criminal justice system was inconsistent in terms of how seriously it considers and punishes different crimes generally; or mentioned society as a cause of crime or the importance of preventative measures for addressing crime in general. Finally, in terms of demographics, non-minorities appeared to be more likely than minorities to treat bias crimes the same. However this is most likely an artifact of the no-college, non-minorities being more likely to treat it the same but not the non-minority college sample and the fact that African-Americans of all the sub-samples were the least likely to treat bias crime the same, in fact never doing so. Unfortunately, the samples are too small to assess possible interactive effects amongst these seeming differences.

But overall, participants, as far as can be assessed from the available data, appeared to be fairly willing to apply their abstract approaches to bias crime to specific, low-level bias crime scenarios. Even when they do appear to be inconsistent, further consideration of their comments serves to offer reasonable explanations.

Citizens' Different Responses to Bias Crime Vignettes

As with participants' different approaches to bias crime in general, their different responses to the bias crime vignettes also took on a variety of forms. Some demonstrated a preference for greater punitive measures towards the bias crime vignettes, others more or different rehabilitative measures, and the rest a combination of both. Also of interest, across the three vignettes the majority of participants, all but eight, were completely consistent in the nature of their approach (for example, being more punitive for all of the bias crime vignettes). Four participants gave responses that could not be fully understood. The other four provided clear responses and were consistent across two of the three vignettes, and their "inconsistencies" were based on differences between V1 compared to V2 and V3, either the former receiving rehabilitation and the others not or the latter receiving punitive measures and the former not, suggesting that minor property crimes may sometimes be perceived as less demanding of a fully different response than crimes against persons. When individual participants' overall approaches to bias crime were assessed, the majority of participants for whom such could be determined applied approaches consistent with those they voiced for bias crime in the abstract.

<u>More Punitive Responses to Bias Crime Vignettes</u>
Based on responses to the individual vignettes, a tenth to a third of study participants, depending on the vignette, included a more punitive component to their sanctioning of a bias crime offender compared to his non-bias counterpart. However, only a small minority of those chose a solely more incarceration-based punitive approach, usually more so for V2 or V3 than V1. For V1, participants supported greater non-incarceration-based punitive sanctions by demanding that biased offenders clean a greater range of properties as community service work and/or for a longer time, pay greater damages, or serve harder community service or simply a "more intense" non-incarceration-based sanction. Increases in jail time for such offenders, if a specific amount was given, ranged from a weekend or two to a year. For V2 and V3, more punitive sanctions included a larger fine or added probation or a short jail time from two days to a couple of months. While some authorized increased jail times above that recommended for the non-bias vignette, in most instances participants were not questioned as to how much more jail time unless they had previously indicated a certain

amount of time for the non-bias vignette. It was discovered early on that those who did not offer specific lengths of time when asked usually did not know or answered in a manner that suggested they were not necessarily committed to the specific time but rather the need for some jail.

When the nature of each participant's overall stance toward bias crime across the vignettes was assessed, only four participants fit the solely more punitive category, two men and two women. One, an African-American man, was the only participant who supported a jail sentence for bias crime longer than an additional year and a day. While supporting hard community service labor (Alabama chain gang type of approach) and some possible rehabilitation for V1, for V2 he said, "It's a hate crime...We stick them under the jail 10-15 years...What business of yours is it what color they are?...It's nobody else's business what they do (gay couple)" and for V3 his end punishment was similarly as harsh (14). An African-American grandmother felt that the punishment for bias crime should be harsher (added/increased jail or greater fine) because it was for two crimes-one the underlying crime and one the bias crime, although she also indicated that the graffiti offenders should receive some appropriate rehabilitation, which fit more with her rehabilitative approach to crime in general (2). A Caucasian man in his thirties, while suggesting that "education may help" in V1, increased the jail time from a weekend (maybe for non-bias crimes) to "a year and a day just to make them mad," for bias crimes, an increase that he supported for all three vignettes. Responding to V2 he also said, "I don't know how long it would take to make the difference. I would check up on them to see if they are getting raped, wait 'til they get popped around a couple different facilities...it might take a while for people of that mind" (15). Finally, a Caucasian female and mother of an interracial family supported "deeper" punishment across the board but she did not know how that could or should be achieved (2). While the two men seemed particularly punitive in their actual sentences or thoughts surrounding them, only the former seemed to be substantially more punitive than participants who supported more punitive measures along with rehabilitation. All but one of these overall solely punitive participants mentioned rehabilitation for one vignette suggesting that even given their punitive response to the others given the option they too might support some rehabilitation along with the increased punishment.

Overall, participants were fairly consistent in their means of providing a more punitive response to bias crime and for the most part it involved non-incarceration-based measures and when it did involve incarceration it did not involve any significant amount of time in jail or prison. Although participants were not directly asked to describe or explain their reasons for authorizing more punitive sanctions, based on the comments shared, a few assumptions seemed reasonable. First, it seemed that when participants were concerned with "changing" offenders rather than just deterring them, they raised rehabilitative issues directly in addition to their desire for greater punishment. Only two participants ever indicated that the need for incarceration was to provide additional rehabilitation. Second, when they seemed interested in deterrence, they generally spoke of incarceration or non-incarcerative measures in terms that made it seem clear that their measures were meant to punish the offender and thus have such an effect rather than an issue of their confusing deterrence based on punishment with rehabilitation. Finally, although a couple of participants did mention the need for some incarceration or probation in terms of the need to keep any eye on offenders who might be inclined toward further similar behavior, the more general sense was that the bias offense was a more serious crime requiring a more seriously punitive response – just deserts. In terms of the non-incarcerative measures, they were assessed carefully to ensure that they were meant as punishment rather than some form of rehabilitation and coded appropriately. These distinctions were maintained across coding of both bias and non-bias responses to allow for accurate comparisons.

<u>Combination Responses to Bias Crime Vignettes</u>
Based on responses to individual vignettes, a range of one tenth to a quarter of participants applied a combination approach to bias crime compared to its non-bias counterpart. Such an approach included a more punitive component, as discussed above, and a different and/or greater rehabilitative component. In terms of overall assessment, eight participants, a mix of minority and non-minority males and females, were coded as supporting such an approach to bias crime. For punitive measures they supported "harsher," "more severe," or longer sentences-although no more than an added or increased year for those who provided amounts-and/or something akin to greater fines and/or damages or more community labor for punitive purposes, etc. In terms of changes in rehabilitation for bias crimes, these participants wanted offenders to receive education, treatment, therapy or training of one

sort or another relevant to the hate-based motivation of their crimes that would provide them with a better appreciation for their victims and/or the wrongness and/or impact of their hate-based acts. Although sometimes such rehabilitation was viewed as taking place in the community and other times in jail (usually more likely for V2 and/or V3), the need for hate-based rehabilitation remained constant.

> 16-(V1) [they need] more education, come to services or something more educated to perceived that those people [Jews] are normal too...Educate them as to who the people are that they did the hate crime against, and that there is no reason why you need to fear these people.

> 13-(V1) You have to treat that a little more harshly...Give them a little more than a dime store tour of what the holocaust was and things of that nature.

Generally, these participants' responses indicated a sense that the bias vignettes deserved harsher "punishment" because they were viewed as bias crimes and because something about targeting a property/person because of "hate" added to it and made it more serious. However, they also believed that in addition to that punishment should be rehabilitation to address the hate and possibly avoid recidivism.

> 16-(V2) I think there should be some time in jail...a harsher penalty...because it was premeditated thought that it was just truly because of hate...they are judging these people and they are just people too.   I think it should be more jail time...maybe a week or two to think about what they did and somehow while they are in there somehow educate them. Make them read some kind of books or something like that...about tolerance.

> 34-(V2) [Instead of just a fine for non-bias crime] I would want to see jail time...because you're singling out a group because you're seeing an individual that you don't like not because of anything that you know about them only that they represent a certain group...maybe just a couple of months in jail and put them through some sensitivity training put them

with a bunch of black dudes for a while. (V3) Completely
different situation [than non-biased version]. Maybe like 11
months in jail or something like that [compared to probation
and fees/fines] and some time on probation cause it's that
serious. It's not something you can just pay off...And you
know really being really harsh on some kind of education with
the result of you trying to learn something about what it is that
you did and why is it you did it...teach them something that
maybe it won't happen again.

13-(V2) It would certainly appear to be a hate crime...And it
needs to be treated a lot more harshly...I think the punitive
needs to be more severe. Maybe more jail time to spend on
corrective treatment perhaps. That way they can get the
punishment of losing their freedom, but it will be spent
working towards something.

31-(V2; same for V3) That would fall under my categorizing
of a hate crime...I think some monetary fines should be higher
and also diversity training and anger management.

Rehabilitation-Oriented Responses to Bias Crime Vignettes
Based on responses to individual vignettes, a range of a quarter to half
of participants applied a rehabilitation-only change to at least one bias
crime vignette, the higher range being for V1. In terms of overall
assessment, nine participants discussed only rehabilitation changes for
biased offenders' sentences compared to their non-bias crime
counterparts. Note that this does not mean that they failed to authorize
miscellaneous and/or incarceration-based punitive sanctions for bias
crime offenders also but rather that such measures were the same as
those they authorized for non-biased offenders. It also should be noted
that it is unclear whether all of these participants themselves would
perceive of such changes as treating bias crimes "differently" although
in application they are. Regardless of how they did or might conceive
of their decision, each of these participants felt that bias crime
offenders' needed hate-based rehabilitation in addition or rather than
how they would respond to a similar non-biased offender. In most
instances they supported rehabilitation for non-biased offenders also
but recognized that the change in the type or motive of the crime for
bias crime required a different type or added type of rehabilitation that

addressed the hate component of the crime. As with participants supporting combination changes to bias crime, these participants supported counseling, education, diversity/sensitivity training etc. - any rehabilitation geared toward helping offenders get past their hate, bigotry or prejudice. Unlike their counterparts, they did not indicate the need for greater punishment and, except for one participant, they did not even raise the need for longer sentences to make the necessary rehabilitation possible, although it may be that they would have acknowledged such a need if pressed on the issue. Even so, they most likely would not support such a measure for its more punitive function as did other participants, who even when mentioning both punishment and rehabilitation did not connect the former as necessary for the latter or if they did also authorized the additional time as a punishment as well.

6-(V2) Probably about the same [punitively], just different types of counseling...I want to send a message that we don't tolerate this...and I want you to understand how your behavior impacted our community and that we don't tolerate that. And if they are just gay guys who don't go to school, we ain't tolerating it in our community outside either. (V3) But now... change our counseling-treatment to anger management and diversity and hate issues because your issue is not only anger but also diversity or hating other people who are not like you.

9-(V2) I would probably say the same thing [punitively] but they need to get some help with their issues with interracial couples. (V3) He's going to need some help, but he's going to need help in different areas. He will have to deal with some anger management and some hate issues.

11-(V2) I think the same kind of thing [punitively] should occur and that they should be given more opportunity to work in integrated environments and get a chance to get to know African-Americans or whoever or whatever the interracial group would be. (V3) Same thing and then force him to work in an environment where there are gays so he gets a chance to know who they are.

21-(V1) Well it would be similar [as far as punitive] and you need to understand why you did this ["bias" crime] and you need to understand why it was wrong and that's the piece I would want to see. (V2) I'd say to me that's more serious because...that's coming from racial prejudice...it's just because you're black or I don't like you because you're Asian or whatever...We have some wonderful one day workshops at the church that are about racial justice and about living in diverse communities...[I'd like to see] helping them out of that space not impose a punishment on them that may be fair but does nothing to change that core seed that's living inside them. (V3) I'd much rather see them somehow receive some help and some sort of changing process rather than put them in jail.

3-(V1) Again, [like non-bias crime] I think they should have to go in and clean it up. And you know some kind of education [should be added] like volunteer at the temple or something like that to get to know the people and how they affected these people's lives and to make sense of themselves. I think just to do that because maybe they don't like really have an idea in their head of like how much they are hurting these people. (V3) Probably the same type of things, like anger management, because its abuse but also some kind of diversity education, something like that.

25-(V1) The same thing with a mandatory education component. Actually I would maybe have some kind of mandatory education component for the first one [non-bias crime] too but I would have this one very geared toward their hate crime. (V3) Same response with again looking at it as a hate crime and if it is the educational component based on the hate issue, some kind of sensitivity training.

While each of the previously quoted participants in one way or another during their interview supported "different" treatment of bias crimes/criminals, the following two never made clear mention of whether their advocating of different rehabilitation for bias crimes might be perceived by them as similar, in the sense that everyone should get rehabilitation appropriate to their crime, or different because it is not exactly the same.

36-(V2) If it were me, I would want them to come live with me and see what we had to live with everyday. Take them out of their environment and put them someplace were they're totally uncomfortable and see how they do with it. Give them a different viewpoint you know because a lot of people are brought up in the good ole boy white male population communities and they don't know anything else. (V3) Again, I think I would just dive that person into the community that he hates.

37-(V2) Well it's the scenario I think I laid out before where it's still an assault and you punish on that basis but also do the pieces where you're contacting the families. You're at least trying to get to the root of the problem maybe.

And the following three participants seemed to make clear during the interview that they felt that bias crime should be treated the same, suggesting that perhaps for them different rehabilitation for bias crime was treating such crime the same as any other crime-with appropriate rehabilitative measures.

18-(V1) Basically the same but I think they should be made to learn the Torah-put themselves in the place of the people they were trying to victimize-learn something about those people. (V2) They should go through the same process but find some kind of way to send them to a black community to maybe clean up a playground...or maybe have them teaching the young black kids how to read...getting them involved in something and see how it feels to be a minority. I think that might help.

19-(V1) Same response but they need to go to the synagogue and need to apologize to the people and take religious classes to educate them. (V2) More severe punishment by making them go to diversity training on top of the other stuff [same medical damages, fine, apologize for non-bias]...Not necessarily put them in prison for a longer time but give them extra time with this training.

29-(V1) Now if they're black and white then still go through the fine, have them do the community service but then you'd educate them about the Jewish faith. You know you need to let them know what they did was wrong, why it was wrong, what the message is they're supporting. (V3) Pretty similar but there you could...give education to the guy because he was doing it on prejudice.

Overall, as previously indicated, these participants, a mix of minorities and non-minorities, for the most part did authorize "punishment" for bias criminals just not more than for non-bias offenders. In general, there was a sense that their emphasis on added or different rehabilitation was not driven by some naïve idealism but rather by a belief that people are not inherently evil, that they can change, there are reasons they come to engage in such crimes, and steps can be taken to try to counter offenders' hate. They offered no strong indication that it would work only that it would be wrong or pointless not to try. Aside from their only changing rehabilitation and their relatively hopeful look at the possible success of corrections, the only other aspect that made this group in some way stand apart was that they were primarily women (73%).

Consistency in Citizens' General Views and Vignette Responses

The best predictor of the type of different responses participants chose to apply to the bias crime vignettes was the approach they advocated in general. Of the 16 participants whose abstract and specific different approach types could be determined, 11 participants (69%) applied to the vignettes the approach they voiced in the abstract. The greatest consistency was shown by those advocating only changes in rehabilitation (80%), and the least by those supporting solely more punitive measures (60%). That said, when partial consistencies are included-those people whose responses to the vignettes were at least in part consistent with their abstract approach (ex. punitive changing to combination or rehabilitation switching to combination etc.), only one participant made a complete change-from an abstract punitive change for bias crime to rehabilitative changes for the vignettes.

Two of the five "inconsistent" participants could be assessed as applying a less punitive response to the bias crime vignettes than they supported in the abstract, another two a no more punitive stance but a change with regard to the need for rehabilitative measures. Only one participant added a more punitive component to bias crime sanctions when responding to the vignettes, for an overall combination approach, compared to his solely rehabilitative discussion of addressing bias crime in the abstract. However, a closer look at these participants' overall discussions suggests they may not be as inconsistent as they might seem.

The two participants applying a less punitive approach to bias crime than they advocated in the abstract included a man and a woman. The former, a Jewish college professor, supported longer sentences such as those authorized by hate crime legislation in the abstract. However, when discussing the vignettes, he chose to discuss non-specific different and/or greater rehabilitation for the bias crime vignettes, not mentioning a more punitive response. However, he did note during his general discussion of sanctioning bias crime that his more punitive approach was more visceral than pragmatic and perhaps this explains his failure to apply it when confronted with a specific scenario as opposed to an abstract crime. The latter less punitive participant was a lesbian college student who supported a combination approach in the abstract but overall responded with changes in rehabilitation when presented with the vignettes. However, she did respond slightly more punitively to V2 implying that she felt a bias-based assault was more serious and thus deserving of a greater punishment than an assault based on mistaken identity, which she described as "dumb, but it doesn't sound....too serious" (3), although she did not make any such distinctions with V3. In addition, her response to the vignettes seemed somewhat in keeping with her overall thoughts on crime and bias crime given that although she broached both punishment and rehabilitation for both, her emphasis was clearly rehabilitation and prevention, and she indicated concern with the current prison system and its tendency to breed crime and/or repeat crime, suggesting perhaps that she might not rely on added "punishment" to accomplish what biased offenders needed. Finally, the more punitive component of her abstract approach to bias crime was demonstrated by her support for hate crime legislation. It is certainly possible that her support for such legislation may not be support for more punitive responses to bias crime across the board or that it symbolizes more than just a more punitive response to such crimes.

Two male participants, one gay the other a non-minority, when responding to the vignettes maintained their abstract support for a more punitive component for bias crime but when asked to respond to the vignettes also had different things to say about rehabilitation. The former, who in the abstract supported a strictly punitive approach, in addition to longer community service and/or greater fines for the biased offenders in the vignettes also advocated extra rehabilitation to address the hate component of the crime. The latter, initially supporting a combination approach, dropped the rehabilitation for the two more serious of the three vignettes and supported jail terms for biased offenders compared to stiff fines for non-biased offenders/vignettes. It might be relevant that this participant indicated both rehabilitation and punishment for crime in general but rehabilitation was reserved for minor and first/second time offenses. Although he stuck to that approach for bias crimes in general, his primary emphasis was longer sentences as he was primarily concerned about the greater likelihood of recidivism with bias crimes. This concern, as well as his belief that prevention and early education are keys to addressing hate, suggesting that rehabilitation in prison is essentially too late, might reasonably explain his focus on more punitive measures for the vignettes.

Finally, the one participant to support a more punitive response, a Jewish mom, went from supporting different rehabilitation in the abstract to both different rehabilitation and advocating jail time or additional jail time for biased offenders in the vignettes. However, her longer sentences ("not years"), while suggested to provide "more than a slap on the wrist" to biased offenders, also were meant to be used wisely for rehabilitation and as a necessary time to allow biased offenders to cool off (implying they would need more time); thus they seemed to serve non-punitive pragmatic and rehabilitative purposes as much as, or perhaps more than, a punitive purpose (17).

Overall, those who seemed to switch their approaches to bias crime when it came to specific vignettes did not appear to be wholly inconsistent in their abstract and specific views. Instead, in many instances they were only partially inconsistent in the truest sense either supporting part of their general views when responding to the vignettes and/or responding as abstractly suggested for at least one of the vignettes, suggesting that their views may be based to some extent on the context of the incident, such as the perceived seriousness of the offense (property versus physical) or comparisons of the specific motivation behind a similar bias and non-bias crime. In addition, given the earlier discussion of the extent to which people may or may not perceive rehabilitation in terms of general approaches to courts handling of convicted criminals, some participants may have been less likely to consider rehabilitation issues in those abstract contexts then when presented with an actual offender, especially perhaps if their general views were based on the possibility of more serious offenders.

Unfortunately, the current study does not allow the truth of these possibilities to be further assessed. It also is of note that 74 percent of participants who provided a clear approach to crime in general and the vignettes were consistent in the focus of their comments, whether they focused on just rehabilitation or punishment with or without rehabilitation.

Factors Influencing Citizens' Responses to Bias Crime Vignettes

Simple cross tabs were run in hopes of highlighting any major distinctions between those participants who chose to approach bias crime more punitively, whether or not also supporting greater or different rehabilitation (punitive or combination), and those who applied a solely rehabilitative change to the bias crime vignettes, a coding that resulted in a nearly even split.[26] Participants' specific approaches to the vignettes were considered in light of their general views on bias and non-bias crime and punishment as well their personal characteristics.

In terms of participants' personal characteristics, sex appeared to be a rather influential factor in the decision to support more punitive measures for bias crime or not. Seventy percent of men, compared to 39 percent of women supported such an approach, and many of the other factors that seemed to affect participants' decisions seemed to differentially affect men and women (as indicated in parentheses below). In addition, non-minorities appeared to be more punitive, although this may be in part because of differences within the minority and non-minority groups. For instance, 83 percent of the Caucasian, college degree sub-sample applied more punitive measures to bias crimes, where as Caucasian participants without a college degree, along with gay and lesbian participants, were more likely to respond to bias crime with solely different rehabilitative measures. Jewish and African-American participants split equally on punitive versus rehabilitative measures. Also, all the men were more punitive towards bias crime, except both Jewish men and one Caucasian without a college degree. On the other hand, both Jewish women were more punitive, while the majority of lesbian and female, African-American participants were more likely to be rehabilitation oriented. Education also seemed to have an impact in that participants with a college degree of some sort were more likely to be punitive, however this effect was stronger for men than women and for minorities, who overall were more likely to support rehabilitation, than non-minorities, a majority of whom across education advocated greater punishment for bias crime. Finally, participants who indicated they were not political or religious/spiritual were more punitive, although the latter held only for women.

Based on participants' crime or bias crime-related views and experiences, several factors appeared to describe participants not only more likely to support a more punitive approach than their counterparts, but also as a group those more likely to support more punitive approaches more often than not. Those participants were more likely to have not indicated a fear of bias crime or personal bias-based victimization (men); mentioned society (both) but not either fear (women) or individual issues (both) as a cause of bias crime; and did not indicate the importance of, or need for, preventative measures for dealing with bias crime (women). In addition, those who mentioned economics or upbringing as a cause of crime in general (men); or did not mention the criminal justice system being inconsistent (women) in terms of its punishments or suggest ways of fixing flaws in the system (both), were similarly more likely to be more punitive towards bias crime and more often punitive than not. Again, because of the very small numbers involved, these influences are speculative at best although they do hit upon some of the same variables that have surfaced earlier as influences on views of bias crime and so may be worth future theoretical and empirical research.

Summary of Citizens' Responses to Bias Crime Vignettes

In all, the findings indicate that the 23 participants whose type of approach to the bias crime vignettes could be assessed were almost evenly split between treating bias crime some how differently in terms of rehabilitation (11 including two who said treat bias crime the same but always wanted different rehabilitation) compared to those who chose more punitive measures with or without rehabilitation (12). Given that another nine participants advocated consistently similar treatment for the bias crime vignettes, the current study sample would seem likely to be less supportive of bias crime sentence enhancements than national samples assuming such support hinges on support for more punitive approaches to bias crime. In addition, of those participants who did authorize more punitive sanctions for bias crimes, either solely or in combination with rehabilitation, only a few supported increases in incarceration commensurate with general bias crime legislation, and obviously for those supporting a combination approach to bias crime, their desire for hate-based rehabilitation would not be directly addressed through such legislation. In addition, the overall consistency in participants' abstract and specific responses to bias crime might suggest that inconsistency in polls with regards to these issues could to some extent be a matter of the seriousness of the crime vignettes or that such surveys simply do not allow for a comprehensive enough understanding of exactly what approach participants prefer to accurately assess cognitive consistency.

CHAPTER 10

Citizens' Views on Bias Crime Legislation

After providing participants with the opportunity to provide their own views on how bias crime and criminals should be handled, they were questioned directly about their views on bias crime legislation, more specifically a bias crime sentence enhancement. Consistent with previous poll research, it was expected that most respondents would favor sentence enhancements. The main interest was what their support would signify, and their abstract and vignette responses to bias crime suggested that a more punitive response to bias crime would not be their sole or primary basis for supporting such legislation. Overall the results bore out that expectation. Although overwhelmingly supportive of bias crime legislation, participants' discussions were more often focused on the need for different and/or greater rehabilitation for biased offenders and/or the need for greater awareness and condemnation of bias crime than punishment. While the possibility that more punitive legislation might deter offenders seemed to be the hope, participants seemed more focused on the need to address hate. Finally, participants seemed aware of the need for, and highly supportive of, measures, particularly education, that went beyond criminal legislation, which many saw as a rather short-term approach to a problem needing a long-term response and commitment.

Overall, 86 percent of participants said they would support, at least conditionally, legislation in Pennsylvania similar to that passed in other states that authorizes more severe penalties for criminals who commit their crimes because of bias or hate, fifty-eight percent supporting such legislation without noted restriction. To go beyond the numbers, all participants were asked to discuss their thoughts behind, and reasons for, supporting or not such legislation as well as other types of legislation or other responses to bias crime they would like to see. In addition, those supporting bias crime legislation were asked how they would make such penalties "more severe" in order to compare their abstract and vignette approaches to those they would specifically advocate through legislation. Although the few characteristics and views that seemed to distinguish participants' views are discussed at the end of the chapter, it should be noted that a greater use of excerpts and participant descriptions are provided throughout the chapter in order to better testify to the diversity of participants within these groups and, while those within categories often shared some generally similar views, to better provide a sense of the diverse expression of those views.

Citizens' Opposition to Bias Crime Legislation

While the majority of participants did, with seeming assuredness, support bias crime legislation, a minority of participants (14%)- representing a diverse cross section of the constituencies interviewed- fell on the side of most likely rejecting such legislation or at least questioning the probability of such support. In the end, three seemed fairly certain they would not support it, while two others simply did not know.   Not surprisingly, all of these participants voiced either consistent support for similar treatment for bias crimes throughout the interview or did so at least for the vignettes, being unsure or unclear in their earlier statements. Together, their justifications for their stances on bias crime legislation included (1) beliefs that bias crime was not different, and/or that such legislation (2) would not likely deter bias crime offenders, (3) could be abused by the public and/or the legal system, and/or (4) might lead to greater anger and more problems than be helpful.

> 29-I don't see what difference it is if I go and shoot someone because I don't like them because of something they've done or say. That's just as hateful as anything else...I don't really think it's going to help anything because they have the death penalty and people still kill people. It's a little different but it's not that big of a deterrent. People don't think they will get caught so people don't think about it. And if you have a deep-seated dislike for someone, rationality goes right out the window...I think legislation, they do it to suck up to the voters, it's popular, it's to get votes...it's something that won't turn very many people off, it will probably turn more people on to your side.   Politicians for the most part, regardless of party, usually do what's in their best interest unfortunately.

40-I don't think so. I still think it should be across the board. I think if we get into the bias we're going to end up back in the 60's segregation and I just think it's going to open it up wide. Not to make less of it but to me it's still a very serious issue but not to be treated differently.

33-There's no room for error whatsoever and if you can't devise a way to do that then maybe until that time I don't think it's possible [to have bias crime legislation]...I can't sit here and tell you that deep down inside that part of me doesn't agree with it and I know what time it is I know like obviously if those two guys got beat up I know what's going on and it makes me that much angrier but at the same time like I don't know that for sure.

33-There was an instance when I had gone to neighbors and they were having a small get together...and it wound up turning into something bigger...and it was actually a straight person who was getting kind of out of control and subsequently they ended up having to call the police. The officers arrived and one of the officers said that he was sick of getting calls from the fags...I think it just makes it worse you know like maybe if say for example that cop has to go to court to testify that he was there and they were charging a hate crime you know it's going to make him even more bitter.

26-I think all crime at some point comes from a horrible hate and the difference between the hate I have for the individual or that group yes it's awful but I don't know its any worse than the hate I feel for a woman and I rape her simply because of what happened to me when I was a child or whatever. But in my mind it's all very horrible and complex...It does seem to me that what's becoming called hate crime-there's a very thin line between that and hate I might feel towards an individual for other reasons...I think I'm a little uncomfortable to say that [bias crime should be treated more severely] because for me you're on a slippery slope then. That is obviously hate but then that one isn't? How could you determine that? I'm uncomfortable with that right now. I'll work that out later...I think it could make people think about it [committing a hate crime] but I also think it could have the exact reverse effect. It could end up very much increasing one's hostility towards those groups because it is going to make them look like they have preferential status of some sort and that's going to be the exact inverse of what you want...I don't know if at the legislative level [it can be addressed] because for me that's treating symptoms not the root. That's not good. That won't work. That's a failed system in my book. What you need to do is get at the children...This legislative thing is adopting a model of coercion...that's a failed system. It breeds tremendous hostility between groups and what was passed to try to help the groups ends up actually increasing the hate for a group.

36-Well that's sort of a touchy topic with me because my way of life could be construed as hateful. Being pagan, Christians can and have understood and said that I am a hateful person. I think that's where personally it goes into the gray area because who's going to interpret the law. And here if the community interprets the law then I'm out of here. I don't think there's enough open-minded people to make those decisions for everyone...The purpose [of such legislation] I think is to try to force the community together as a whole and to stop hate crime but in my opinion all crimes are hateful...I'd like to think that intentions [behind such laws] are all good but with my experience it's not. Speaking personally, on the surface it's good...but underneath when it gets reported "oh maybe you should see a therapist maybe this is bothering you too much...you're being a little too sensitive about this."...In order to make our laws work we have to make sure every step along the way is on the up and up...but in my opinion...it's not going to happen. There's no place recently that I've felt it.

Overall, these participants either indicated that bias crime should be treated the same, to which bias crime legislation would be antithetical, or identified major flaws with the form, enforcement and/or possible negative consequences of such legislation that seemed to interfere with their ability to support such legislation. While most recognized some good intentions behind bias crime legislation-the desire to protect minority communities, bring people and communities together, and stop hate, it also was noted that the passing of such legislation might be a political tool used to garnish votes or, in some communities, a potential tool to be used to protect one's own. Although a few of these participants mentioned the difficulty in essentially legislating people to change, they did seem to think a difference could be made through non-legislative measures such as public and school-based education, seminars and rallies, advertising and the mere passage of time, which some thought might bring with it more tolerant attitudes towards those who are different. In all, these participants did not simply reject the existence of a problem, and thus the need for a legislative response, but rather questioned the ability of a bias crime sentence enhancement to address it.

Citizens' Conditional Support for Bias Crime Legislation

A quarter of participants thought that a legislative response to bias crime might be an appropriate means of addressing bias crime, however they were willing to support bias crime legislation only under certain conditions or restrictions. Given that in many cases their conditional stance is based in part on their reasons for supporting bias crime legislation, the two are discussed together. For the most part, they indicated the desire for further information or assurances as to the exact nature of such legislation before supporting it. They seemed particularly concerned with the nature, severity, and/or purpose of the more severe penalties authorized under such legislation.

> 37-I don't know. I'd like to see more specifics associated with it…it's just a pretty general thing to say that there should be more penalties added on for bias crimes. How do you define bias crime, what were the penalties in the first place…and what would be the goal of adding more penalties on there? Does it really accomplish what you wanted or is it just being punitive?

For one African-American participant, the key question was whether the penalties authorized in such legislation would be harsh enough-double or triple the non-bias sentence-in which case he would support it. To him severe enough sentences might be a deterrent whereas sentences that were too lenient would be but a "slap on the wrist" for offenders and in insult to law-abiding citizens. Not surprisingly this participant was consistently solely punitively-oriented throughout the interview and was the most punitive and comparatively extreme member of the sample.

> 14-Yes, if the penalty is harsh enough…[otherwise] it is a slap on the wrist, a slap in the face of the average citizen who is going to work, paying the taxes, keeping out of trouble and you have this person who commits a heinous act –give them an extra year?!?! What's a year? We could do a year, in the scheme of things a year isn't too long… If the penalty is harsh enough I think it could serve as a deterrent…For an assault…if it was a hate crime I would say double, maybe triple that. I like triple.

However, the rest of the participants were concerned that the penalties might be too severe and thus would be antithetical to the purpose they felt such legislation could or might serve, which for the most part did not emphasize punishment. One Jewish woman wanted offenders to take their crimes seriously and understand the damage they caused and so would support more severe penalties for misdemeanors but not crimes already treated seriously, fearing that it would only increase perpetrators hate and thus not help decrease the number of hate crimes committed.

> 27-What's it actually going to say–hate crimes are serious and we have to take them seriously or is it going to say mandatory life imprisonment for a hate crime I mean I guess it would depend…I find it very confusing because my basic feeling is when we like put in the news guess what they committed the same crime so they are going to go to jail for 10 years other people who believe the same way just get angrier at the group, so I'm not sure it brings down hate to do that. But I don't know what kind of punishment you get if you go on someone's property and you put a burning cross on there or you put hate on their car or something like that. I mean if that's like a misdemeanor I definitely think it should be considered a serious crime. Now if it's already considered a serious crime I don't think it needs to be made more serious…I think somebody who has never been the victim of a hate crime may not realize just how much damage they do by it, so if it was a misdemeanor I would bump it up.

Two other female minority participants, while wiling to accept slightly more severe punishments, seemed more interested in seeing a more severe penalty in terms of rehabilitation. As raised by other participants, one lesbian participant was concerned that additional punitive measures for very minor [non-jail] offenses might increase hate-based resentment, and she thought that small jail increases for more serious crimes [such as murder] would probably not have much effect. However, she felt such legislation would be good in that it would ensure that the issue would go on an offender's record and provide an opportunity for rehabilitation. The other, a member of the Jewish faith, was willing to support such legislation so long as it did not violate anyone's rights and hate crimes could be "objectively measured" to avoid emotional rather than legal reactions. But again, she too preferred to see minimal "lock up" and greater focus on rehabilitation with the hopes of reducing the number of hate crimes.

9-It depends on what the penalties are. If the penalties are just imprisonment for like 5,000 years-the first number that came to mind, I don't think that's going to help. I don't think really severe imprisonment sentences are going to help. Sentences that follow some sort of rehabilitation on the issue would probably be more effective - trying to help somebody to deal with something, not just punish them...If it were too severe I would probably actually vote against it...If it were only like one additional year, sure; 30 years no. One additional year I don't think is such a big difference. If you murder someone and you get 25 to life and you get one additional year on top of that frankly it's not going to make a big difference but it will at least leave something on the person's record so that people will know in the future. Should something happen again, they'll see that they have previously been convicted for a hate crime, maybe we better take into consideration this guy's motivation for whatever he did now...If [the crime is] something minor [no prison usually], I don't think that [legislation] would help. It would probably make them more resentful because they would resent the fact that the government sided on the side of the person they hate, so they just hate them more and now they hate the authority that punished them on top of that...[To make sentences more severe] it should require additional rehabilitation.

17-I think I probably would [support bias crime legislation] as long as it is clear and it has gone through the proper channels to make sure that we are also not disturbing the rights of the people who committed the hate crime. It is such an emotional issue that there has to be a very objective way to measure it…I wouldn't want to see them in a maximum security prison. Something more minimum where they maybe can still go out to work during the day, come back at night and be going through education, some kind of education classes; something that again is going to start discussions, movies, whatever it will take to try to educate them…I would hope it would deter the number of hate crimes …I think restricting someone's freedom when they create crimes like this is probably fairly effective.

An African-American woman was similarly concerned about penalties that might be too severe and possibly mandatory for fear that they would not fit the crime, which in her opinion required case-by-case consideration of mitigating circumstances. However she did feel that additional time would be appropriate for hate crimes given their greater seriousness.

18-It depends on what the penalties are. If you are going to send them to jail for 50 years, no I wouldn't support it because I think that the punishment should fit the crime…If it was taunting them or maybe assaulting them but not killing them or causing any severe injury of throwing rocks in their window or cutting their tires or something fifty years is too much. I think maybe [I would support such legislation] as long as they did take a look at mitigating circumstances …Even though they knew that [a crime] had been done as a hate crime, it would be kind of hard to explain to the black woman [who committed the crime] why she got more time than the white woman did for the same crime [non-bias]. [But if they could prove] the fact that she did it purely for the reason that you are white…she needs a little more time than the white woman…I just think it is a more serious crime…The intended purpose would be to curtail these types of crimes. I don't know if it would work out that way, in fact I feel you might get involved because of the supposed unfairness of the different sentences. But I don't think there should be a blanket anything. I think everybody should be on a case-by-case basis.

Another issue frequently raised by such participants was concern with the legality or legal application of such legislation. As suggested by the earlier statements concerning the rights of offenders and the need for objective hate crime measures, issues of law led to hesitant support from some participants. A college-educated, Caucasian man was willing to support bias crime legislation to add more time to make the punishment fit and deter the crime but only if it were legal to punish someone for having a hateful belief, which he was not sure about.[27]

> 20-I would say yes, I would say no. To me it is going back to does the punishment fit the crime. Can you punish for someone hating something? You can punish them for killing somebody or burning their house down or whatever the physical thing is. Can you punish them for having a hateful belief too? I don't know...I don't know if you can do that. If they could, I could see that I would agree with that. I don't know if they could ever do that...I don't know if they could do it because how do you punish that...They are found guilty and if it is proven that they killed the person, then they should be thrown in jail for the maximum they can for killing a person whatever the reason is. I don't know if that can be increased. I think judges in some states put that in because they are trying to deter that too. I would like to see that happen, I would like to see that [hate] go away. Would I want to see that in Pennsylvania? Sure. I would like to see people like that not influence other people...I would make sure the punishment fit the crime. If that meant that I was allowed to add more time to it based on the facts that this was a hate crime or whatever then yeah I would add on to it.

Two non-minority participants, while raising penalty-related issues similar to those above-whether a more severe penalty should be mandatory and for what crimes (more or less serious) it would be appropriate, also raised the legal issue of proving a bias/hate crime.

The first, a male college student, felt that unless a bias crime was obvious-ex. swastika involved-it would be hard to prove. On top of that he was not sure how much could be done with such offenders. However, if the crime was proven he was willing to support longer sentences along with some type of education or rehabilitative program, although he seemed only interested in a mandatory response to extremely serious crimes. The second, a female high-school graduate and salesperson, was highly focused on the proof issue and was not willing to provide more severe punishment without ample proof and even then was not willing to support legislation that she thought would provide punishments that were too harsh. In addition, she was not convinced as to the deterrent effect of such punishment but was willing to support bias crime legislation it seems primarily for the message it would send.

> 28-I think so long as it could be proved. I mean just evidence. I mean if a swastika was painted on a Jewish temple I mean I think that's proof enough but if somebody is assaulted I think it would be harder to prove so I'm not sure...I guess maybe just longer sentences and maybe admission into a program or something. I don't know how much you are going to be able to do with someone whose that driven against a group...but I think just to try to keep them like behind bars for longer and maybe more time to think about it and being behind bars they might experience like the other group...I don't know if there should be a mandatory more severe sentence. I think it depends on the severity. I think if you are going after a group like more leaning towards terrorism than I think it would be more severe than if just on an individual.

> 22-I'd have to now exactly what it meant...and when you say more severely what that meant too...with hate crimes I think people really thought about why they wanted to hurt these people and they have very in-depth feelings on why they believe they should be hurt. They should be more severe but I think that would be very hard to prove...I would be very strict about it. You would definitely have to know this is why it occurred; it could not be assumed. Witnesses would have had to have heard it or there would have to be evidence from someone's past that this might have been a problem and in that case there would be reason maybe to believe that but I

think you would have to be very careful because you wouldn't want to convict someone unless you were absolutely sure that that's why...If maybe I felt that punishment was too harsh [I would not support it]. I would have to know that really it was justified to make a specific law saying well if the bias crime was based on that it's a hate crime, I would really want to know that it was justified to add that on....I think that some people might feel that it would help prevent this, knowing that there is a harsher penalty out there for hate crime. I don't know because I don't know that when criminals do these kinds of things that they put that much thought into it. So yeah they'd be getting a harsher penalty but would it necessarily prevent them, I don't know. [I'd still support it] because it still might give a message to people that it's wrong that you can't do that. No matter what you feel, you are entitled to what you feel but that doesn't mean that you can feel that way so strongly that you're causing harm to someone else.

Interestingly, both of these participants in their general bias crime comments were unclear or unsure exactly how they would handle bias crime, the former providing unclear statements the latter suggesting she would treat it differently but she did not know how. When presented with the vignettes, they treated bias crime for the most part the same. Their responses overall might suggest that the vignettes, except for V1 for which they were both willing to support different or greater rehabilitation, may not have provided the clear proof necessary to justify a different response. In addition, the former participant's concern about the potential negative consequences of treating bias crime more punitively and the latter's primary interest in sending a message might explain their inability to clearly indicate or determine their general stance on the appropriate approach to bias crime.

The final participant to offer conditional support for bias crime legislation was a gay business owner who was only willing to do so if he thought that the current laws could not be changed to treat bias crimes equally to their non-bias counterparts and additional legislation was necessary to get judges to treat crimes based on the underlying crime and not their own values or agendas. However when asked how he would design such legislation, he indicated his concerns regarding more punitive sentences and suggested he would create legislation that while raising awareness would ensure that bias crimes were treated the same as non-bias crimes. However, it would seem that in order to get to that point he was willing to support more punitive legislation along the way.

8-That's an interesting situation because that's like creating strategy. I mean, if you want to change a larger law, what do you do?...So if I saw there was no hope of refining present laws, I probably would support some type of hate crime legislation even though they make me uncomfortable...I like the idea of creating public awareness, more awareness that a lot of crime stems from hate. I'd also like to create a situation where you are creating a climate where it makes it really difficult for people in visible roles, such as judges, within our society to back peddle and impose their political agendas or values on a particular situation. But it makes me very uncomfortable to increase penalties because something has been deemed to be a hate crime. I think the penalty should be the same...I'm trying to see the pros and cons of it and why you could use it and why you couldn't use it and how you could use it in a strategy. I'm not sure that people look at it closely. I think it is like the Patriot Act. We passed it immediately based on our response to what was happening-9/11. People react emotionally...It's like we can't be the only state without a hate crime act because everybody else has one...We have to say that we totally support all these individuals within our voting sphere...Will it deter a crime? I don't know...It certainly makes people more aware that there are consequences associated with it...but we are talking about situations where people are killed, there is an impulse control issue going on there, there is premeditation going on there. To what degree does an awareness of the penalty influence premeditation or impulse control? I don't think it does but I do think in some cases it possibly could.

In all, it would seem that participants who were unwilling to support a generic bias crime sentence enhancement without further conditions or restrictions were more concerned with responses to bias crime aside from punishment-such as rehabilitation, doing something to try to reduce hate crime, sending messages, and/or issues of legality and proof than with the need for more severe punishment that such legislation might offer. In addition, many seemed concerned with the potential negative consequences more severe punishment might have. However, excluding bias crime legislation with extremely more severe punishments, they seemed willing to support it as an available potential means to their own ends. Though not said directly, these participants seemed to imply that supporting something was better than nothing as long as it was not illegal or too extreme in nature. Of course these comments do not apply to the one participant who would only support punishment he deemed severe enough to make a difference, although again he was only willing to support legislation that he viewed as capable of meeting his preferred approach to bias crime.

Citizens' Support for Bias Crime Legislation

Of course even those who indicated that they would support such legislation without offering such conditions might share similar thoughts if asked directly, however they seemed to authorize more severe penalties without consideration of such issues. Instead their comments focused primarily on the reasons or justifications for their support. They also were asked to discuss how they would make penalties "more severe." To provide a sense of participants' thoughts on these issues as well as the extent to which their comments were in keeping with their earlier views, discussion of those who would support bias crime legislation are broken down by how they treated the bias crime vignettes.

Citizens Who Treated Bias Crime Vignettes the Same

Six participants who originally indicated that bias crime should be treated the same as similar non-bias crimes (except perhaps with different rehabilitation) still supported the generic bias crime legislation with which they were presented. However, the comments of two of those participants, a non-minority high school teacher and a lesbian mom, made clear that their support for the legislation was not support for greater punitive measures towards bias crime but because of the need for society to start doing something to address the issue or at least keep track of the problem. In fact, the former, when asked how he would design such legislation, described legislation more in line with the Hate Crime Statistics Act than a sentence enhancement, preferring tracking to punishment.

24-Well I guess it would go against everything I've said-any crime is a crime whether it's a hate crime or not a hate crime-but yeah I would probably support it just so we can start identifying particular groups and their actions, however whatever they do, hate crimes are equivalent to a normal crime. But I think acknowledging it would be a good thing to make people more aware.

19-[why support] Because for too long we have done nothing...If we educate them along with the punishment, then it would become more effective. Not just give them more jail time. I really believe in rehabilitation of some kind. [Earlier comments made by this participant also indicated that she supported tougher laws/punishment for all crimes-so her supporting bias crime legislation would essentially address both her concerns but not with a desire to treat bias crime differently.]

Two other participants indicted not only that they would support bias crime legislation but also that additional punishment would be appropriate and that they would authorize legislation that served to double the sentence. However, they also mentioned the importance of, or difficulty in, proving that a crime was a bias crime. In fact, one was the participant previously discussed who thought that bias crime generally should be treated more punitively but seemed to think that it was near to, if not, impossible to prove it and then treated the vignettes the same, again emphasizing the fact of how difficult it is to actually prove a crime is a hate crime. So although he indicated he would support such legislation his application of it would likely be very rare.

10-I would [support it], but the problem is proving it gain...Probably the easiest way to do it would be to double whatever the regular sentence is. It might be a little extreme but it probably would deter a little bit of it.

A non-minority female participant also was willing to increase the penalty for hate crimes for the purposes of its message and deterrence. However after her formal interview she mentioned that she realized that her support for legislation might seem inconsistent with her previous remarks, and she justified her earlier comments that advocated treating bias crime the same by indicating that she thought it would be very difficult to prove something to be a hate crime and thus in most instances probably would treat otherwise similar crimes the same.

> 5-I would [support bias crime legislation] because I think it's something that needs to be done to open people's eyes and just try to make them see that it is not a good thing...I would approve a more severe penalty, severe enough that they wouldn't do it again...If the normal penalty is two years, I think they should have an additional three years for a bias hate crime...I would hope that it would make people think. I hope it would lesson the amount of bias crimes because of the severe penalties.

The final participant, a Jewish business owner, indicated that she would support such legislation and additional jail time because bias crime is wrong. However, she also reiterated an earlier concern that such legislation would have to be careful not to infringe on rights such as freedom of speech. In fact during both her general comments and her responses to the vignettes she indicted that she was not sure that treating bias crimes differently would be legal and that she assumed that it was only appropriate to respond to people's actions not their reasons for doing so except in the extreme cases of perhaps terrorism. Although earlier she indicated that she thought that it should be treated the same for those reasons, it may be that when that issue was essentially resolved for her-by a hypothetical law authorized by a government-she would support bias crime legislation. In all, she seemed to want more severe punishment for such crime but was somewhat torn by her sense that doing so might somehow be infringing on civil liberties.

> 30-[I would support it] because it's wrong, its just wrong to prejudice yourself against something just because of an idea and that someone should receive damage mentally or physically because you know I don't think people should have the right to decide a person's quality of life, their happiness or whatever, and you know why should someone else be allowed to infringe upon that...I don't know that additional time would be such a bad thing other than the fact that it would cost us more. I don't disagree with it until it would infringe I mean you have the civil liberties and you have to be careful of

your freedom of speech even though it comes back to kick
you in the pants.

Overall, these participants seemed to either support bias crime
legislation for reasons not particularly punitive in nature or supported it
with doubts as to its legality or the ability to prove it. Therefore, under
the circumstances it is not that surprising that they supported bias crime
legislation while voicing support for similar treatment for the bias
crime vignettes overall and most similar treatment for bias crime in the
abstract.

Citizens Who Offered More Punitive Responses to Bias Crime Vignettes

Aside from the one previously discussed participant who indicated that
he only would support bias crime legislation if it was harsh enough, the
other three participants who treated the vignettes more punitively were
willing to support such legislation primarily it seemed because of some
hope or belief that more punishment might deter such crimes. At the
same time, one such participant, a non-minority correctional officer,
indicated that the nature of the severity should be determined on a case-
by-case basis because of the number of different factors involved, and
another, the mom of an interracial family, indicated that she was
actually torn as to whether such legislation should require longer
sentences because she was afraid that it might lead to more anger.

> 15-Yes [I would support it]. [It would serve as] more of a
> deterrent than anything. It's going to be hard to educate
> that…I think it would help. I'm not going to say it's going to
> eradicate it but it definitely will help…[I would make it more
> severe] case by case because every situation is different.

> 32-Yes…perhaps more people would take it more seriously
> and not you know just do it because they could. I don't know
> cause I don't understand why people do that kind of stuff. So
> I don't know what kind of thing will help handle it…Although
> I'd support longer sentences, I'm torn by the fact-maybe you
> should just leave things the way they are because it might just
> anger people more. It might make people's [potential
> victims'] situations worse.

Thus, although not overwhelmingly staunch advocates of strong punishment, these participants were willing to support their previous stance of treating bias crimes differently by supporting generally more punitive bias crime legislation in the hopes of its deterrent effect.

Citizens Who Offered Combination Responses to Bias Crime Vignettes
Five of the six participants who chose a combination approach to the bias crime vignettes-all but the one who indicated it depended primarily on issues of proof and legality-indicated that they would support a generic bias crime sentence enhancement. They provided a host of justifications including that bias crime is worse because of its targeting, premeditation, or potential cyclical threat and/or that such legislation might be a deterrent, it might stop the cycle of hate, and/or could send a message that intolerance is simply not accepted. When discussing how they would operationalize more severe penalties, participants, as expected, mentioned punishment as well as rehabilitation and education. Interestingly, while a couple of participants suggested the need for punishment seemingly in and of itself, in several instances participants directly indicated or implied that more severe penalties were necessary to provide the education or intervention that bias crime offenders should receive.

> 7-Hopefully the fear of harsher punishments is going to deter people from doing these things. But gosh, hopefully it will stir up some dialogue and people will start taking a look at what they are doing, reflect a little bit on their behavior. I think most of these things are to deter behavior...Not like life in prison or anything but I think it should be a bit more severe...it would be interesting to look at the research on how long the offender would have to be in, whether longer does make any significant difference in terms of rehabilitation or whether they commit another crime. But...I definitely think that if somebody assaulted somebody because they had just shoved their girlfriend down on the ground and then another assaulted somebody because he is black, I definitely think that should be a worse punishment...I think there is going to be some trial and error in figuring it all out what works and what doesn't, but I definitely think it is a good idea.

13-Hate crimes are just idiocy at its worst...the only reason Hitler killed 6 million was because he could. What's to say you can get away with one, maybe you can get away with two...It [bias crime legislation] might scare a couple people out of it but there's gotta be education with it. Part of that legislation has to have funding to give to education [before and after crimes are committed]. Punishment is short term. Education is long term. I have no reason to believe that stiffer penalties for hate crimes is going to deter it, although I did say earlier that they should be stiffer which I still believe...I think it is important to keep it [such legislation even if it doesn't deter] until you can adjust it to make it more effective which would include more preventive stuff, more education, stuff like that...I guess [the more severe penalty] would be a theoretical educational program, I think you would have to set the punitive consequences over on that. You just can't say two years and throw the book at him, there's gotta be a reason for the more [severe penalty]. It's gotta work with the educational aspect of it. Someone who does a hate or bias crime, they need more intense, more in-depth, more emotional corrective things.

16-Definitely [would support bias crime legislation] because hate crimes I feel are more premeditated. You think about it. You don't pick out the average person, you pick out a specific person that you are doing a crime against. I think that makes more thought and I think that we need to do more severe punishments because they need to do more severe intervention to have that person's mind changed...Either more jail time or maybe a program, like for instance when we have three tickets, they have to go to driver's school. Well, why not have some type of school system...some type of educational program where they learn about differences in people or whatever...I am open to anything if they [lawmakers] think that it is really going to solve the problem.

31-[I would support bias crime legislation because] At the very least it will show the community that bias and hate is not something that the community will support and that's the very least that will happen. Hopefully it will reduce the number of hate crimes...whatever the normal punishment would be just to increase it longer sentences though I don't like the idea of locking people up unless they're an immediate threat to the community. Like someone who's like doing harassment I don't like to see them go into jail. I'd like to see them go to therapy or something-whether it's a crime or bias crime but more of it for the bias crime and different....Well from what I've learned about politics...you're never going to get it perfectly the way you want it so you do have to compromise. And I think that anti-bias legislation is important enough that you deal with what you can get.

34-[I would support bias crime legislation] Cause of the cyclical potential of hate crimes. I mean what it can really cause and how volatile it is-some kind of retaliation by another group that is very dangerous...I think just longer prison sentences, I don't now it's difficult in how you'd do it. But also I think on the other hand I would set up...maybe just educational camps I mean programs that would teach them...Without the legislation you don't get the education. Without the legislation you don't get the adequate punishment for these crimes nor do you get the identification of these crimes. So it all starts with the legislation. And I think if people can see how these crimes are punished I think they'd be less apt to do them. Somebody can still have the hate, I mean people are going to have hate...I'm not trying to eradicate hate I'm trying to eradicate the products of it.

Overall, this mixed group of male and female, minority and non-minority participants seemed to support bias crime legislation because it offered an opportunity to treat bias crime differently, primarily it would seem in terms of the greater intervention its offenders could receive through more severe-longer and more intense-penalties.

Citizens Who Offered Rehabilitative Responses to Bias Crime
Vignettes
Participants who advocated rehabilitative changes for bias crime vignettes, a group made up predominantly of minority females, were overwhelmingly supportive of bias crime legislation-all but one woman who indicated it would depend on whether the sentence was too severe. True to their vignette comments, these women advocated for different and/or greater rehabilitation/education for bias crimes through bias

crime legislation, however for the most part they also were not completely opposed to longer sentences either to accommodate such rehabilitation or as increased punishment because of the perceptions that bias crime was worse or such punishment at least might serve as a deterrent. Several members of this group, seemingly more so than others, also offered as justification or explanation for supporting bias crime legislation the message it would send to communities as well as potential victims of bias crime that society deems prejudice and hate, and particularly crime based on it, as unacceptable and a serious matter that it is willing to address.

11-I think I would [support bias crime legislation]. I don't know to what extent but I think it would help people who are the victims of hate crimes to feel a lot more comfortable that the state itself, our state government, is looking unfavorably at those kinds of things...I think it would be a message but I also think it would lead to a reduction especially with young people. I don't think it would make that much difference after you get a certain age when nothing changes. I do think that it would have a more positive effect on what happens in the minds and behavior of young people...I think you can have all the rallies, and churches and synagogues and all talk against it but it seems that in order to get things to change it has to be legislative...I probably would not increase the length of time in prison. I still think that the educated populace is what we are after more than a punishment. So where the crime would ordinarily carry five years, this person [biased offender] would be in an educational kind of experience for the next two years. Interaction and educational experiences-a socialization process...I suspect I would [still support legislation that just increased jail time] because I think it [hate] has the potential to so divide us as a group or a nation; therefore, it has to be dealt with in some way.

21-Yes because do I think a hate crime is worse than just a robbery-I do. More punishment? Well I don't see the punishment we're giving them now is changing any thing so more punishment what good does that do? I would say more appropriate punishment and if it was based on hate that would take more work. It would take more time-more severe rehabilitation more extensive-so that makes sense to me...I probably would vote for it just on principle [even if just regular incarceration] but I would continue to work for a better criminal justice system to promote some healthy change. It sends a message. If the legislature in PA passes a law that says hate crimes are worse than other crimes that sends a message to our community and this is such an insidious and systemic problem that its not going to get fixed over night and there might be different levels of change so just saying it's worse might be ok-one step. So now we say it's worse and we're putting them in jail and incarcerating them for a longer period of time now lets work on what we do with them there that can help them I guess is what I'm saying.

3-I think that [bias crime legislation] is important...I think it says we don't accept crime but we also don't accept bigotry, bias towards people for no reason other than that they are different. I think it says a lot about how we view prejudice. In making these laws I think it protects people who might be victims of these crimes but it also just makes a general statement saying we don't accept this...I just think the statement itself is a huge part in changing people's minds a little, and I think that if the penalties for those crimes are harsher than if it were just vandalism or just assault, that kind of thing, it might be a deterrent.

6-It needs to be handled more severely and needs to be understood we will not tolerate this...More severe including if there's a way to do a monetary thing, increase the jail time, definitely some education in there of some form. We provide it and if you don't utilize it you ain't never going to leave...You need to get double the time-not by itself but in addition to some other things that I don't necessarily know what would work. But not by itself, but definitely it would send a "you don't know how to act now then we will treat you like an animal and lock you up." Not that that's not good but not by itself. It needs to be in conjunction with some other things.

25-I think it's [bias crime legislation] appropriate. It's a good thing. I think it doesn't change the event it doesn't change the likelihood of it happening again...I don't think it's a deterrent but I still think it should come with a heavier punishment because it's maliciously targeting a person or group rather than meeting a need for money or something like that. Whether it's jail that should be added, added time and also get a mandatory education component...I don't think it would be a deterrent for other people but maybe that individual would be slightly rehabilitated with a different education...I think it [education] can be done in jail in fact I probably think it should because the person still has this issue...I would also be for subsequent monitoring, parole being geared at those issues in some way.

Overall, this group seemed perhaps slightly more message-oriented in their support for bias crime legislation and a little less optimistic on it's potential as a deterrent than the previous group-those who supported combination measures to address bias crime. However, both seemed willing to support bias crime legislation even if they questioned its deterrent effect or thought that the particularly important component of such legislation should be education and/or rehabilitation rather than punishment per se.   While for a few participants the extra "punishment" was advocated in its own right, in general they seemed to accept more severe "punishment" in the form of longer sentences as part and parcel of getting the message of anti-hate out and/or rehabilitating bias crime offenders. As such, it would be particularly interesting to see if given the option of a non-punitive, intensive rehabilitation-based sentence in lieu of a traditional jail or prison sentence such participants would support it over bias crime legislation offering only the more punitive element of a longer sentence. Even two participants who throughout the rest of the interview were not clear or sure how they thought bias crime should be handled in terms of sentencing, supported bias crime legislation but emphasized the real need for distinct "punishment" or rehabilitation more than just more severe penalties.

38-Well I would support it just because it does acknowledge the existence of a hate crime. It gets the ball rolling in terms of the system handing hate crimes at all so I would immediately support it. There is that fuzzy piece of more severe penalty. I don't know that it's necessarily a more severe penalty…I would like to see distinctive punishments for hate crime, clearly defined punishments that fit the crime and consider the dynamic that there is a hate involved.

35-Yes. I would hope it would be a deterrent from people being ignorant and inflicting violence or pains on any other person because of their differences…I would hope that it would set the standard for what is deemed acceptable behavior and what is not…I guess the penalty…should be longer I guess but I really again I would really like to see real changes in the system itself. To say that would be the ultimate solution to my problem as a gay person being targeted for crime I don't think that's really the answer [longer sentences]…I'd like to see a more integrated approach to true rehabilitation and that's where I would say the sensitivity training or some kind of thing…So if you can somehow get at that I'm wondering if that would be helpful in addition to or in conjunction with the criminal penalty…I would say I guess we have to start somewhere and we start with small steps and if that's where you're willing to go that's good but I intend to also want to see really radical changes and transformation in the society and I wonder to what extent those little steps are creating real change…But you know I think I would still probably say if that's what you can get that's what you can get and at least that's better then where we are now.

This last comment, offered by a lesbian college student, seems to sum up what a number of participants seemed to be getting at-something needs to be done and whatever might help is probably worth trying. Thus, perhaps many participants, though not for the most part adamant about more severe "punishments," supported more punitive bias crime legislation in the form of a sentence enhancement because 1) they thought it would include or at least provide the opportunity for a distinct education/rehabilitation based response to such crime, or 2) because doing so would acknowledge the existence of bias crime, condemn community-wide both the crime as well as the bigotry, and/or at least offer a first step toward doing something meaningful about it. In the meantime, given that most participants felt that bias crime was a different and to some extent worse crime deserving of a different response, longer sentences seemed fair and justified especially if they might serve as a deterrent. This left only those participants with concerns that in some way such legislation might: be illegal or abused- either by violating civil rights or by judging guilt without real proof of bias; made too punitive so as to no longer "fit the crime;" or even potentially lead to negative consequences to question support for bias crime legislation, and only those who did not feel that bias crime should be treated different because it is not a different crime and who questioned the potential for positive effects of such legislation to reject it.

Influences on Citizens' Support for Bias Crime Legislation

To further explore any breakdown in support for bias crime legislation, three dependent variables were run against participants' characteristics and views. The first set of cross tabs compared those who supported bias crime legislation, fully or at least conditionally, to those who were most likely to oppose it. The second looked at differences between those who supported bias crime legislation outright versus those who offered more conditional support. The third examined differences between supporters who chose a punitive rather than more rehabilitation-focused "more severe" penalty for bias crime legislation. As with cross tabs presented in earlier sections, the small numbers involved make these findings questionable and cross comparisons that might divulge interactive or spurious effects impossible. As such, explanations are kept to a minimum and are based on theoretical assertions rather than on study responses, which did not provide such insight. More than anything, these differences are provided as a means of more specifically describing participants and their support for bias crime legislation and provide possible directions for future investigation.

<u>Distinctions Between Citizens Who Support and Oppose Bias Crime</u>
<u>Legislation</u>
In terms of support versus failure to support bias crime legislation, several general bias crime variables could have been used to predict responses. Participants who indicated that bias crime was a different crime, felt that a judge or jury should be privy to the biased nature of a crime, or felt that bias crimes should be handled differently than non- bias crimes were more likely to support bias crime legislation, outright or at least conditionally, than their counterparts. Participants mentioning bias crime legislation before being directly asked about it also were more likely than those who did not to support such

legislation. Potential explanations for this finding may be that such participants, given their familiarity with such legislation, may have given more previous consideration to the issue and thus were more capable of a more definitive answer and/or that those who would raise it unprompted might be those more likely to think favorably of it. In addition, participants who mentioned ignorance as a cause of bias crime showed a greater willingness overall to support bias crime legislation, perhaps identifying an issue so potentially amenable to rehabilitation through education it made the law, and particularly the criminal justice system, seem an appropriate response. Participants who generally indicated problems related to proving bias crimes were less likely to support bias crime legislation, perhaps having difficulty getting around application problems with such legislation. Finally, although alone fear and victimization of bias crime did not appear to influence support for bias crime legislation, further examination (although based on very small numbers) revealed that fearful physical or property victims of bias crime were less likely than non-victims (fearful or not) and victims of verbal bias incidents to support such legislation. This is most likely a result of their concerns regarding the negative potential consequences of bias crime legislation, specifically its ability to create more hate and increase the likelihood of victimization and their sense of fear.

A few other differences between those who did and did not support bias crime legislation were based on participants' crime-related views or their personal characteristics. In terms of crime views, all participants who indicated they feared crime in general supported such legislation compared to 70 percent who did not. In addition, all study participants who mentioned crime prevention supported such legislation compared to only three quarters of those who did not. Finally, participants' status and level of education seemed to influence their response to bias crime legislation. Participants with a college degree were more likely than those without to support bias crime legislation. It would seem that the status differences found are likely an artifact of education level. Non-minority participants without a college degree were less likely than the other groups to support bias crime legislation overall, although the majority still did so. In addition, the sole minority to fail to support bias crime legislation was a gay participant without a college degree who rejected such legislation because of concerns related to defining and proving bias crimes, the possibility of it just making hateful people angrier, and the potential abuse of such a law both by citizens and the system. The only participant with a college degree to fail to support bias crime legislation was a college professor whose concern with the thin line between "bias crime" and other crime caused him difficulty in making an absolute decision but who thought he would probably not support bias crime legislation. Although the numbers do not allow further examination, it is plausible that some of the potential influences previously mentioned are also a factor of education.

<u>Distinctions Between Conditional and Non-Conditional Supporters of Bias Crime Legislation</u>
In terms of participants who supported bias crime legislation, only a few factors seemed to distinguish those whose support was conditional compared to those whose support was without such restrictions. Jewish participants and non-minorities without a college degree were more likely to be conditional in their support than non-minorities with a college degree who were least likely to offer restrictions. However, findings regarding participants' education levels suggest that those with post-graduate degrees may be more likely than those with bachelor's degrees to offer such conditional responses, a finding that seems to hold across sub-sample categories and thus may explain the substantially lower conditional support for the college sub-sample. This would leave participants with bachelor's degrees or high school diplomas (although only 1 participant) the least likely to offer such conditional support. In addition, though not surprising, individuals who mentioned bias crime legislation prior to being asked about it were less conditional in their support, a finding likely explained by possibly greater prior consideration of the issue. Those who indicated in the abstract that bias crimes should be handled differently based on rehabilitation tended to be more conditional in their support than those preferring a more punitive or combination approach to bias crime perhaps because of a concern that needed and desired rehabilitation might not be addressed and/or that additional punishment was not needed and might be problematic. Participants who acknowledged bureaucratic flaws in the criminal justice system also were more conditional in their support, perhaps because of a perceived inability to actually accomplish what legislation would require. Non-victims and property or physical victims of bias crime who indicated that they feared bias crime also were more conditional, leaving low-level victims as the most unconditionally supportive of bias crime legislation. Finally, participants who failed to mention the economy as a cause of crime in general were more likely to offer conditional support and were

the only group to do so more often than support bias crime legislation outright, although this would appear to be an artifact of victims of low-level bias crimes being substantially more likely not to address this cause of crime.

Distinctions Between Supporters of Punitive Versus Rehabilitation-Focused Bias Crime Legislation

Finally, participants responses were broken down by whether they indicated that bias crime should be punished more for the sake of punishment-whether or not in addition to rehabilitation, or rehabilitated differently and/or given a greater punishment to allow for such rehabilitative changes during their discussion of their views of bias crime legislation or how they would operationalize or design such legislation. Given the few participants who advocated solely punitive legislation and the number of participants who seemed to support longer punishments solely or primarily for its ability to allow for greater rehabilitation such a breakdown seemed to provide a more informed and clearer view of which participants were more truly punishment oriented when it came to bias crime. Under this coding, participants were fairly evenly split, and a number of differences between the two groups were found.

Minorities appeared to be more rehabilitation-oriented than non-minorities however this seems to be a result of the non-minority, no college sample being solely punitive. Non-minority participants with college degrees were primarily rehabilitation-oriented as were Jewish and gay/lesbian participants, the latter being the most inclined toward rehabilitation. In addition, participants with a post-graduate degree were more likely to focus on rehabilitation than those with a college degree or some college (the one participant with a high school degree only was least likely). Not surprisingly, those who discussed rehabilitative or combination approaches to bias crime in general and/or in response to the bias vignettes were less likely to be punitive in their discussion of how to operationalize "more severe" penalties for bias crime legislation than those who were solely punitive in such views.

Participants who identified problems with the criminal justice system in general or with regards to bias crime were more rehabilitation-oriented in their views, particularly those who felt that the criminal justice system was inconsistent in its punishment within and across crimes as well as those who believed there were enforcement problems related to bias crime or that bias crime was not treated as seriously as other crimes. Those who indicted a fear of bias crime or who had been victims of bias crime were similarly inclined, although as noted in the previous two sections, these factors seem to be interactive and apply only to fearful victims of low-level bias crimes. In addition, participants who mentioned society as a cause of crime, or ignorance or human nature as a cause of bias crime were more rehabilitation oriented, perhaps because these in large part externally generated causes could not be blamed as much on the individual offender, lowering to some extent his culpability, and could in some part be addressed by education-based rehabilitation. On the other hand, those who blamed parenting/upbringing in part for crime, perhaps a less society-based factor and less amenable to fixing, were more punitive.

Interestingly, other more punitive groups were participants who supported bias crime legislation but indicated that bias crime was not different than non-bias crime, was difficult to prove, was irrelevant to a judge or jury, or should generally be treated the same generally and in regards to the vignettes compared to those who did not. This could indicate a general willingness by such participants for the criminal justice system to be more punitive in general, including bias crimes; a desire to treat bias crimes more punitively but reservation because of issues of proof; or, as indicated in an earlier section, a failure to consider legislation as addressing rehabilitation-oriented measures in addition to or rather than just punitive ones.

Approaches to Bias Crime Beyond Bias Crime Legislation

After discussing their overall thoughts on bias crime legislation, participants were asked whether there was any other type of legislation or other approach they would like to see used to address bias crime. While a couple of participants simply voiced the need to do something...

> 16-I just think it needs to be addressed and I have no idea if it
> is being addressed or in what realm it is being addressed. I
> think in this day and age, it definitely needs to be addressed.

...most had suggestions that while somewhat varied tended to focus on three, often interrelated, key areas: law and the criminal justice system, education, and public diversity, education and awareness.

In terms of the law and the criminal justice system, some participants continued to focus on issues of legislation. They voiced several issues from the nuts and bolts of the laws we need, to their enforcement, to their prosecution and the sentencing of offenders. In terms of the laws, a couple raised the need to simply clearly identify and acknowledge people's rights and/or to avoid creating laws that serve to negate those rights and essentially legitimize bias.

28-I don't know what else we can do cause it seems like we've tried a lot and its taken decades and it still goes on...I don't know. I think just like putting the civil rights in place, basic individual rights. I think that's helped but I don't know if it still goes on so I don't know what else there is to do.

35-I don't know if this is going to answer your question...I think the whole issue of [same-sex] marriage is really a big one for me...This is the law legitimizing institutionalizing heterosexism...and if we set the standards a little differently and we start legitimizing these deviant or different relationships and we looked at the structure of the family differently and understood the family differently, then perhaps you know hate crimes would be less likely to occur...you know work on rights.

One participant, while expressing a desire to create more legislation to stop those who hate, commented on the need to allow free speech so as to allow for the better identification and vigilance toward those who might commit hate crimes. He also supported general community programs that would provide education and/or sensitivity training and would push for attempts to force it where possible, such as in schools and at the workplace, on those who may need it.

25-I find that very difficult because my visceral response is yes [additional legislation to address the problem] but I think being aware of those [who hate] is through allowing free speech and being able to identify those and be more weary of them. How would you know this person, their past, their beliefs might cause them to commit a crime a hate crime if you didn't have access to that...I would like to see...if there is a group of individuals that that person [hate-based perpetrator] associates with that that group be identified by the community as being in need of having some kind of community programs to do some community work or cohesive education or sensitivity training. I would be in favor of forcing it in contexts in which that can be done like with kids in school...mandatory at the work place. I think in general it should be in place but I think when there's a group that can be identified that may be at high risk, I think there can be more specific measures taken.

A few participants addressed actual hate crime laws, in particular their scope and enforcement. They indicated interest in such laws existing nationwide, and they expressed the need for such laws to be followed up with solid enforcement, which they believed would require better training of police to identify hate crimes, the political financial support to provide it, an updated interrogation process, and a higher, perhaps Federal, level of complaint for citizens who felt their local or state governments' handling of the issue or enforcement of the laws was not on the "up and up".

38-I'd like to see the law put in place. I'd like to see it in every state. I'd like to see the federal government put it there. But what really would have to be done differently I'm sure in every place where the laws even exist is that the enforcement would have to occur.

27-With the police, we can't just tell them to be sensitive. We actually have to help them learn about it. We can't do it on the cheap...I think they're [bias crime laws] crucial because I think when you make a social statement like I think technically we probably didn't have to say that black people had a right to vote because we had a law saying people had a right to vote but they were trying to make a point...but I don't know sometimes they [politicians] think it's like this cheap fix and it's not going to do anything about the problem–it's like no child left behind, it's crap. They didn't give any money or support to make that work so if passing the legislation is part of the package where they're going to provide money to public forces to learn more about recognizing hate crimes and intervening then it will be great but if it's you want the Jewish vote for the next election kind of thing then it will be worthless.

11-I think probably we need to update our interrogation process. I don't know how you would do that but I do believe that most people are willing to share when it is a hate crime.

36-In order to make our laws work we have to make sure every step along the way is you know on the up and up...I think when you get a broader audience to be able to see what's going on I think more light is shed then...I think overall our laws need to be more concise from state to state. And I know history shows that we're trying to do that but with a lot of government being handed back to the state governments that is somewhat difficult because if there's something that's happening within the state...and its not handled to the extent that you feel it was necessary then its best always to have you know the next step to go to.

A couple of participants addressed issues related to the prosecuting and sentencing of bias crime cases. Their comments included the need for a case-by-case handling of such cases rather than mandatory or uniform responses, the need for stiffer penalties, and/or the desire for greater diversity on juries, as well as the Supreme Court.

15-It seems like what they are doing right now, it seems to be going in the right direction. Again, it seems that the case-by-case basis is the way to go but nobody wants to look at it that way. We have a uniform crime code and I am sure nobody is going to want to get away from it because it makes life easier for the lawyers, the prosecutors...If you were to ask me that would be the way to go-case-by-case. It doesn't seem they need a uniform crime code for that situation.

14-We need some stiffer, much stiff penalties for hate crime. If we could get a handle on it I might consider relaxing the laws but not until then...

34-I think juries should be more ethnically diverse. It's usually all white or all black juries. They just ought to be more sympathetic to the plight of the criminal or there should be opposing views and that's more likely with a diverse jury...You should be talking about the Supreme Court, that's

the key...you know they judge how the law should be defined
and it ain't looking to good as far as that's concerned. It's
looking all white and all right...That's where the real change
happens; we need diversity there.

Some participants recognized that the law was essential to the
education that they believed necessary to address bias crimes. Bias
crime laws were seen as crucial to informing, enforcing and reinforcing
education; education not only about diversity and tolerance but hate
crimes themselves and the laws that punish them.

34-Just a push toward teaching it in schools. In high school
we learned nothing about hate crimes other than that it was so
far in the past that nobody would really connect it because
they assume people who did it are dead...I'd push for that and
at younger ages...we should have legal knowledge of what
constitutes a crime...And I think that's a key that we really
should not make this ethnic sensitivity or anything like that
but schools should definitely push toward eradicating some
biases. I think they both are necessary [law and education].
They're intertwined. Without the legislation you don't get the
education. Without the legislation you don't get the
appropriate punishment for these crimes nor do you get the
identification of these crimes. So it all starts with the
legislation. And I think if people can be educated about how
these crimes are punished I think they'd be less apt to do
them.

19-We need laws and education. Use the laws to enforce the
education.

11-I still believe in the power of education so I would really
and truly increase the kinds of experiences for young people
in schools. That would be the first, first, first thing...And I
believe we if we did it more effectively by getting a lot more
sincere people working with kids in school who totally believe
in the process of change happening that way. Not just as a
simple activity but a continuing kind of value system that is
built into the programs in our schools... I am convinced [it
would be more effective than legislation] but then I think
about all of the times that we marched and fought and talked

in schools; we did all those things but until the Civil Rights Bill of 1964 came around it didn't make a difference...until they passed that law, we didn't get any changes.

13-Punishment is short term. Education is the long term...Just as with any other issue dealing with personal bias and human emotion, it's going to take a long time to evolve and legislation for punishment is only going to fix the now but not the future...I wonder if community improvement programs wouldn't help with the integration of society...I don't think one [cjs/law or education/community programs] can replace the other. I think they have to work together.

Many who did not make any direct connection between education and the law mentioned both the need for legislative as well as educational measures to address the problem. In fact the need for, or importance of, education, especially for the young and through the schools, was the most often raised "other" method for addressing bias crime. The majority of participants, whether they felt the law was necessary and effective or not, felt that young people needed to be taught about differences, about tolerance and sensitivity, about being tolerant if not accepting of all, about being essentially open and caring people. Some participants also stressed the importance of sincere and trained teachers willing and capable of providing lessons of tolerance perhaps not just through a class but throughout the educational environment, as well as the necessary financial backing that politicians would have to provide, requiring them to accept that reducing hate is not a quick fix but one worth addressing across the long term.

18-I think a lot of good things could be done if they were done in schools-preventative things that were done at the elementary level. If there is more done to show that the diversity of the class is good that would be good. I think that could carry on...up through the grades...If the teachers are taught sensitivity training so that they would go out of their way to find teaching aids that would help minimize the differences while still celebrating the differences...you gotta start someplace. If more of this is done, let these kids know that you don't have to be a white male that you can be anybody and be anything that you want to be and if this could start and go through the elementary schools across the country this is the only thing I think is going to help.

22-I think this is more true for big cities but I think this should be addressed in schools like sensitivity training on why this stuff can't go on.

27-I think since it's an issue of education and people learning to understand people it would be great if we integrated it more in the curriculum-more diversity and I think we tend to do things the wrong way. Like we make it this separate chunk course and then we give it to someone who has no training in it and the curriculum is boring and then the kids just think it's a joke...and I just think you know if people just developed more of an awareness and kind of small little steps all through their life versus this one course.

26-I don't think at the legislative level it's going to work because for me that's treating the symptom not the root. That's not good. That won't work. That's a failed system in my book. What you need to do is get at the children. And you need to educate the children to be merciful and loving people and I think if you've taught children a warm humanity toward all people then in time you wouldn't have to pass legislation where you're throwing people in jail because the heart will have changed...I think the legislative thing is adopting a model of coercion...it breeds tremendous hostility between groups and what was passed to try to help the group ends up actually increasing hate crime.

8-Education and it would actually be a more effective approach but it would be more costly and it would take more effort. We are talking about changing the way people think and you are talking about pouring tons of energy and money into our education system. We are talking about not disenfranchising people but enfranchising people.

15-Education, Education, Education from the time they are little. You figure half these kids are probably going home teaching their parents how to read anyway, hopefully they can take that home with them too. It's a start. Politicians have to bite down and be able to accept that they are not going to see the results that they want the public to see for 20 years.

A few participants recognized difficulties in the educational approach or skepticism regarding its effectiveness but still seemed to think that education might hold a partial solution to the bias crime problem.

17-I guess through the schools...unfortunately I'm not sure it would be effective especially like places that this that are so homogenous. But I think if we could come up with some type of national campaign that gets us into the schools, especially at the middle school level that would be good.

10-Actually I don't know if there is anything that would be helpful. I mean, if kids are young maybe you could educate them and get some of them to play together and things like that but I don't even know that that really works.

20-Obviously trying to do it through education but again with the rules and regulations of those things, what you can and cannot teach in school it is very difficult. You would like to be able to teach moral values. You have to teach right and wrong, but I don't know what those kids go home to at night...How do I look in their eyes and can I actually look at something a little differently than maybe they ever thought about looking at it and get them to consider it? I would like to bc able to say that could happen.

Participants also raised the importance of diversity in the classroom, suggesting that a book lesson alone might not be enough, that children need to be exposed as part of their education to the diverse range of people and cultures in our society to better understand who those people who are different from them are so as to be less likely to fear them.

39-I think education is a piece. I think what people don't know is always what people fear. You know what people don't know, what's different than what they know people are afraid of...One of the disadvantages here is the lack of diversity...When we were in the city the kids went to nursery school and the holidays they celebrated were Christmas, Hanukah, and Kwanzaa you know. They got a little bit of everything. And the nursery school was pretty culturally diverse.

9-Start when they are young. Programs in schools, more education, serious education, funds for education, real funds...if you get to them before their cognitive mapping is complete, before they have grown into adults and molded that all into their systems. They should have a wide experience, a lot of diversity in their lives. That makes them more accepting of people and more well-rounded people because they are better able to come up with new ideas and more innovative ways of doing things because they can see from different angles.

Even when participants did not focus directly or solely on schools and/or children they seemed to reach primarily to education and diversity as essential tools for addressing bias crime.

33-Educating society like I mean there's not much else you can do.

24-Just probably as much awareness as possible, making people aware is the key. The more people are aware I think the less inclined they are to make judgments on particular groups...I think it would be more effective than criminal legislation.

37-It's tough to legislate morality. I think it's education. I don't think that you can ever fully educate everybody anyway to the same kind of degree because people are going to have built in biases and it's going to be reinforced by families. But I think that that's the best hope for changing people's attitudes...Seeing things, sampling things, you really learn a lot about being with different kinds of people when your put in the same situation, you find out people are people and it doesn't matter how they're physically different from you.

For some participants, awareness, and thus greater understanding and tolerance, could be achieved through public education via media. They spoke of the role of television, radio and print media in addressing the problem through advertising, diversity in news broadcasts, and exposure to differences in entertainment-based programming. They seemed to suggest that greater exposure to people who are different, whether through the media or personal knowledge, could provide the information necessary to counter misgivings that perpetuate fear and perhaps hatred.

31-I would like to see...especially in the media, more diversity and equal time. I see the shift in especially the news media as a radical right wing shift. I found the liberal media on the internet...you don't hear about this stuff in the news...I think that when more people really understand the issue...if there's more information out there and people realizing that these people are the same...it would be more helpful than the laws even though I think the laws are very important. I think just getting the information. There's been some research...that people are more likely to react favorably to anti-bias legislation and pro-gay and pro-pagan laws if they know somebody that's gay or pagan or black etc...A lot of time it's people basing their misgivings to a whole group based on their little bit of exposure...I don't know, I think more than even the anti-bias crime legislation-it would help but the more people that are out as far as the gay issue...would help more than the laws.

29-Just have TV ads, people on TV and radio ads, magazine ads. Advertising does wonders. [Advertising regarding] tolerance; try to change the culture.

38-You know nothing has been more effective than Will and Grace on TV for ten years and I don't think it's done much for my mother's generation but the kids for future generations it's like water flowing over rocks. It takes that long for things to change. But just the more freedom and expression that are there it will just mount up. I'm not sure what can really be done. You can't really force people...I don't think it's right to really impose on them when they are believing something differently. But everyone has the burden of trying to live with other people who are different...Everybody has to learn some bit of tolerance.

Religion also was mentioned as an avenue for providing public education, information, and awareness. Although some participants recognized the potential for some religions/religious leaders to perpetuate bias, they stressed the importance of religious commitment to lessons of tolerance.

> 21-Well I think it needs to be addressed in the churches and sometimes it is and sometimes it is not... and they find a validation for allowing hate to exist and I don't think it should.

> 30-I think our religious books, I think the religious leaders have to be very, very sensitive to what they read and preach because a lot of our religions, the older religions, tend to perpetrate a lot of bias and so I think our religious leaders and teachers have to make a commitment to be careful about what they want to teach to their young people. And at the same time, whereas I don't think it's the place for education to teach moral values I think in the religious as well as the parental environment that's where it needs to be stressed.

> 40-I'm sure there's plenty of like ways-seminars maybe a rally or churches speak about it synagogues whatever but again its still a choice and there's going to be that one bad seed that's going to do what they want to do no matter what you say and they're not going to be swayed, they are what they are...I have a gay housekeeper and there's people who make pretty crude remarks but they don't know him. So to me they're being biased, they're being prejudice. So I think until you know what the situation is, it's tough.

In all, study participants seemed to support the need for a community-wide educational endeavor to counter bias and hate. While in several instances recognizing the difficulty in doing so, the inability to legislate morality or coerce people to change, and for some participants the impossibility of eradicating hate, participants seemed to acknowledge the need for social change that would allow people to be "free to be who they are" with confidence that their differences would at least be tolerated.

27-I guess the only other thing I can think of is that we seem to have a really hard time hitting like a happy medium. We tend to either go you know for the throat or we ignore it and I don't think-you can't make a person accept the idea that a Jew isn't a bad person or that a gay person isn't a bad person, you can't make them. You have to create an environment that has information where they get to see people as real individuals and so have like the medium sell. The hard sell never works and I guess in the back of my mind I worry that we are going to bob back and forth between the extremes and never be successful.

21-Well I think safe zones, I always think of those types of things...but at least stating that that's the desire of the community for this to be a safe zone...people are free to be who they are on this street. But then it's in a more positive way, positive goal - a desire to create that community atmosphere or culture.

21-If we continually approach diversity from all aspects of our community, I think we are doing good work...I think that it's such a systemic issue that change is going to have to come on a number of different levels. There's going to have to be individual change, institutional change. So I think anytime any group or individuals are working for that bigger picture, I think it is good.

When asked why educational measures had not yet taken strong root, one participant, a Jewish mom and former school teacher indicated, "I think that 9/11 has made us open our eyes a little bit more about hate crimes that exist all over...but I think that maybe we just haven't seen it as an issue up to now because it is not affecting the majority" (17).

A final participant suggested that the only way to probably stop bias crime is "if we were all the same color. If in our hearts there were no colors, there were no gender, there were no barriers" perhaps explaining his almost sole focus on laws authorizing stronger punishment for crimes and bias crimes. Although he did add "that would get monotonous" (14) highlighting a feeling shared by the vast majority of participants that diversity was an amazing and rewarding characteristic of the United States that, it seemed, surpassed the difficulties of bias and hate that it at times brought with it but that could not be ignored and needed to be addressed either through legislation and/or more preventive, educational measures.

Summary of Citizens' Views on Bias Crime Legislation

Overall, participants seemed highly supportive of education and other preventive measures throughout society's institutions that might more effectively attack the root of the bias crime problem-the ignorance and fear that perpetuates it-rather than relying solely or primarily on what was seen by some as the short-term criminal justice punishment-legislative approach to the issue. Although overwhelmingly supportive of bias crime legislation, participants' discussions were more often fixed on the need for different and/or greater rehabilitation for biased offenders than punishment per se. Some participants' support for bias crime legislation seemed grounded more in the need to make a social statement to raise awareness and condemn such crime and the bias that perpetuates it or to simply take some measure to recognize and address the issue than to increase the "punishment" for bias crimes. While the deterrent effect of greater punishment was often mentioned, it seemed for most a hopeful possibility more than a predominant justification for such legislation. In all, study participants' support for bias crime legislation seemed less about punishing biased criminals than countering hate.

CHAPTER 11
Findings and Implications

Though obviously limited by its sample, the study's strength is that it offers a somewhat broader perspective than previously available of a group of citizens' views on bias crime and bias crime legislation. Though skewed toward a more educated citizenry than originally hoped, it describes the thoughts of a more diverse group than the heretofore studies of predominantly college undergraduates or community leaders. Though the exploratory nature of the study makes comparisons to prior literature and research difficult, the study did reveal some similar issues while offering a better opportunity to capture the breadth of citizen opinion related to them. Finally, the current study provides some of the first research-based insights into the meaning behind majority support for bias crime legislation and lesser support for its actual application.

Summary of the Findings

Overall, participants demonstrated substantial familiarity with the concept of bias crime even though not fluent in relevant terminology, the presence of bias crime legislation in their own state, or statistics. Comments across the interview revealed that their views were grounded in at least a basic understanding of bias crime, including the nature of its predicate crimes and the range of its traditional victims. Though participants certainly were not of one voice on the issue, their views offered fairly clear themes. First, they overwhelmingly perceived bias crime as a problem, primarily as a result of its inherent hateful or biased nature. Second, not surprising given national poll findings, the majority of participants supported treating bias crime differently than non-bias crime either in the abstract, through their support for a bias crime sentence enhancement, or in their responses to hypothetical vignettes. However third, for the most part they did not advocate the solely punitive approach taken by current bias crime legislation.

Participants' decisions whether to support differential treatment of bias crime were strongly related to how they viewed bias crime relative to similar non-hate based crime. Participants who viewed both as the same generally maintained that "a crime is a crime" and/or that most crimes are "hate" crimes in the sense that they involve hate or at least anger. They concluded that it would be difficult to distinguish between different types of hate and any such distinction would be an inappropriate basis for sanctioning bias crime differently. They viewed bias crime as a serious problem and had strong negative feelings towards it but seemed to think that its sanctioning should be based on its underlying crime not its motivation.

Participants who viewed bias crime as "different" offered reasoning similar to that offered by Levin (1999) and Lawrence (1999). They contended that bias crime is different and more serious because of its motivation, providing support for Vogel's (2000) finding that hate-based motivations may be viewed as more serious. Though several were unable to verbalize why a biased motivation was more serious, many offered explanations related to its victim selection and greater harm. They viewed biased victim selection as demonstrating greater premeditation and coldness and a motive crueler and less justified. Consistent with the scholarly greater harm argument, they indicated that biased selection might make for a more personal and emotional victimization and thus a more painful one psychologically. They also raised the possibility of bias crime resulting in greater harm to the larger victim community and society, usually in terms of retaliation and greater likelihood of recidivism. Participants failed to mention any specific greater physical injury resulting from bias crime often noted in pro-bias crime legislation literature. In all, such participants would seem to support the Supreme Court's contention that motive is a valid means of distinguishing between crimes and its conclusion that bias crimes might "provoke retaliatory crimes, inflict distinct emotional harms on their victims, and incite community unrest" (*Wisconsin v Mitchell* 1993, 488-489). In addition, the issues they raised were similar to many raised by elite respondents in Iganski's (2001) research, although the views of the latter were much more precise and as a group they viewed the issue to some extent from a more social and often value-oriented perspective, perhaps reflecting their greater knowledge of the issue and their role as community leaders. Interestingly, these findings suggest that citizens are able to voice some version of the issues presented by those in the know, suggesting the ability to engage a wider segment of the public in the discourse of bias crime and how best to address it.

Participants who supported a different response to bias crime were evenly split on whether it should include greater punishment, more or different rehabilitation, or both. While those advocating more punitive measures supported harsher, heavier, more severe sentences or conditions of incarceration, those emphasizing rehabilitation felt that bias crime demanded treatment or education aimed at combating its biased motivation. Their comments suggest that differential views on the purpose of punishment may influence support for punitive measures coinciding with Gaubatz's (1995) conclusions concerning instrumental concerns and punitiveness. Participants supporting a solely more punitive response to bias crime were more focused on the retributive and/or deterrent function of such a sanction than those whose responses emphasized a more rehabilitative approach. In addition, the fact that study participants overwhelmingly noted causes of crime and bias crime external to the offender may indicate the presence of a tempering effect on their punitiveness consistent with Gaubatz (1995).

In terms of participants' willingness to apply their preferred approaches to hypothetical bias crimes, they were more consistent than national polls on application of bias crime legislation would suggest. The vast majority of participants consistently applied their choice of a similar or different sanction for bias crime and one similar in nature to their general approach. Considering a combination approach to the vignettes as "more punitive", participants were fairly evenly split between more punitive versus more rehabilitative responses to bias crimes. However, only four participants offered solely more punitive responses, the vast majority adding the need for a change in rehabilitation to reform the perpetrator and reduce the chances of recidivism. In addition, more punishment often took the form of non-incarceration-based sanctions such as greater fines, damages, or punitive-based community service. When incarceration for biased offenders was deemed necessary, the time added rarely surpassed six months, much less than authorized by the typical bias crime sentence enhancement. While participants who changed only the nature or extent of rehabilitation for bias crimes did often authorize punishment of some sort for biased offenders-usually not incarceration-it was the same as for non-biased offenders.

Participants whose vignette responses initially appeared inconsistent with their general views seemed reasonable given their overall comments. In particular, a number of "switchers" mentioned concern with proving that a vignette was a bias crime, the seriousness of the predicate crime, and the possibility of changing the offender. It may be that the vignettes presented, although designed to be easily identified as bias crimes, may not have provided all the facts necessary to convince certain participants. In addition, given that the predicate crimes for the vignettes were not perceived as overwhelmingly serious by participants, as well as the public's propensity to base general responses to crime on rather extreme criminal circumstances, it is possible that the bias crime vignettes did not rise to the level justifying a different response, or if different as punitive a response, to the crime (changes in type of different approach generally involved less punitive responses to vignettes). It is also possible that the more specific questions led to a shift toward greater consideration of the offender. In at least a couple of cases participants were quite pessimistic about the ability of biased offenders to change when offering their general approaches to bias crime and partly for this reason advocated similar treatment for bias crime. However, given a situation with an actual offender, they seemed to figure a rehabilitative change was worth trying. Though it is not possible to directly assess, these findings may reflect participants' greater concern with proportionality in more specific contexts as suggested by research (Cullen et al. 2000; Hutton 2005). Finally, given that most switching concerned the added consideration of rehabilitation, their may be some discrepancy in the extent to which some participants view a change in rehabilitation as treating bias crime "differently" than non-bias crimes or perceive criminal courts as directly involved in rehabilitative measures. Either of these could account for participants not mentioning a different approach or rehabilitation in their response to the question of how the courts should handle convicted perpetrators of bias crimes generally but mentioning rehabilitation when asked for their preferred responses to the bias crime vignettes.

Overall, given the quarter of participants who treated bias crime similarly to non-bias crime and the rehabilitation-focused nature of the preferred responses to the vignettes by those who chose to treat it differently, the participants might have been expected to be less supportive of bias crime sentence enhancements – a solely more punitive approach to bias crime – than national samples. However, over 86 percent of the sample at least conditionally supported bias crime legislation, 58 percent supporting it without noted restrictions. This suggests that support for bias crime legislation may not hinge on actual support for an approach to bias crime focused primarily on greater punishment.

Participants who were willing to support bias crime legislation authorizing more severe punishment without noted conditions seemed primarily to do so because of its general social benefit. They saw it as a necessary step to acknowledge and address bias and bias crime in society, issues they felt generally were not being taken seriously or seriously enough. At the same time, given that most felt that bias crime generally was different, more serious and thus deserving of a different response, the fairness of longer sentences likely was not a consideration, especially given that they might serve as a deterrent, again protecting society. Most participants who supported bias crime legislation conditionally also generally viewed bias crime as a distinct crime deserving a different response and recognized the potential social benefits of such legislation. However, they also recognized its potential negative consequences. Specifically, they were concerned that punishments that were mandatory or too severe would not be fair and might only cause greater hate or that such legislation might be illegal. As a result, their support for bias crime legislation was contingent on factors not captured in general favor/oppose survey questions but that could become relevant in the context of more specific questioning. Finally, a slight majority of individuals who viewed bias crime as similar to non-bias crime were still willing to support bias crime legislation although their conditional support was based on its more symbolic power or ability to track such crime rather than its punitive emphasis. They seemed to recognize it as a lesser of two evils, a necessary response the nature of which needed changing.

Participants who rejected bias crime legislation viewed bias crime as not distinct from non-bias crime, at least for the purposes of sentencing, and held strong reservations about its potential positive effects and strong concerns regarding its potential negative uses/abuses and consequences. Similar to Jacobs and Potter (1997, 1998), they were concerned with making the problem worse by creating an unjustified or unnecessary distinction that could too easily be abused by the public, criminal justice actors or politicians and lead to greater tension and hostilities against potential victims of bias crime. As a result, they felt that such legislation offered little hope of deterring bias crime or reducing hate. In general, they seemed to be concerned with the fairness of the legislation and its implementation and as a result its ability to benefit/protect society. Unlike the scholarly research, no participants rejecting bias crime legislation directly raised the possibility of such legislation being illegal, perhaps because most citizens are unfamiliar with the precise nature of such issues or are not moved by them, or because the courts have ruled in its favor.

Consistent with recent research, participants did seem generally concerned with broader social impact, benefits, and protection when generally questioned as to their support for punitive legislation. And without the opportunity to provide commentary on their support or their own general responses to bias crime, for some their support for bias crime legislation would have seemed quite at odds with their lack of a more punitive response to the bias crime vignettes and for some their preference for treating bias crime the same as non-biased crime. However, providing that opportunity revealed that general support in some instances is based on an assessment of the social benefits assuming contingencies for fairness, since without them many recognize the benefits may be lost, or for some the more symbolic value of such legislation even in light of the need to change its solely punitive focus. In such instances, it seems that participants' desire for or belief in social benefits is allowed to outweigh their concerns, which have no concrete basis until they are provided with an actual crime and criminal. Those who rejected bias crime legislation also seemed concerned with its greater social benefit. However, they seemed to determine that given that the general nature of the legislation would be unfair – because it focused on a difference that they deemed unacceptable for general sanctioning purposes – it would not be capable of achieving such benefit. In all, it seems that those who viewed such legislation as pragmatically fatally flawed rejected bias crime while those who could envision a beneficial application supported it, regardless of whether it matched their sanctioning preference for addressing such crime.

Beyond support or opposition to bias crime legislation, there was a strong consensus amongst participants on the need for a community-wide educational endeavor to counter bias and hate. While recognizing the difficulties in doing so, participants were confident in the need to support tolerance of social diversity, especially in the classroom. However, they also believed that this could be accomplished through more general public education and awareness via advertising, news and entertainment, and the rejection of law and institutions that indirectly promote or perpetuate fear or hatred.

Interestingly, participants' views did not appear directly influenced by their sub-sample status. While it is difficult to tell whether or not this is a result of the specific participants within these groups or the inability to fully analyze the relevance of status based on the small sample sizes, in all, participants across status seemed more similar in their views than different. However, a number of seemingly interacting factors resurfaced throughout analysis suggesting their potential relevance to participations' views, sometimes differentially impacting certain sub-samples. Several such factors have either been identified by prior research as potentially relevant to public opinion on crime or bias crime or at least hold seemingly reasonable theoretical basis for their potential influence. However, based on the study size, such findings should be viewed with caution and are offered more to suggest factors worthy of future consideration rather than strong evidence of effect.

In terms of personal characteristics, minority status, education and sex seemed to distinguish participants' core views on bias crime and bias crime legislation, although which factor might be primarily or solely responsible was impossible to assess. Minorities as a whole appeared more likely than non-minorities to view bias crime as different, prefer a different approach to bias crime and support bias crime legislation. However, the findings may be partially explained by the impact of education given that participants possessing a college degree were more likely to think of bias crime as different and to support bias crime legislation across status, and also to explain some differences across status groups. There also appeared to be differences based on participant sex with women more likely than men to view bias crime as different and women much more likely to be rehabilitation oriented in their responses to bias crime. Such personal characteristics also seemed to impact other variables relevant to participants' views, namely fear and victimization. Perhaps not surprisingly, minorities were more likely to fear bias crime and to be the victims of bias crime. Although minority women were twice as likely to be victims, minority men, who were more likely the victims of physical or property crime rather than verbal incidents of bias, were more fearful of bias crime. In addition, minority participants with college degrees were more fearful than those without even though they were less likely to claim bias victimization.

Fear of crime and criminal victimization are staple factors in literature and research on public opinion of crime with evidence to support the prospect of either or both increasing the likelihood of a punitive response to crime (Langworthy and Whitehead 1986; Warr 1995, 2000). The study findings seem to suggest that both factors likely influenced participants' views, although fear and victimization related to crime generally or both crime generally and bias crime seemed more influential than fear and victimization related only to bias crime. Victims who reported general and bias victimization were more likely to view bias crime as different and advocate a different response. Those with fear of crime in general or both crime and bias crime were more likely to believe that bias crime should be treated differently. In all, neither fear of bias crime or bias-based victimization were apparently essential for participant support of bias crime legislation. This may be in part explained by the fact that many participants' support for bias crime legislation seemed to relate to its motivation at least as much as, if not more than, the crime per se meaning they may be responding based on their views regarding bias and hate more so than crime or personal safety. The findings related to fear of crime in general might suggest that it alone is enough to push individuals to support crime control measures such as bias crime sentence enhancements. However, both fear and victimization seemed to increase the likelihood of bias crime being viewed as different and/or requiring a different response. Although fear of bias crime or bias-based victimization alone seemed less influential than that related to crime in general or a combination of the two, this could be a by-product of the fact that the majority of bias "crime" victims experienced verbal incidents that may not have been crimes and that it was men, who had been the victims of more serious crimes, who were more fearful.

In terms of the nature of different responses to bias crime, as indicated previously, the vast majority of participants were not staunch advocates of more punishment. However, there did appear to be distinctions between those who in response to vignettes authorized more punitive measures, with or without rehabilitation, for bias crimes and those who supported only changes in rehabilitation. Once again, minority status, sex and education seemed influential. Men were more punitive than women, the majority of women supporting rehabilitative changes only, particularly those who did not fear crime. In addition, participants with bachelor's degrees also were more punitive, although this seemed to make more of a difference for men and minorities, who otherwise overall were more likely to support rehabilitation than non-minorities, the majority of whom supported greater punitive measures. Minorities, when supporting bias crime legislation, also were more likely to operationalize it in terms of different or increased rehabilitation rather than punishment. However, this may be the result of non-minorities without college degrees being solely punitive, as were African-Americans. Jewish participants and non-minorities with a college education were primarily focused on rehabilitation and gay and lesbian participants were the most inclined toward rehabilitative changes for bias crime.

In addition, there does seem to be some connection between fear of victimization and a more punitive response to crime as suggested by inconsistent and weak findings of prior research (Langworthy and Whitehead 1986). It also seems that such connections may be influenced by perceived seriousness of the offense and perception of it occurring (Warr and Stafford 1983). In particular, men who had been the victims of more serious bias crimes were more fearful of such crime and more punitive than others towards it. On the other hand, minority women who were more rehabilitation oriented were less fearful than minority men and when victims most likely to have experienced lower level incidents and likely non-crimes. However, non-minorities were less likely to fear bias crime or be its victims and were still more likely to be punitive than minorities. Although this may somewhat be a reflection of the greater punitiveness of non-minorities without college degrees, perhaps suggesting that more educated and/or minority citizens may have a better appreciation for the need for education to address the attitudes underlying bias crime but the data are inconclusive.

In all, study participants clearly want bias crime addressed at least as seriously, if not more seriously, than other crimes, which many do not think is currently occurring. Although they are not ignorant to problems with the criminal justice system and more specifically with enforcing bias crime legislation as well as potential negative consequences with bias crime legislation, the majority of participants are willing to support a bias crime sentence enhancement, at least as a step in that direction, even if they do not support its punitive component or its potential magnitude or mandatory nature. Although most hope it will serve as a deterrent, the majority seem more confident in the need for and potential success of different or increased rehabilitative measures to reduce recidivism and combat the attitudes, views and emotions behind bias crimes. While many participants feel that punishment may be necessary and increased punishment justified given the crime's motivation, based on the interviews overall it would seem that interpreting support for bias crime legislation as an indicator of strong support for a more punitive approach to bias crime would be disingenuous if not inaccurate.

Study Strengths and Weaknesses

The strengths and weaknesses of the study are in large part interchangeable. Its exploratory nature obviously limits the ability to assess components of theories, perspectives or hypotheses suggested by the literature or discovered in earlier research since the data is driven in large part by the freedom given participants to discuss the issues broadly rather than through the researcher's narrowly defined expectations. Its non-random sample nullified the possibility of statistical analysis that possibly could have provided a clearer end picture and one with generalizeability. In addition, even within the confines of a non-random sample, the diversity of participants was less than hoped for particularly regarding education. The highly educated nature of the sample suggests the possibility of very different findings with a representative sample. In particular, the more educated sample might in part explain the greater familiarity with the concept of bias crime, focus on rehabilitation, and consistency between abstract views and their application. Also, although the study, for the most part, revealed no glaring distinctions between minorities and non-minorities, a sample with more representation of non-minorities, especially those without college degrees, might capture a greater diversity of views. Unfortunately, the nature of the current study makes speculation difficult. However, prior research suggests that the views captured might be more punitive in nature. Finally, the study's scope and size, while providing patterns and themes across a host of issues relevant to bias crime, often failed to provide great enough depth or a large enough sample of participants holding particular views to offer much analysis beyond description and possible avenues of interest for future research.

That said, the research design allowed for a very open-ended qualitative study helpful for beginning to fill in the gaps left by current information and research on the topic. It allowed for a potential range of opinions by sampling not only minorities and non-minorities but a fairly diverse range within each. In addition, more so than prior studies, it permitted citizens with more of an opportunity to choose their own path of discussion by offering a range of rather broad/vague questions, allowing them to provide a glimpse into their view of the issue rather than their "view" shaped by those of academics or researchers through the questions asked and specific issues raised. Finally, the exploration of participants' views on crime and punishment as well their responses to bias and non-bias crimes provided a better set of data from which to examine whether and to what extent bias crime is perceived and/or responded to as a distinct type of crime. In essence, the methodological limitations were in large part the accepted consequences of an attempt to open the floodgates of public opinion on bias crime and capture as much as possible given the minimal study resources available. However, I would be remiss to not also acknowledge the limitations placed on the study by this being my first foray into qualitative research. On reflection, I often stayed silent when further questioning may have provided greater insight into participants' views and on occasion prompted responses on issues not first raised by participants. In addition, my desire to explore the issue as fully as possible led me perhaps to try to focus on too much where a narrowing of the interview protocol may have been more beneficial to the study's descriptive and explanatory capabilities. In particular, questions designed to explore the symbolic perspective, discussed earlier in this work, were too vague on their own and inappropriately placed-at the end of a lengthy interview and after long discussions of bias crime-to offer anything more than the general conclusions that participants generally felt social diversity to be beneficial and greater tolerance a worthy goal. In all, this researcher learned the importance of restraining ambition to further the goals of the research.

Implications of the Research

When initially discussing this research with friends and colleagues a concern often raised was that citizens' opinions might be quite unstable given their likely lack of prior reflection on the issue of bias crime, and without replication it is impossible to know to what extent this might be the case. However, my sense from the current interviews was that while the participants for the most part were new to the experience of being sincerely asked to share their views, they responded positively and seriously to the opportunity. While sometimes acknowledging their lack of prior reflection on the issue, they seemed to be conscientious in their answers, often taking the time to stop and think before answering, to reword their comments to ensure that I understood what was being said, and to even note when they recognized that their views might be more emotional than rational. In all, the extent to which they were willing, usually unprompted or only minimally prompted, to provide ample discussion of their general and specific views suggested that whether informed or not they thought the topic worthy of discussion and took seriously their role in the study as an opportunity to personally play some part in helping to address bias crime.

Although the sample was less diverse in educational background than desired, which may have influenced participant interest and responses, its findings imply that at least members of society with perhaps greater ability and opportunity to make a difference do not fit the vengeful punitive label with which American citizens are often tagged when it comes to crime and punishment. Instead, while perhaps automatically assuming an initial criminal punishment, whether incarceration based or not, their thoughts more strongly reflect the need for greater rehabilitation. Even in the case of bias crime, which seemed to provoke more intense feeling than crime in general and which many participants feared and at least believed they may have been victims of at least in low-level forms, participants' discussions turned primarily to addressing the bias or hate that motivated such crime and the education and/or exposure criminals or the public generally needed to serve that purpose. Even though the majority of participants viewed bias crime as a distinct crime deserving of a different response, a solely more punitive approach was rarely at the forefront.

The implication that some citizens are likely highly supportive of more rehabilitation-based approaches to bias crime, and seemingly more so than purely more punitive measures, is insightful particularly in light of the general public's and the current participants' support for bias crime legislation. The research suggests that such support does not directly equate to support for solely more punitive action against bias offenders. Although many participants were not opposed to such measures, especially in the hope of a deterrent effect and the available justification of such steps given their perception of bias crime as a more serious crime, their overall comments imply that their support for bias crime legislation is more support for the taking of at least some action to acknowledge and take seriously bias crime. It is support for the general concept of a response to bias crime, and when taken in light of participants' other views, it is not for the most part backed by a strong desire to get back at such offenders or punish them harder or longer but instead to protect society from the commission of such crime-a goal not it seems reached by locking biased perpetrators up and throwing away the key, or locking them up for longer periods of time, but rather actually addressing the bias or hate of which their crime is a byproduct. Thus, the public's lack of willingness in polls to apply bias crime sentence enhancements that they support in the abstract may be consistent with their belief that something needs to be done but reflect their view that "more punishment" isn't necessarily the answer to the bias crime problem, and for some that a more severe punishment would simply be unfair.

These suggestions imply that given the choice, and similar to recent findings with regards to the death penalty, the current study's participants, and perhaps at least some segment of the general public, might support less punitive bias crime legislation than the bias crime sentence enhancements on which their opinions are currently requested. They also indicate that to the extent that any legislators, activists or criminal justice actors might use public support for bias crime legislation as a justification for passing, advocating or supporting more punitive measures may be an inaccurate use of such data and one that may stifle perhaps more promising avenues for addressing bias crime, especially if Grattet and Jenness (2001) and Jacobs and Potter's (1997, 1998) negative predictions of bias crime legislation come to pass. At the same time, findings concerning participants who fail to distinguish between crime and bias crime taken with those regarding participants who do might suggest that different responses to bias crime could be developed that would satisfy both. If the former are seemingly concerned with the "punishment" fitting the underlying crime and not the motivation, perhaps they would support responses to bias crime similar in punishment but varying in rehabilitation – an approach that a few participants did in fact apply to bias crime vignettes while claiming to treat them the same and that many supporters of different responses to bias crime also would be likely to support.

Interestingly, the overall focuses of participants' preferred responses to bias crime are fairly consistent with those for crime in general implying that, as discovered in prior research, rehabilitation is not dead in the eyes of the public. That said, it is perhaps foolish to think that a public who is taught to turn to the criminal justice system-a system predominantly based on use of force and punishment-in the face of crime would sidestep its expert conventions when asked to respond to crime. In addition, as the current research suggests, it is not enough to accept the public's general statements of, or support for, more punishment as a necessary indicator of greater fines or longer sentences-because sometimes they mean a simple change in rehabilitative measures. It could be that bias crime provides a more obvious focus for rehabilitation than crime in general with its more varied or less obvious motivations or social causes. Unfortunately, the current data does not provide straightforward implications regarding these matters. However, it does perhaps imply that given the opportunity or option, the public may support rehabilitation even for a crime that they fear and/or that seems to touch a widely-held social norm or value. Given the current state of corrections in the U.S., any possibility for public support for a non-incarceration-based, potentially less costly and perhaps more effective approach to crime would seem to warrant future research.

Future Research

The study's findings and implications offer a whole host of interesting lines of investigation for future studies on bias crime as well as other criminal justice issues. However, of particular interest is the implication that given the chance, the public might support bias crime legislation focused more on rehabilitation and/or general prevention than more severe "punishment." National polls seem to leave little doubt that the majority of the public wants something done about bias crime but to question only their support for a punitive bias crime sentence enhancement and their faith in deterrence puts them in an all or nothing position that does not allow them to express their sincere opinions. In essence, it creates a situation that makes them look from afar either punitive or potentially bigoted.

If the public's opinion on such matters is to be seriously considered in the development of criminal justice policies or legitimately used to advocate for or justify them, it is incumbent on research to fully explore the range and depth of opinions. That suggests that at its most basic level, investigation into public opinion should offer citizens a range of possible approaches and justifications from which to choose as well as an opportunity to present any concerns related to such approaches. Beyond that, issues raised must be explored qualitatively to ferret out exactly what they mean to individuals. In the current study, participant-raised issues included social causes of bias crime, seriousness of crime motivation and its appropriate role in criminal sanctioning, definitional and proof-based concerns related to bias crime, discriminatory/abusive enforcement of bias crime legislation, and problems with the criminal justice system including discrimination and inconsistency. Each of these areas presents a host of components that could influence views on how the system should be used generally and more specifically to address bias crime. In addition, as suggested by prior research, fear of crime and victimization did seem to impact participants' views on crime and punishment but perhaps in a much more complicated way than a mere yes/no response would provide. Finally, it is highly possible that issues within each of the aforementioned areas and personal characteristics created additive or interactive influences on participants' views. In all, each of these areas seems ripe for further qualitative examination in order to create the background necessary to determine whether more quantitative research on the issue should include it and how so.

In addition, each of the aforementioned issues offers a venue for potential public ignorance and/or misinformation or, in some instances, genuine issues if not problems within the criminal justice system. Their investigation and confirmation could provide key areas in which to educate the public in ways that could serve to better inform their views of the criminal justice system and their opinions of and possibly support for criminal justice policies. In instances in which the problem may be the system rather than misinformation, such research could be used to advocate the need for specific system evaluation and possible change, again with the prospect of influencing the public and potentially creating and/or improving attempts at public-system endeavors to address crime in general or specific offenses.

Finally, although the substantive and procedural issues with the current study made it impossible to explore, Tyler and his colleagues' perspective on symbolic crime concerns and how such concerns might influence public opinions on criminal justice policies offers an interesting avenue for future research. Given the inherent relevance of social diversity and tolerance to bias and prejudice, public opinion on bias crime would seem a perfect context for such research.

Conclusion

In the end, the purpose of public opinion research concerning the criminal justice system or the policies it is designed to implement and enforce should be to inform and progress. Its findings should be used to inform legislators, researchers and system actors as to the will, concerns, and ideas of the public, which with its mass holds the possibility of benefiting the system through support, cooperation or an outsider's perspective that may offer an insight lost by those in the trenches or cripple it via disregard/disrespect or direct resistance. Thus, opinion-based findings should be used as a means of improving the system. That said, the public's view of bias crime and bias crime legislation or any criminal justice issue is irrelevant and/or wasted if used merely to fill academic journals or worse as a tool to loosely measure the safety of political action or inaction or inaccurately justify the views of policymakers and/or system actors.

According to the current research, public support for a general bias crime sentence enhancement may not indicate support for a more punitive approach to bias crime or the belief that a more punitive approach is the answer to the bias crime problem. In addition, support for bias crime legislation may coincide with concerns regarding its legality, enforcement, and potential for unintended negative consequences, all of which might interfere with the successful implementation of bias crime legislation as a primary response to bias crime. Thus, these issues seem worthy of further investigation and its results, serious consideration by those who develop, pass and implement criminal justice policy.

Interview Protocol

A. Consent Form

Thanks again for agreeing to participate. Before we get started I just need to go over the informed consent form with you, answer any questions you might have about it and have you sign it if you agree with all of it. [Read consent form and answer any questions.]

Do you have any other questions before we start the interview?

B. Domains and Questions

1. Crime and Punishment

First, I'd just like to get a sense of your thoughts on crime and punishment in the U.S.

If someone from another country asked you about crime in the U.S. what would you tell them? How would you describe it?

How do you feel about crime in the U.S.? Have you had any experience with crime in the U.S.? Would you say you fear crime or becoming the victim of a crime?

How would you describe the US approach for dealing with crime? How effective would you say that approach is? How would you like to see the US deal with crime?

How would you describe how the US courts handle people found guilty of committing a crime? How effective would you say that approach is? How would you like to see the courts handle convicted criminals?

Do you have any other thoughts you'd like to share regarding either the issues we've been discussing or perhaps issues that I did not ask you about but that you feel are important to the topic of crime and punishment in the US?

2. Bias Crime and Punishment
In some instances, crimes are committed against other people because of who they are or what they believe. (They are often referred to as bias or hate crimes).

Are you at all familiar with this type of crime, or have you or anyone close to you had any experience with it?

If someone who had never heard of bias crime asked you about bias crime what would you tell them? How would you describe a typical bias crime? How, if at all, would you say you feel about bias crime? Would you say you fear bias crime or becoming the victim of a bias crime?

How would you describe the U.S. approach for dealing with bias crime? How effective would you say this approach is? How, if at all, would you like to see the U.S. deal with bias crime?

Is it necessary for a judge or jury in a criminal case to know whether a crime is a biased crime or not?

How do you think the courts handle people found guilty of committing a bias crime? How effective would you say that response is? What, if anything, would you like to see happen to a person convicted of committing a bias crime?

Do you have any other thoughts you'd like to share regarding either the issues we've been discussing or perhaps issues that I did not ask you about but that you feel are important to the topic of bias crime or its punishment?

3. Crime Vignettes
Now I would like to shift gears a little and ask you to listen to and react to some hypothetical situations. (Questions will remain the same for scenarios A-C.)

A. Property Damage
Two 19-year-old boys decide to go on a vandalism spree in their neighborhood causing about $400 in damage (to remove the graffiti).
What if: a) they spray paint Metallica (the name of their favorite rock band) on a local business

What, if any, action do you think should be taken against them?

Assuming they are arrested and convicted, what, if any, action do you think the court should take?

What if: b) they spray paint a swastika on a local Jewish temple

If their response does not indicate anything regarding the crime being a bias crime, I will ask....

Do you think this crime would or should be considered a bias crime and why or why not?

B. Personal Violence
A couple of male college students are sitting on a bench watching people go by. A (variations) couple walks by holding hands. Believing it to be their best friend's girlfriend with another man, the two students jump up, accost the man, and shove him to the ground. Realizing their error (it was not their friend's girlfriend), they let the couple run off. The man receives only minor scratches to his hands.

What if: a) woman looks like their best friends girlfriend (mistaken identity)
What if: b) interracial couple (black guy, white woman) w/out mistaken identity wording
What if: c) gay couple w/out mistaken identity wording

C. Discrimination versus Racial
A middle-aged construction worker is fired from his job and goes to a local bar to let off some steam. At the bar...
What if: a) he runs into his former boss, picks a fight with him and breaks his nose
What if: b) he notices a guy at the bar, who he thinks is gay, figures he can take him and so picks a fight with him and breaks his nose

4. Bias Crime Legislation
Now, I'd like to switch back to some more general questions. Some States have passed legislation that authorizes more severe penalties for criminals who commit their crimes because of bias.

Would you support the passing of such legislation in Pennsylvania?

Different states include different types of groups and penalties in their legislation. If you had the opportunity to determine the details of such legislation, what would you want them to include?

Do you have any other thoughts you'd like to share regarding legislation on bias crime?

5. Social Cohesion and Diversity
Some people think that our country benefits from the fact that it is made up of so many different types and kinds of people while others believe it to be a problem. How do you feel about the social diversity in the U.S.?

Generally speaking, how would you describe the current state of the country in terms of how well people get along and treat one another? What do you think contributes to that state?

Some people believe that our country needs to more tolerant of people who are different, others say we have become too tolerant, and some believe we have reached a good middle point. How do you feel about the level of tolerance in our society?

Do you think the government does or should promote tolerance of people who are different or believe differently than the majority of citizens in the U.S.? (If yes) How does or would you like to see the government promote tolerance?

Do you have any other thoughts you'd like to share regarding social cohesion and diversity or social tolerance and protection for minorities?

Do you have any other thoughts you'd like to share regarding any of the issues we've discussed today?

Background Questionnaire

Should you choose to skip a question, please write "skip" on the answer line or next to the answer categories. All answers will be kept confidential.

1. In what year were you born?
2. Have you always lived in western PA? (Yes or No)
   If no, please indicate how long you have lived in western PA.
   If no, please indicate where you lived most of the time before western PA.

3. What is the highest level of education you have obtained?
   _____ less than high school education
   _____ high school diploma or ged
   _____ some college
   _____ college degree - please indicate degree
   _____ post graduate degree - please indicate degree
4. How would you describe your occupation?
5. What is your current marital status?
   _____ single, never been married
   _____ married
   _____ separated/divorced
   _____ widowed
6. How many, if any, children do you have?
7. Which category best describes your average annual household income?
   _____ less than $20,000
   _____ $20,000 - $39,999
   _____ $40,000 - $59,999
   _____ $60,000 - $79,999
   _____ $80,000 or more
8. How would you describe your race.
9. How would you describe your ethnicity.
10. How would you describe your sexual orientation?

11. How would you describe your religion, if any?
    Do you consider yourself a religious person?   _____yes

                                               _____ no
12. How would you describe your political affiliation in terms
    of political party?
    How would you describe your political ideology?
    (conservative, moderate, liberal, other - please write in)
    Do you consider yourself a political person?   _____ yes

                                               _____ no
13. What, if any groups or organizations are you a member of or belong to in
which you regularly participate or feel very committed to?
14. In five words or less how would you describe yourself to someone who did
not know anything about you?

APPENDIX C

Recruitment Card

(For this and all other appendices, contact information has been removed and marked by an asterisk to avoid identifying the study region.)

Volunteers Needed for a Study on Public Opinion on Crime, Punishment and Bias Crime

Hi! My name is Terrylynn Pearlman and I am a student at the State University of New York at Albany, currently completing a Ph.D. in Criminal Justice, and a new faculty member at * University. I am conducting a study on public opinion on crime, punishment and bias crime. I hope that the knowledge gained from this study will provide a better understanding of how the public feels about such issues and may be used to evaluate public satisfaction with current and future criminal justice policies. People of all races, religions, sexes, sexual orientations, educations and occupations are being asked to participate. No expertise is necessary but participants must be 18 or older and speak English fluently. Participation involves an in-person, taped, 1.5 hour interview on your opinions concerning crime, punishment and bias crime and a short written questionnaire about yourself. Please contact me at * or pearlman@*.edu at your earliest convenience if you have any questions about the study or would like to participate. Participation is completely voluntary and will be kept confidential. Should you wish to verify my identity or the authenticity of the study please contact Alissa Pollitz Worden, my faculty advisor, at 518-442-5213 or the * University Department of Criminology at *. Thank you.

APPENDIX D
Invitation Email

Dear ....:

As you are aware, my name is Terrylynn Pearlman and I am a student at the State University of New York at Albany currently completing a Ph.D. in Criminal Justice and currently a faculty member of the Department of Criminology at * University. I am conducting a research study on Public Opinion on Crime, Punishment and Bias Crime. Please accept this email as an official invitation to participate. Below you will find details regarding the nature and logistics of the study and your role in it should you decide to participate. Please feel free to contact me at * or pearlman@*.edu should you have any questions or concerns. Should you wish to verify my identity or the study itself, please contact Alissa Pollitz Worden, my faculty advisor, at 518-442-5213 or * University's Department of Criminology at *.

Your participation in the study would involve an in-person, audio-taped interview with the purpose of obtaining your general opinions on crime, punishment, and bias crime, your opinions regarding specific hypothetical crimes, and some personal demographic information such as age, education, and race. There are no right or wrong interpretations or answers to any of the questions I might ask. The goal of the research is to obtain an understanding of how people think and feel about these issues. The interview is expected to take about 1½ hours, although its length ultimately will depend on what you have to share. Interviews will be conducted at a time and location convenient for you.

I cannot promise you any direct benefits from your participation in this study. However, it will provide you an opportunity to share your views with someone very interested in them. In addition, this study will provide a better understanding of how the public feels about crime and punishment and may be used to evaluate the success of criminal justice policies. At the same time, this study is not expected to put participants at any risk, although for some people the topics to be discussed may be upsetting. In addition, your participation in this research would be completely voluntary and confidential, meaning I alone will know you participated and the content of your interview.

If you chose to participate and have not already scheduled an interview, please contact me at * or pearlman@*.edu to do so. If you choose not to participate, contacting me with your decision will help to avoid any follow-up contact. The success of the study depends on people such as yourself being willing to share their views. Thus, I hope the research will pique your interest and your schedule will allow you the time to participate.

Sincerely,
Terrylynn Pearlman

Filtering Questions

Questions to be asked after I provide potential participants with basic information/requirements of the project (entailed in the recruitment card) and they indicate they would like to participate.

"Just one additional thing, as the recruitment card you received indicated I am attempting to interview a diverse group of people including people of different races, religions, sexual orientations, educations and occupations. Would you mind answering a few background questions that will help me ensure that I am maintaining a diverse group of people? Please know that your answers will not be kept or shared with anyone whether or not you participate and you are under no obligation to answer any questions if you do not wish to." If they do not mind.....

1. Are you 18 years or older?
2. How would you describe your race?
3. How would you describe your religion, if any?
4. What is the highest level of education you have obtained?
5. How would you describe your occupation?
6. How would you describe your sexual orientation?

If they complete the questions and are appropriate participants: "You should fit into the study very well, if you are still interested in participating would you like to set up an interview at this time?" (I will also ask them for a contact number or email in case interviews have to be changed.)

If they refuse...."I am sorry but without knowing how you compare to the group of people I have already interviewed, I cannot determine whether your participation would help maintain the diversity I am trying to achieve. But I thank you for your interest." - Never had to use

Consent Form

You are being asked to participate in a study on <u>Public Opinion on Crime, Punishment and Bias Crime</u>. This study is being conducted by Terrylynn Pearlman, a doctoral student at the State University of New York, School of Criminal Justice. Potential participants have been suggested by acquaintances and been recruited with any eye towards interviewing a diverse group of people.

<u>Participation involves a 1-11/2 hour, in-person interview</u> with the purpose of obtaining: your general thoughts, <u>feelings and opinions on crime and punishment and bias crime, your opinions regarding specific hypothetical</u> crimes, and some personal demographic information ·such as age, education, and race.

Voluntariness
<u>Your participation in this research is completely voluntary.</u> Should you choose to participate, <u>you may also choose to not answer any question(s) you do not wish to for any reason -</u> indicate such, the question will be skipped and the interview will proceed. In addition, <u>you may discontinue your participation at any time without penalty</u> - notify me of your desire and the interview will be canceled or discontinued.

Confidentiality
<u>Your participation in this research and the content of your interview will be kept confidential.</u> Your identity and any identifying information will be stored separately from the tape(s) and transcription of your interview, which will be labeled only by a number, and all will be kept under lock and key. All information identifying you as a participant will be destroyed when the study and all related publications are completed.

Audio Taping
Your interview will be tape recorded. Any reference to your opinions or use of your words in reports or publications will not include your name or information that reasonably could be used to identify you.

Benefits and Risks
I cannot promise you any direct benefits from your participation in this study. However, it will provide a better understanding of public opinion on crime, punishment and bias crime that might be help design and evaluate criminal justice policies to address such issues. This study is not expected to put you at any risk although some people may find the topics to be upsetting.

Contact Information
If you have any questions regarding the study, please contact me, Terrylynn Pearlman at * or   pearlman@*.edu or Alissa Pollitz Worden, my faculty advisor at (518) 442-5213. If you have any questions regarding your rights as a participant, contact the University Compliance Office, Office for Sponsored Programs, The University at Albany, at (518) 437-4569.

PLEASE SIGN BELOW IF YOU ARE WILLING TO PARTICIPATE IN THE STUDY.

I, (print name) _____, agree to participate in this study on Public Opinion on Crime and Punishment and Bias Crime and Punishment.

Sign: _____   Date:_____

Notes

1. Substantive bias crime legislation received its first Federal constitutional challenge in 1992 in response to the conviction of a young white boy for the burning of a wooden cross by several white youths on a black family's lawn. In *R.A.V. v. City of St. Paul* (1992), the Supreme Court reviewed the constitutionality of the Minnesota ordinance that stated:

    Whomever places on public or private property a symbol, object, appellation, characterization of graffiti, including but not limited to a burning cross or Nazi swastika, which one knows or has reasonable grounds to know arouses anger, alarm, or resentment in others on the basis of race, color, religion, or gender, commits disorderly conduct and shall be guilty of a misdemeanor (379).

2. In the case of *Virginia v. Black et al.* (2003) the Supreme Court was asked to decide the constitutionality of a statute making it a felony 'for any person..., with the intent of intimidating any person or group..., to burn...a cross on the property of another, a highway or other public place" (1541). It presented the questions whether such behavior is the conduct of illegal intimidation or the expression of an idea protected by the First Amendment and whether cross-burning in and of itself can be "prima facie evidence of an intent to intimidate a person or group" (154). Both questions seemed to request further application and/or clarification of *R.A.V. v. City of St. Paul*. The Court ruled:

    ..a State, consistent with the First Amendment, may ban cross burning carried out with the intent to intimidate...The protections the First Amendment affords speech and expressive conduct are not absolute...The First Amendment permits Virginia to outlaw cross burnings done with the intent to intimidate because burning a cross is a particularly virulent form of intimidation. Instead of prohibiting all intimidating messages, Virginia may choose to regulate this subset of intimidating messages in light of cross burning's long and pernicious history as a signal of impending violence (1549).

It also stated that nothing in *Black* contradicts their ruling in *R.A.V.*, which "did not hold that the First Amendment prohibits all forms of content-based discrimination within a proscribable area of speech...[but rather] that a particular type of content discrimination does not violate the First Amendment when the basis for it consists entirely of the very reason its entire class of speech is proscribable" (1549). So long as the intent to intimidate exists the statute does not run the "risk of the suppression of ideas" (1551). However, the Court ruled unconstitutional VA's provision authorizing cross burning as prima facie evidence of an intent to intimidate arguing that to do so would be to permit a shortcut that blurs the line between a person engaging in "constitutionally proscribable intimidation or core political speech" (1551).

3. *Wisconsin v Mitchell* (1993) challenged a Wisconsin statute that authorized enhanced sentences based on a perpetrator's "intentional selection of a victim because of" an enumerated prejudice. Mitchell was convicted of racially-motivated aggravated battery after inciting a group of young black men to attack a passing white youth after viewing the film Mississippi Burning. He was sentenced to seven years for a crime that absent biased motivation would have permitted a two year maximum sentence. Upholding the enhancement, the Court held that "the First Amendment does not prohibit a state from providing enhanced punishment for a crime based on the actor's discriminatory purpose in committing the crime" and indicated that "the First Amendment...does not prohibit the evidentiary use of speech to establish the elements of a crime or to prove motive or intent" (489). In distinguishing *Mitchell* from *R.A.V.* the Court emphasized the difference in more severely punishing specific conduct (aggravated battery) rather than speech. The court also approved the use of motive as a sentencing factor and the use of associational and speech-related activity to demonstrate that motive when such factors are directly relevant to the crime.

4. The case of *Apprendi v. New Jersey* (2000) concerned the enhanced sentence of a white man who fired several shots into the home of an African-American family. After pleading guilty to a firearms charge, which authorized a five to ten year sentence, the State filed for enhancement under its hate crime statute, which allowed a judge to enhance a sentence if it could be demonstrated by a preponderance of the evidence that "the defendant committed the crime with a purpose to intimidate a person or group because of...race." Based on the enhancement, Apprendi received a 12-year prison sentence. Based on the rights afforded the 5th, 6th and 14th Amendments, the Supreme Court held that "the Constitution requires that any fact that increases the penalty for a crime beyond the prescribed statutory maximum, other than the fact of a prior conviction, must be submitted to a jury and proved beyond a reasonable doubt" (2362). It further stated that the State's placement of the "enhancer within the criminal code's sentencing provisions does not mean that

it is not an essential element of the offense" (2365). In essence, after *Apprendi* little distinction between the hate element of a substantive bias crime and a sentencing factor of hate that would increase the maximum penalty of the underlying offense remained. The only time now in which the process for substantive offenses and sentence enhancements can legally differ is when the latter permits an enhancement only within the minimum-maximum penalty range of the underlying substantive offense.

5. Since the first official reporting of bias crime statistics in 1993, the annual number of incidents has fluctuated from a low of 5,932 in 1994 to a high of 9,730 in 2001 with an average of approximately 7,500 bias crimes per year. A general increase was documented from 1991 to 1996 with a decline in the late 1990s (Partners Against Hate 2002, 2004; U.S. Dept. of Justice 1993-2001). A general lack of trust in these numbers and the trends they might suggest results from a host of administrative and crime-related concerns.

To some extent administrative concerns hinge on the relative newness of the issue and data collection methods. In particular, the relative recentness of both awareness and understanding of the bias crime issue has resulted in what Frederick Lawrence (1999, 23) identifies as a "mutual-feedback relationship" between bias crime and its official response. In essence, once initial concern translated into a legislative response-namely the official reporting of bias crime, the data collected provided evidence as to the quantitative extent of the problem that had previously not been available and that led to a perceived increase in the problem, justifying an expanded response that led to an increased capturing of the number of such crimes, once again supporting a perceived increase and so on. In reality it becomes difficult to tell whether perception is the proverbial tail that wags the dog or the increases reflect an actual rise in bias crime or a combination of the two.

The answer is hindered by the administrative nature of the Hate Crime Statistics Act. Participation in the Act's data collection program is voluntary leading to a host of problems of validity and reliability. In 2001, 11,987 state and local law enforcement agencies reported to the FBI, up from roughly 6,000 in 1993 when official reporting began, 17.6 percent of which reported one or more bias crimes. However, even the highs leave unknown the prevalence of bias crime in the jurisdictions of over 4,000 state and local law enforcement agencies eligible for participation but that do not report. While the increase in participating agencies certainly has improved, the representative nature of the official data (participation in 2001 representing 49 States and the District of Columbia and 85% of the population), year-to-year fluctuation in the number of agencies reporting has made analysis of trends based on incident numbers alone invalid. However, even if full participation were achieved and maintained such that a base line for comparison could be established, the ability of official bias crime statistics to measure the magnitude of the problem still would be in question.

The FBI's complete dependence on state and local reporting means acceptance of great variation in the concept being measured, the methods used and the overall accuracy that could result in the under- or over-reporting of bias crime. The first issue involves differences in the definition of bias crime. While the FBI definition requires "manifestation of prejudice in whole or part," it is undocumented how or even whether jurisdictions with differing motivational standards such as the "because of" form address such distinctions when reporting to the FBI (Jacobs and Henry 1996; Jacobs and Potter 1998). While some might argue that the distinction is irrelevant, it would be folly to ignore, or at least fail to acknowledge, the potential difference between crimes based on racial animus and those reflecting discriminatory selection. Future research might suggest that the two are not interchangeable in terms of prevalence, causes, influences and successful preventative measures. Unduly combining what might be distinct although similar phenomena might severely slow, if not make impossible, any progress toward addressing and reducing either, or both, form(s) of bias crime.

Beyond variety in definition, the FBI's data collection program reflects varying law enforcement policies and procedures. Guidelines for labeling a crime as a bias crime may differ not only as a result of definition but by the evidence police are willing to accept as indicative of such a crime. Individual departments and their officers also may have different incentives or disincentives for recognizing a crime as prejudicially motivated and documenting and charging it as such. A 1998 National Law Enforcement Survey with a stratified sample of 2,657 and a response rate of 30 percent found that: 37.5 percent of officers surveyed indicated that their department had an official hate crime policy; three-quarters of those officers indicated they were willing to support that policy; 25 percent of agencies had a specialized hate crime unit or officer, and while 67 percent of agencies reported providing hate crime training most programs were limited to two hours. In addition, once a hate crime is identified as such the infrastructure available for recording that incident and properly submitting it to the FBI may affect overall bias crime data. The 1998 Survey also found that 37.1 percent of officers from non-HCSA-participating agencies believed they had reported 1 or more hate crime incidents as did 31 percent of those from participating agencies that actually reported no hate crimes. Such findings suggest not only disparities between police perceptions of, and the actual, prevalence of bias crime in their States or locales but an overall lack of focused emphasis on the issue likely to result in a rather haphazard enforcement of bias crime laws between and within departments. In essence, the structure necessary for more valid and reliable enforcement and reporting is not present, although a move toward it has been developing since 2000 owing in part to the strengthening of the bias crime concept by both legislatures and courts (Lawrence 1999).

However, the accuracy of official statistics is dependent not only on the administrative policies and practices of departments and their offices. Research has shown that victim-related factors can have substantial impact on crime figures because of their effect on reporting. Many bias crimes may be reported as only their underlying crimes. Factors leading to such under reporting of bias crimes may include victims' inability to understand the crime committed; lack of knowledge as to the possibility of a bias-motivated crime and the legal relevance of such; or inability to express such a concern/perception to law enforcement. However, in addition, those capable of recognizing their victimization as bias motivated might be unwilling to solicit law enforcement assistance at all or to report the underlying crime's biased nature. Much under-reporting may be attributed to the generally low-level nature of most bias crimes leading victims to deem them "too minor to report." In addition to the reasons given for victim failure to report crime in general, such lack of action by victims of bias crimes may relate to a perceived or actual negative relationship between the victims' groups and the police or victims' unwillingness to identify themselves as a member of a protected group so as to avoid the personal, social and/or legal ramifications of such disclosure (Lawrence 1999).

6. Unofficial statistics, while suggesting significant under-reporting of bias crimes as reflected in official data, do little to provide any more reliable a picture of the phenomenon. The collection of bias crime statistics by independent advocacy groups documents a well-accepted increase in bias crimes from the mid 80's to the early 90's with a general decrease in the late 90's. However, the ability of such statistics to pinpoint the nature of the bias crime problem remains elusive. The Anti-Defamation League leads the way in unofficial reporting of bias crimes, having compiled annual statistics since 1979. The ADL actually publishes figures of "overt acts or expressions of anti-Jewish bigotry or hostility," relying on local law enforcement, newspapers, community groups and victims for the reporting of such incidents. The breadth of their definition and sources means that not all such incidents are actually crimes or if crimes not necessarily identified or charged as bias crimes by law

enforcement. In addition to ADL, the Southern Poverty Law Centers' Klanwatch also collects statistics on "hate crimes" but only those motivated by racial and ethnic prejudice. Although focusing only on crimes, Klanwatch includes in their audit any crime reported by newspapers or electronic media "if its motivation seemed to be race-related" (Jacobs and Potter 1998). Similar problematic issues are raised regarding numbers produced by other advocacy groups and surveys that either fail to precisely define the nature of the acts their figures cover or admit to including "biased or insensitive speech or literature" and/or "psychological violence." Such discrepancies in the reporting of unofficial statistics lead to questions as to their value in terms of identifying the scope of bias crime. In addition, the advocacy role of many groups that collect such data leads to skepticism of their figures and interpretations of the problem because of their undeniable desire to address all biased-motivated behavior so as to serve the well being of their constituents. This is not to suggest that figures presented by advocacy groups are faulty only that their collection is designed to "call attention to their members' victimization, subordinate status, and need for special governmental assistance" (Jacobs and Potter 1998, 63). To such groups the exact number and type of hate or bias-motivated acts perpetrated do not define their cause, for any amount of such behavior is unacceptable, but rather provide the evidence necessary to provoke and maintain a general awareness and response to the issue.

7. Culpability, or the level to which an individual merits condemnation or blame for an action, is an essential building block of legal guilt and serves as a primary mechanism for the assignment of punishment by setting the general severity level of a crime. Lawrence (1999) argues that culpability for a bias crime exceeds that of its underlying crime because it combines the mens rea of the latter with what he refers to as a second-tier mens rea-the purpose of bias crime of either "furthering hostility towards the target group" in a racial amicus model or selecting the victim on the basis of race in a discriminatory selection model. In essence, the distinction in culpability between the bias and non-bias crime lies not in what the actor did but in why-the motivation. Whether the relevance of culpability to crime seriousness depends on the retributive notion of blameworthiness or the utilitarian concern with social welfare, Lawrence claims the prejudicial motivation of bias crime makes its offenders more culpable. For the former, bias crime violates the deeply held equality principle and thereby fits a deontological justification for punishment, and for the latter, bias crime is by nature more likely to involve greater consequences and less social value than its underlying crimes.

8. A 1994 national victimization survey discovered that victims of ethnoviolence, compared to non-victims, group defamation victims and non-bias personal crime victims, experienced a "greater average number of symptoms and behavior variations on a scale of 19 psycho-physiological symptoms of posttraumatic stress and 12 social and behavioral changes" including nervousness, anger, loss of friendships, interpersonal skills and ability to sleep and concentrate (U.S. Dept. of Justice 2001; Ehrlich et al. 1994, 700). In addition, a convenience sample of 2000 gay, lesbian and bisexual respondents found that those who in the last five years believed they had been victimized because of their sexual orientation were significantly more likely than non-bias crime victims to report anxiety, depression and traumatic stress that tended to last more than three years longer for bias than non-bias crime victims (Herek, Cogan and Gillis 1999). Data from a survey of Bostonian assault victims reconfirmed the greater psychological sequelae previously reported as experienced by bias crime victims and demonstrated its severity in terms of number, intensity and duration. In addition to more anger, which reflected the largest difference between the compared groups, nervousness, depression and lack of will to live, bias crime victims experienced more difficulty dealing with, and recovering from, their victimization than non-bias crime victims (McDevitt, Balboni, Garcia and Gu 2001).

9. They provide as examples the anguish of uninvolved parents after child abduction and murder cases, and commuters following car-jacking and public transportation crimes, and they cite research findings in support of vicarious victimization, including "enhanced feelings of vulnerability and fear" for general crimes (Skogen and Maxfield in Wright 1985 qtd in Jacobs and Potter 1998, 87).

10. Categories reflect researchers' groupings rather than legally-defined categories.

11. Respondent characteristics included age, gender, religion/religiosity, violent/property crime victim, opinion of hate crime legislation, political philosophy and level of crime concern. Vignette characteristics included offender age, socioeconomic status, race, gender and victim-offender relationship and criminal record.

12. Seven hundred students from universities in six states (Florida, Georgia, Indiana, Kentucky, Ohio and Virginia) were divided into two categories, criminal justice majors or not, and provided with twenty hate crime incidents/scenarios that had been provided by the FBI or the Southern Poverty Law Center.

13. Both samples were provided a scenario involving a shooting between two motorists with varied details based on the experiment. The incident involved the shouting of racial epithets and the firing of six rounds, one of which grazed the victim's ribs without serious injury. The scenario indicated no provocation on the part of the victim.

14. Experiment three offered to the same sample as experiment two a scenario in which an African American or Caucasian male had racial slurs yelled at him, was chased, and sustained serious bruises on his arms and face from a baseball bat. The primary variant was the nature of the peer influence on the perpetrator. Ratings of crime severity and jail sentence were measured.

15. This also may be a factor for other crimes for which people perceive a very specific type of victim.

16. It should be clarified that as used in the current study "symbolic" is not meant to suggest non-instrumental concerns or responses to crime. Indeed, laws that intend to promote social control are, strictly speaking, instrumental. Rather, symbolic is used to differentiate the focus of participants' thoughts when responding to crime. In this context, instrumental refers to participants' primary concern for controlling individual criminal behavior either through deterrence, incapacitation or rehabilitation-the crime and criminal is the immediate focus. On the other hand, symbolic denotes participants' concern for the current state of society with crime and criminals serving as but a symbol of that state – the condition of society being the immediate focus. So while support for legislation under either type of concern is in fact instrumental, the basis for that legislation may be either concern for crime directly or indirectly as a symbol of the condition of society.

17. Level of education, primarily through its impact on people's political understanding and knowledge of the concepts of freedom and equality, is likely to influence their commitment to libertarian values, and thus members of society in a better position to take advantage of educational opportunities are more likely to be tolerant. For this reason, individuals with greater wealth and higher occupational status, especially those who live in more urban areas, are expected to be generally more tolerant. Because of differences in cultural expectations and opportunities, biological factors such as race, gender and sexual orientation are expected to influence these characteristics as well as have influence on the type of issues individuals take interest in. In addition, generation is expected to influence education and political knowledge in that each generation is exposed to varying degrees, interpretations, and examples of libertarian values. (McClosky and Brill 1983).

18. It should be noted that the distinction between punitive and rehabilitative used throughout the analysis may not reflect some readers' general conception or use of such terminology. Technically any criminal penalty is by nature punishment and therefore punitive, including rehabilitative criminal sanctions. However, as used in the current study, the distinction between "more punitive" and "more or different rehabilitation" is meant to distinguish participants who advocated penalties for biased offenders as a source of "retributive suffering, pain or loss" – the dictionary definition of punishment – from those who advocated punishment as a means to "restore to good health or condition" – the dictionary definition of rehabilitation. In other words, the current use of the terms reflects a layperson's conception of such terms. A "more punitive" response reflects a participant's desire to provide an offender the punishment necessary to get his just deserts and/or suffer for his behavior generally through a longer and/or harsher penalty. A more or different rehabilitative response reflects a participant's desire to use punishment as a means to address the reason for an offender's behavior through counseling, treatment, education etc. Though more precise terminology was sought, none was found that quite as succinctly distinguished participants' views.

19. Given the nature of the study and its sample, these findings obviously are meant to serve as further description of the current sample rather than to suggest the predictive capabilities of any particular variables. Although the data were examined for any particular patterns that might emerge, cross tabs identifying a 20 percentage difference were given greater consideration in an attempt to identify true patterns rather than simple artifacts of the small samples. In addition, only participants who made a clear choice between whether bias crime is different or not and whether it should be treated differently or not were included in the analysis, leaving out those who were unsure or whose comments could not be clearly coded.

20. Participants advocating a more or different rehabilitative approach to bias crime also were more likely to: mention enforcement problems surrounding bias crime but not that is was to taken as seriously as other crime; have a college and/or post graduate degree; mention that the system was unfair/discriminatory in some way or that politics were too involved; or were opposed to or didn't mention the death penalty.

21. In addition, switchers also seemed to be more likely to include: those who mentioned economics, society or individual factors as causes of crime, those who had something positive to say about the system before critiquing it, and those who mentioned the politics involved in the system.

22. One was a middle-aged, college-educated African-American male who worked a blue-collar job and was very punitively oriented when asked to discuss his general thoughts on crime and punishment. One was a college-educated gay man who owned his own business and offered no real discussion of his general thoughts on crime and punishment choosing instead to discuss his concern with the influence of politics on both. The third was a 19-year-old, Caucasian college student whose crime and punishment discussion focused on the need for greater rehabilitation whether in or out of jail/prison.

23. Some people accidentally were not asked this question and after reviewing the interviews did not make it absolutely clear that they were handling it differently because of the bias or not (3, 13 and 10 missing for the vignettes respectively) and thus the statistics are only for those who were specifically asked or indicated/made it clear on their own that it was a bias/hate crime.

24. Although participants were not asked directly whether they would treat the bias vignettes "similarly or differently," initially their language, particularly their use of "same" or "different" in introducing their response to bias crime was considered a feasible first method of assessment. Based on the roughly 75 percent of participants who used such language, the following percentages suggested they would treat bias crime "differently" for V1, V2 and V3 respectively and went on to discuss how: 28%, 42%, and 33%. Those who said "same" and did not say anything to contradict that statement accounted for 22%, 28%, and 31% respectively. However, the next two findings strongly suggested that such a measure was probably not appropriate. First, a handful of participants for each vignette suggested they would treat bias crime "the same but," 19%, 6% and 11% respectively. Second, after reviewing participants' responses in full and across the vignettes, it became clear that their language did not always necessarily match their response and/or was not always capable of describing their approach as the same as, or different than, non-bias crime. This issue seemed reserved to those participants whose responses to bias crimes focused on adding or changing the rehabilitative response to bias crime compared to non-bias crimes. It seemed that across vignettes, these participants, even when in the end they chose the same outcome-added more or different rehabilitation-used different language to describe their overall approach, some calling it the same approach to bias crimes others different and for some it was not possible to tell.

25. Two of those participants could have been coded as consistent based on the rehabilitation issue mentioned above. These two individuals, who varied on all the primary personal characteristics considered in the study,

originally indicated that they would treat bias crimes the same as other crimes. However, when presented with the vignettes they indicated similar punishment but either added hate-based rehabilitation, where for the non-bias vignette no rehabilitation had been indicated, or added more or changed the nature of the rehabilitation when it had been. These might be considered consistent responses in that it cannot be ruled out that some participants may conceive of changing rehabilitation as an inherent and necessary part of any criminal sanction and thus would consider giving bias crime different rehabilitation as treating it similarly to any other crime. As one of these participants stated "all punishment should include learning, just different learning for different crimes" (19). It is also possible that some participants might consider rehabilitation as a separate entity from or add on to a court's criminal sanction and thus when asked how the court's should handle bias crimes generally did not consider variations in rehabilitation as relevant. It also should be noted that four or the five participants who initially indicated that in the abstract bias crime should be treated differently in terms of rehabilitation used "but for" language in expressing their responses to the vignettes and advocated changes in rehabilitation only for those vignettes. This suggests that some participants most likely did perceive changing just rehabilitation to be a "different" response to bias crime. Thus, it could be that the two "inconsistent" participants reconsidered their thoughts and if asked directly would have called their rehabilitation change to the bias crime vignettes "different," or they may have considered it similar given the fact that they were generally in favor of rehabilitation and it would be normal for it to change based on varying types or motivations behind crimes.

The two participants who did not maintain consistency provided clues as to their seeming switch. The first, a Caucasian male in his earlier thirties with some college experience, initially indicated that he generally believed that bias crime should be treated more punitively if it could be proved "100 percent," "beyond the shadow of a doubt" (10). Although he didn't really believe that it was a "different" crime, he felt that treating it more harshly might deter people from engaging in it. However, he also indicated skepticism that a hate crime could be proved, concern that he reiterated when responding to the vignettes, indicating that they are "just too hard to prove" and therefore they should be treated the same as the non-bias crimes. While it is possible that if given a detailed and blatantly hate-based vignette he might respond differently, and thus his responses would not be truly inconsistent, the general nature of his comments seemed to suggest that aside from a confession he would be uncomfortable with delineating a hate crime for the purposes of additional punitive measures. Even when acknowledging V1 as a hate crime, he still supported a similar response.

On the other hand, the second, a male, Caucasian school teacher initially said that bias crimes should be handled the same because "if someone gets killed or murdered, that is the crime itself...if a punishment is what a punishment is supposed to be for the crime that is okay" (20). However, when responding to the vignettes he indicated, "That is where education comes into play. V2-It really changes when you add that little thing to it...and punishment might be a little harsher because they went after someone because they didn't like what they saw (interracial couple)...they need a little jail time (unlike non-bias scenario) with the counseling. V3-I would like to see the court come down on the guy because he jumped to a conclusion...it is another innocent person being hurt because of someone's perception of what they are (gay)." However he also, both when discussing bias crime in general and the vignettes, indicated some question as to whether anything would really change the hateful perpetrator. "What else do you do to that person (besides the same)? Can you change that way of thinking? I don't know if that would happen in jail or not... I would have to say they need a little jail time, but again, what is that going to do? Is that going to change their opinion or their attitude?" Thus, his inconsistency may be an artifact of his questioning whether a different approach would actually do any good leaving him actually torn on the issue. It is possible that the specificity of the vignettes provided him with stronger incentive to at least try something given that he seemed to be more expressive in his comparative difference given the vignettes: "that is crossing the line (V1)," 'that was a crime that crosses the line of individuality, people not being able to do what they want (V2)" (20).

26. As a result of the small sample involved, only percentage differences greater than 20 percent are noted and any suggested interactions are speculative at best. The decision to combine punitive and combination approaches was based on the small number of solely punitive cases (4) and a personal interest in identifying factors that might influence more punitive approaches to crime, particularly bias crime. Based on the 23 participants with a clear vignette approach to bias crime (excluding those who treated bias crime the same and those with unclear responses), after combining participants with more punitive or combination approaches, 48 percent of the sample supported solely rehabilitative changes to bias crime and 52 percent a more punitive change either with or without rehabilitative changes.

27. This concern, along with his earlier stated issue concerning the ability to change hateful perpetrators, might in part explain the seeming inconsistency

between his statement that bias crime should be treated the same and his different approach to the bias crime vignettes. Individuals such as he might feel the need to do something while at the same time questioning whether there is anything that legally or pragmatically can be done leaving them in state of flux concerning what to do.

References

ABC News Poll. 1999, August 16-22. *Question 27.* Roper Center at University of Connecticut Public Opinion Online. http://www.ropercenter.uconn.edu (accessed April 1, 2002).

Adams, D.M. 2005. Punishing hate and achieving equality. *Criminal Justice Ethics* 24(1): 19-31.

Adams, M.S., and R.C. Toth. 2006. The unanticipated consequences of hate crime legislation. *Judicature* 90(3): 129-135.

American Fact Finder. 2006. *White Township, Indiana County, Pennsylvania.*

Anti-Defamation League. 2007. *Hate crime laws.* Anti-Defamation League http://www.adl.org (accessed Sept. 7, 2007).

Applegate, B.K., F.T. Cullen, B.G. Link, P.J. Richard, and L. Lanza-Kaduce. 1996a. Determinants of public punitiveness toward drunk driving: A factorial survey approach. *Justice Quarterly* 13: 57-79.

Applegate, B.K., F.T. Cullen, M.G. Turner, and J.L. Sundt. 1996b. Assessing public support for three-strikes-and-you're-out laws: Global versus specific attitudes. *Crime and Delinquency* 42(4): 517-534.

Apprendi v. New Jersey, 120 S. Ct. 2348 (2000).

Association of American Religious Bodies. 2002. *Religious congregations and membership in the United States: County report (Indiana, PA).* Nashville: Glenmary Research Center.

Barnes, A., and P.H. Ephross. 1994. The impact of hate violence on victims: Emotional and behavioral responses to attacks. *Social Work* 39(3): 247-251.

Blakely v Washington, 542 U.S. 296 (2004)

Booker v United States, 543 U.S. 220 (2005).

Center for Survey Research and Analysis, University of Connecticut. 2000, November 9-19. *Question 10.* Roper Center at University of Connecticut Public Opinion Online. http://www.ropercenter.uconn.edu (accessed April 1, 2002).

Civil Rights Violations. 42 Pa. C.S.A. 8309.

Cohen, M.A., R.T. Trust, and S. Steen. 2003. *Measuring public perceptions of appropriate prison sentences, final report.* U.S. Department of Justice.

Colomb, W., and K. Damphousse. 2004. Examination of newspaper coverage of hate crimes: A moral panic perspective. *American Journal of Criminal Justice* 28(2): 147-156.

Cowan, G., B. Heiple, D. Khatchadourian, and M. McNevin. 2005. Heterosexuals' attitudes toward hate crimes and hate speech against gays and lesbians: Old fashioned and modern sexism. *Journal of Homosexuality* 49(2): 67-82.

Craig, K.M., and C.R. Waldo. 1996. 'So, what's a hate crime anyway?' Young adults' perceptions of hate crimes, victims and perpetrators. *Law and Human Behavior* 20(2): 113-129.

Cullen, F.T., Fisher, B.S. and BK Applegate. 2000. Public opinion about punishment and corrections. *Crime and Justice: A Review of Research* ed. M.Tonry. The University of Chicago Press 27: 1-79

Cunningham v California, 127 S.Ct. 856 (2007).

Desecration of Venerated Objects. 18 Pa. C.S.A. 550.

Dunbar, E. and A. Molina. 2004. Opposition to the legitimacy of hate crime laws: The role of argument acceptance, knowledge, individual differences, and peer influence. *Analyses of Social Issues and Public Policy* 4(1): 91-113.

Ehrlich, H.J., B.E.K. Larcom, and R.D. Purvis. 1994. *The traumatic effects of ethnoviolence.* Towson: Prejudice Institute, Center for Applied Study of Ethnoviolence.

Ethnic Intimidation Act. 18 Pa. C.S.A. 2710.

Ethnic Intimidation Statistics Collection Act. 71 P.S. 250.

Fernandez, J.M. 1991. Bringing hate crime into focus: The hate crime statistics act of 1990 pub. l. no. 101-275. *Harvard Civil Rights-Civil Liberties Law Review* 26(2): 261-293.

Flanagan, T., and D.R. Longmire. 1996. *Americans view crime and justice: A national public opinion survey.* Beverly Hills: SAGE Publications Inc.

Frase, R.S. 2007. The Apprendi-Blakely cases: Sentencing reform counter-revolution? *Criminology and Public Policy* 6(3): 403-432.

Gallup/CNN/USA Today Poll. 1999. August 16-18. *Buford Furrow Questions 1 and 2.* Public Agenda Online. http://www.publicagenda.com (accessed April 1, 2002).

Gallup Poll. 1999a, February 19-21. *Are you worried about becoming the victim of a hate crime?* Polling Report http://www.pollingreport.com (accessed April 1, 2002).

Gallup Poll. 1999b, February 19-21. *Question 28.* Roper Center at University of Connecticut Public Opinion Online Lexis-Nexis Academic Universe http://web.lexis-nexis.com/univers (accessed April 1, 2002).

Gallup Poll. 1999c, February 19-21. *Question 31-34.* Roper Center at University of Connecticut Public Opinion Online, Lexis-Nexis Academic Universe http://web.lexis-nexis.com/univers (accessed April 1, 2002).

Gallup Poll. 1999d, February 19-21. *Would you favor or oppose this type of hate crime law in your state?* Public Agenda Online http://www.publicagenda.com. (accessed April 1, 2002).

Gallup Poll. 2000a, August 29. *Question 31.* Roper Center at University of Connecticut Public Opinion Online, Lexis-Nexis Academic Universe http://web.lexis-nexis.com/univers (accessed April 1, 2002).

Gallup Poll. 2000b, September 11-13. *Question 32-35.* Roper Center at University of Connecticut Public Opinion Online, Lexis-Nexis Academic Universe http://web.lexis-nexis.com/univers (accessed April 1, 2002).

Gallup Poll. 2000c, October 25-28. *Question 14.* Roper Center at University of Connecticut Public Opinion Online, Lexis-Nexis Academic Universe http://web.lexis-nexis.com/univers (accessed April 1, 2002).

Gallup Poll. 2001, Oct. 11. *Question 12.* Roper Center at University of Connecticut Public Opinion Online, Lexis-Nexis Academic Universe http://web.lexis-nexis.com/univers (accessed April 1, 2002).

Gallup Poll. 2007, May 10-13. *Poll: Favor or oppose Federal hate crime legislation.* Polling Report http://www.pollingreport.com (accessed July 8, 2007).

Garin-Hart-Yang Research Group. 2000, Aug. 28-31. *Poll: Support a candidate based on hate crime support.* Polling Report http://www.pollingreport.come (accessed April 1, 2002).

Gaubatz, K.T. 1995. *Crime in the public mind.* Ann Arbor: The University of Michigan Press.

Gerstenfeld, P.B. 2003. Juror decision making in hate crime cases. *Criminal Justice Policy Review* 14(2): 193-213.

Glynn, C.J., S. Herbst, G.J. O'Keefe, and R.Y. Shapiro. 1999. *Public opinion.* Boulder: Westview Press.

Grattet, R., and V. Jenness. 2001. The birth and maturation of hate crime policy in the United States. *American Behavioral Scientist* 45(4): 668-695.

Hamilton College-The Arthur Levitt Public Affairs Center. 2002, August 27. *Poll: Favor or oppose laws to protect gays against hate crimes.* Polling the Nations 1986-2002 http://silverplatter.com (accessed September 1, 2002).

Harel, A., and G. Parchomovsky. 1999. On hate and equality. *Yale Law Journal* 109: 507-539.

Hart and Teeter Research Companies. 1998, October 24-27. *Question 50.* Roper Center at University of Connecticut Public Opinion Online, Lexis-Nexis Academic Universe http://web.lexis-nexis.com/univers (accessed April 1, 2002).

Hart and Teeter Research Companies/NBC News/Wall Street Journal Poll. 1999, June 16-19. *Poll: Favor or oppose increasing punishment for hate crimes.* Public Agenda Online http://publicagenda.com (accessed April 1, 2002).

Herek, G.M., J.C. Cogan, and J.R. Gillis. 1999. Psychological sequelae of hate crime victimization among lesbian, gay and bisexual adults. *Journal of Consulting and Clinical Psychology* 67(6): 945-951.

Herek, G.M., J.R. Gillis, J.C. Cogan, and E.K. Glunt. 1997. Hate crime victimization among lesbian, gay, and bisexual adults: Prevalence, psychological correlates, and methodological issues. *Journal of Interpersonal Violence* 12(2): 195-117.

Hurd, H.M., and M.S. Moore. 2004. Punishing hatred and prejudice. *Stanford Law Review* 56: 1081-1131.

Hutton, N. 2005. Beyond populist punitiveness. *Punishment and Society* 7(3): 1243-258.

Iganski, P. 2001. Hate crimes hurt more. *American Behavioral Scientist* 45(4): 626-638.

Indiana County (PA) Statistical Demographics. 2004. http://www.indianapa.com/chamber/county_profile.pdf (accessed September 1, 2005).

Institutional vandalism. 18 Pa. C.S.A. 3307.

Jacobs, J.B., and J.S. Henry. 1996. The social construction of a hate crime epidemic. *Journal of Criminal Law and Criminology* 86(2): 366-391.

Jacobs, J.B., and K. Potter. 1997. *Hate crimes: A critical perspective.* Crime and Justice: A Review of Research, ed. M.Tonry. 22: 1-50. Chicago: University Chicago Press.

Jacobs, J.B., and K. Potter. 1998. *Hate crimes: Criminal law and identity politics.* New York: Oxford University Press.

Jenness, V. 1999. Managing differences and making legislation: Social movements and the racialization, sexualization and gendering of federal hate crime law in the U.S. *Social Problems* 46(4): 549-577.

Johnson, S.D., and B.D. Byers. 2003. Attitudes toward hate crime laws. *Journal of Criminal Justice* 31(3): 227-235.

Kaiser Family Foundation. 2000, September 7-17 and October. *Poll: Federal law to protect gays and lesbians.* Polling the Nations 1986-2002 http://silverplatter.com/c48312 (accessed April 1, 2002).

Kiley and Company. 1998, October. *Poll-Tougher sentences for hate crimes.* Polling the Nations 1986-2002 http://silverplatter.com/c48312 (accessed April 1, 2002).

Langworthy, R.H., and J.T. Whitehead. 1986. Liberalism and fear as explanations of punitiveness. *Criminology* 24 (3): 575-591.

Lawrence, F.M. 1999. *Punishing hate: bias crimes under American law.* Cambridge: Harvard University Press.

Levin, B. 1999. Hate crimes: Worse by definition. *Journal of Contemporary Criminal Justice* 15(1): 6-21.

Levin, J., and J. McDevitt. 1993. *Hate crimes: The rising tide of bigotry and bloodshed.* New York: Plenum Press.

MacNamara, B.S. 2003. New York's hate crimes act of 2000: Problematic and redundant legislation aimed at subject motivation. *Albany Law Review* 66: 519-545.

Maguire, K., and A.L. Pastore. 1997. *Sourcebook of Criminal Justice Statistics 1996.* U.S. Department of Justice. Bureau of Justice Statistics. Washington, DC: Government Printing Office.

Marcus-Newhall, A., L.P. Blake, and J. Baumann. 2002. Perceptions of hate crime perpetrators and victims as influenced by race, political orientation, and peer group. *American Behavioral Scientist* 46(1): 108-135.

Martin, S.E. 1996. Investigating hate crimes: Case characteristics and law enforcement responses. *Justice Quarterly* 13(3): 455-480.

McClosky, H., and A. Brill. 1983. *Dimensions of tolerance: What Americans believe about civil liberties.* New York: Russell Sage Foundation.

McCracken, G. 1988. *The long interview.* Beverly Hills: SAGE Publication Inc.

McDevitt, J., J. Balboni, L. Garcia, and J. Gu. 2001. Consequences for victims: A comparison of bias- and non-bias-motivated assaults. *American Behavioral Scientist* 45(4): 697-713.

Messner, S.F., S. McHugh, and R.B. Felson. 2004. Distinctive characteristics of assaults motivated by bias. *Criminology* 42(3): 585-619.

Miller, A.J. 2001. Student perceptions of hate crimes. *American Journal of Criminal Justice* 25(2): 293-305.

National Institute Against Prejudice and Violence (NIAPV). 1986. *The ethnoviolence project* (Institute Report No. 1). Baltimore, Maryland.

National Institute Against Prejudice & Violence (NIAPV). 1989. *The ethnoviolence project* (Institute Report No. 2). Baltimore, Maryland.

Newport, F. 2007. Public Favors Expansion of Hate Crime Law to Include Sexual Orientation: Majorities of republicans, conservatives, and frequent church attenders in favor. *Gallup News Service* http://www.galluppoll.com (accessed August 2, 2007).

Partners Against Hate. (2002). *Hate Crimes Around the Country.* http://www.partnersagainsthate.org (accessed July 8, 2002).

Partners Against Hate. (2004). *Hate Crimes Around the Country.* http://www.partnersagainsthate.org (accessed February 2005).

Pennsylvania Uniform Crime Reporting System. 2004. http://ucr.psp.state.pa.us (accessed April 20, 2005).

Princeton Survey Research Associates. 1998, Nov. 4-Dec. 6. *Question 23.* Roper Center at University of Connecticut Public Opinion Online, Lexis-Nexis Academic Universe http://web.lexis-nexis.com/univers (accessed April 1, 2002).

Princeton Survey Research Associates. 1999, Aug. 12-13. *Question 18.* Roper Center at University of Connecticut Public Opinion Online, Lexis-Nexis Academic Universe http://web.lexis-nexis.com/univers (accessed April 1, 2002).

Princeton Survey Research Associates. 2000a, Jan. 20-Mar. 19. *Question 14.* Roper Center at University of Connecticut Public Opinion Online, Lexis-Nexis Academic Universe http://web.lexis-nexis.com/univers (accessed April 1, 2002).

Princeton Survey Research Associates. 2000b, Feb 7-Sept. 4. *Question 43.* Roper Center at University of Connecticut Public Opinion Online, Lexis-Nexis Academic Universe http://web.lexis-nexis.com/univers (accessed April 1, 2002).

R.A.V. v. City of St. Paul, 505 U.S. 377 (1992).

Rayburn, N.R., and G.C. Davison. 2002. Articulated thoughts about anti-gay hate crimes. *Cognitive Therapy and Research* 26, 431-447.

Rayburn, N.R., M. Mendoza, and G.C. Davison. 2003. Bystanders' perceptions of perpetrators and victims of hate crime. *Journal of Interpersonal Violence* 18(9): 1055-1074.

Roberts, J.V. 2003. Public opinion and mandatory sentencing: A review of international findings. *Criminal Justice and Behavior* 30(4): 483-508.

Roberts, J.V., and M. Hough. 2005. *Understanding public attitudes to criminal justice.* New York: Open University Press.

Roberts J.V., and L.J. Stalans. 1997. *Public opinion, crime, and criminal justice.* Boulder: Westview Press.

Roberts v. United State Jaycees, 104 S.Ct. 3244 (1984).

Rubenstein, W.B. 2004. The real story of U.S. hate crime statistics: An empirical analysis. *Tulane Law Review* 78: 1213-1246.

Saucier, D.A, T.L. Brown, R.C. Mitchell, and A.J. Cawmen. 2006. Effects of victims' characteristics on attitudes toward hate crimes. *Journal of Interpersonal Violence* 21(7): 890-909.

Sebba, L. 1980. Is mens rea a component of perceived offense seriousness? *Journal of Criminal Law and Criminology* 69: 124-135.

Sellin, T., and M.E. Wolfgang. 1964. *The measurement of delinquency.* New York: John Wiley and Sons.

Sentencing for Criminal Mischief. 42 Pa. C.S.A. 9720.

Skogan, W.G., and M.G. Maxfield. 1981. *Coping with crime: Individual and neighborhood reactions.* Beverly Hills: SAGE Publications.

Stafford, M.C., and O.R. Galle. 1984. Victimization rates, exposure to risk, and fear of crime. *Criminology* 22: 173-285.

Steen, S., and M.A. Cohen. 2004. Assessing the public's demand for hate crime penalties. *Justice Quarterly* 21(1): 91-124.

Tyler, T.R., and R.J. Boeckmann. 1997. Three strikes and you are out, but why? The psychology of public support for punishing rule breakers. *Law & Society Review* 31(2): 237-265.

Tyler, T.R., and R. Weber. 1982. Support for the death penalty: Instrumental response to crime, or symbolic attitude? *Law & Society Review* 17(1): 21-45.

U.S. Congress. 1968. *Federally Protected Activities.* 18 USC 245.

U.S. Congress. 1990. *Hate Crime Statistics Act of 1990.* Pub. L. No. 101-275 (April 23, 1990).

U.S. Congress. 1994. *Violent Crime Control and Law Enforcement Act of 1994. Sec 280003 Direction to US Sentencing Commission Regarding Sentencing Enhancements for Hate Crimes.* Pub. L. No 103-322 (September 13, 1994).

U.S. Congress. 1995. *Hate Crime Sentencing Enhancement Act.* 28 USC 994 (November 1, 1995).

U.S. Congress. 2007a. *Hate Crimes Against the Homeless Statistics Act of 2007.* HR 2216, 110th Cong., 1st sess. (May 8, 2007).

U.S. Congress. 2007b. *Hate Crime Statistics Improvement Act of 2007.* HR 1164, 110th Cong., 1st sess. (February 16, 2007).

U.S. Congress. 2007c. *Local Law Enforcement Hate Crimes Prevention Act of 2007.* H.R. 1592., 110th Cong., 1st sess. (February 16, 2007)

U.S. Congress. 2007d. *Matthew Shepard Local Law Enforcement Hate Crimes Prevention Act of 2007.* S. 1105, 110th cong., 1st sess. (April 12, 2007).

U.S. Department of Justice. 1993-2001. *Hate crime statistics.* Washington, D.C.: U.S. Government Printing Office.

U.S. Department of Justice. 2001. *National crime victimization survey.* Bureau of Justice Statistics. Washington, DC: U.S. Government Printing Office.

U.S. Department of Justice. 2006. *FBI-uniform crime reports 2004.* Washington, D.C.: U.S. Government Printing Office.

U.S. v. Morrison, 120 S.Ct. 1740 (2000).

Virginia v. Black et al., 123 S.Ct. 1536 (2003).

Vogel, B.L. 2000. Perceptions of hate: The extent to which a motive of "hate" influences attitudes about violent crimes. *Journal of Crime and Justice* 23(2): 1-25.

Warr, M. 1995. Poll trends: Public opinion on crime and punishment. *Public Opinion Quarterly* 59: 296-310.

Warr, M. 2000. Fear of crime in the United States: Avenues for research and policy. *Criminal Justice 2000,* Vol. 4: *Measurement and Analysis of Crime and Justice,* ed. D. Duffee. Washington, DC: National Institute of Justice.

Warr, M., and C.G. Ellison. 2000. Rethinking social reactions to crime: Personal and altruistic fear in family households. *American Journal of Sociology* 106(3): 551-78.

Warr, M., and M.C. Stafford. 1983. Fear of victimization: A look at the proximate causes. *Social Forces* 61: 1033-43.

Weiss, R.S. 1994. *Learning from strangers: The art and method of qualitative interview studies.* New York: The Free Press.

Weisburd, S.B., and B. Levin. 1994. On the basis of sex: Recognizing gender-based bias crimes. *Stanford Law and Policy Review* 21.

Wexler, C., and G. Marx. 1986. When law and order works. *Journal of Crime and Criminology* 32: 205-227.

Wisconsin v. Mitchell, 508 U.S. 476 (1993).

Wilson, M.S., and R.B. Ruback. 2003. Hate crimes in Pennsylvania, 1984-1999: Case characteristics and police responses. *Justice Quarterly* 20(2): 373-391.

Yankelovich Partners/CNN/Time Poll. 1998a, Oct. 14-15. *Poll: Favor or oppose federal hate crime law to protect homosexuals.* Polling Report http://www.pollingreport.com (accessed April 1, 2002).

Yankelovich Partners/CNN/Time Poll. 1998b, Oct. 14-15. *Poll: Seriousness of violence against gays and lesbians.* Polling Report http://www.pollingreport.com (accessed April 1, 2002).

Yankelovich Partners/CNN/Time Poll. 1998c, Oct. 14-15. *Poll: Attack of a gay Wyoming student.* Polling Report http://www.pollingreport.com (accessed April 1, 2002).

Index